# The White Rose
# OF STALINGRAD

OSPREY
PUBLISHING

Dedicated to all the young people, male as well as female, who aspire to break the bonds of earth to soar among the clouds.

# The White Rose
# OF STALINGRAD

## The Real-Life Adventure of Lidiya Vladimirovna Litvyak, the Highest Scoring Female Air Ace of All Time

BILL YENNE

First published in Great Britain in 2013 by Osprey Publishing,
Midland House, West Way, Botley, Oxford, OX2 0PH, UK
43-01 21st Street, Suite 220B, Long Island City, NY 11101, USA

E-mail: info@ospreypublishing.com

A CIP catalogue record for this book is available from the British Library.

ISBN: 978 1 84908 810 7
PDF e-book ISBN: 978 1 78200 913 9
Epub ISBN: 978 1 78200 912 2

Page layout by Myriam Bell Design, UK
Index by Zoe Ross
Typeset in Minion Pro and Univers
Two maps have been redrawn by Mapping Specialists Ltd.
Originated by PDQ Media, Bungay, UK
Printed in China through Worldprint Ltd.

13 14 15 16 17    10 9 8 7 6 5 4 3 2 1

Osprey Publishing is supporting the Woodland Trust, the UK's leading woodland
conservation charity, by funding the dedication of trees.

www.ospreypublishing.com

Cover photos © Anne Noggle collection and Bill Yenne Collection

# Contents

# Introduction

T his is the story of a woman who dared to aspire to be a warrior, in part to defend the reputation of her family name, dishonored by lies which had shamed her father, and in part to save her beloved Motherland from a dark beast who came out of the west on leathery wings to consume and subjugate a land whose soil runs in the veins of its people.

The fact that popular culture has portrayed her as the "White *Rose* of Stalingrad," when it was actually a white lily that she painted on the side of her Yak-1 fighter aircraft is illustrative of how, in death, the story of her short life has become more myth than legend.

In the making of myths, factual details can be an intrusive nuisance. In the making of history, the myths, in the literary sense, are the elements of the story that elevate certain events and certain people to prominence above others. Throughout history, great warriors, heroines as well as heroes, are remembered as such as much for the light reflected from their armor as for the deeds they did and their true accomplishments. This is the story of a woman about whom little is known, a story that is seen through the window of her times, as well as through the window into the dimly lit room that was her life.

The documented facts about her life are few, the recollected information fleeting. In the mythology that surrounds her, she is at once a victim of circumstance and a feminist hero. She is both a shy girl and a skilled warrior. She is seen as representing many, and symbolic of much.

Yet she is both far simpler than all of this and far more complex. She would probably never imagined herself as allegorical, but rather as an unpretentious girl who simply wanted to fly airplanes, and who, when given the chance, was exceptionally good at it.

Lidiya Vladimirovna Litvyak was universally known as "Lilya," or "Lilia," meaning "Lily," and known intimately to her closest friends by the diminutive "Lil'ka." Her father's given name, Vladimir, is memorialized, as is Russian custom, in her middle name. For Lilya, this is especially poignant because, as a teenaged girl, she suffered the humiliation and the torment of watching her father be arrested, executed, and erased by the state for which he had served as a civil servant and she would later serve as a warrior.

She was born in Moscow in 1921, specifically on August 18, the day that, on her twelfth birthday, became "Soviet Air Fleet Day," also called "Soviet Aviation Day." This coincidence is especially auspicious, given Lilya's eventual prominence as one of the Soviet Union's most outstanding military aviators. They still hold the Moscow International Aviation and Space Salon (MAKS) air show at Ramenskoye (Zhukovsky) Airport near Moscow during the week of Lilya's birthday.

It is important to underscore the fact that Lilya grew up with the Soviet Union, an immense empire of a new kind, born of a violent revolution, rising out of the ashes of an empire of the old kind. As Vasily Vitalyevich Shulgin, a member of the prerevolutionary government, wrote in retrospect, this vast place, which had cut itself off from the rest of the world, "was no longer a monarchy, but nor was she a republic. She was a form of state with no name."

The story of the birth throes and tumultuous adolescence of this empire is thickly intertwined with Lilya's own story. This state, and its leader, the cruel and enigmatic Josef Stalin, became the governing presence throughout her entire life.

Lilya grew up in a Janus-headed state which, in many ways celebrated and molded its youth into idealized components of the society which it was inventing, while at the same time, compelled an older generation— ironically, the generation who fought to make the state possible—to live with fear and suspicion. As young people like Lilya grew up with campfires and patriotic songs, dark and sinister shadows lurked beyond the warm glow of their fire circle.

Beyond that warm glow, the days and nights of her youth in the Soviet Union were a dark and tempestuous time, the history of which is composed of half-truths and is cheated of facts that were deliberately omitted, intentionally erased, or never recorded out of fear, or for more sinister purposes.

Lilya Litvyak grew to prominence in a time of war, the time of the "Great Patriotic War." Like the original "Patriotic War" fought against Napoleon in 1812, the Great Patriotic War of 1941–45 was a war of national survival, and one in which the very essence of national identity was at stake. The rest of the world was embroiled in World War II, but to the Soviet people, this global conflict was merely a sideshow to their mighty, and very personal, struggle against the "Hitlerite fascists." Even today, Russians still refer to the war they fought against the Germans between 1941 and 1945 as the Great Patriotic War, and not as World War II.

In the beginning of those years, a groundswell of popular support for this great and patriotic war emerged from the youth of Lilya's generation who had grown up with the idealism and the patriotic songs. They came by the millions to form the great body of the armed forces that ultimately saved their Motherland. Among them were not just the young men of Lilya's generation, but also the young women—and a great many of them, too.

Among the tens of thousands of young women of that generation who fought and died in the Great Patriotic War were those special ones who did so as aviators.

The story of Soviet women in military aviation during the Great Patriotic War began with the vision and tenacity of a single exceptional officer. She was nearly a decade older than Lilya, but she was still a young woman, just twenty-nine years old, when the Great Patriotic War began.

Marina Mikhailovna Malinina Raskova was an aspiring opera singer turned pilot who had achieved international prominence in the world of aviation in the 1930s, the same era when women such as Amelia Earhart were capturing headlines and world records—and becoming household words. Marina Raskova was one of the household names in the Soviet Union. She was the woman whose picture was carried—like that of a pop star—in the school bags of young schoolgirls like Lilya Litvyak.

A woman of great beauty and charisma, Marina Raskova was also a great visionary. She inspired the women of Lilya's generation to fly and fight, but beyond that, she also succeeded in realizing the impossible dream of creating all-women combat regiments in which that generation of flying fighters would have the opportunity to shine—and how they shone!

Among the Allies in World War II, only in the Soviet Union were women deliberately sent into combat—and only in the Soviet aviation regiments formed by Marina Raskova did they serve in all-women units. While thousands of other young Soviet women would serve in uniform in ground combat roles from snipers to tank drivers, they served as small minorities within mostly male units.

Woman warriors have always been a part, albeit small and often overlooked, of military history. From ancient times through the Middle Ages, there have been numerous instances of individual armed women going into battle alongside male warriors. These have ranged from warrior queens, such as Tomyris of Persia and Boudica of Wales, leading troops in battle; to women warriors, from the fifteenth-century French heroine Jeanne Hachette to the American Revolution's Molly Pitcher, both of whom rose from the nonnobility to take up arms. Among these, France's Joan of Arc, the "Maid of Orleans," is an outstanding example.

From the eighteenth and nineteenth centuries, there are many well-documented instances of specific women who either took up arms in time of war to defend their homes or homeland or who disguised themselves as men in order to join the armed forces of their country. Indeed, there are numerous cases of women who enlisted in the Union Army or the Confederate Army during the American Civil War and who served for a year or more without it being known that they were women.

Well-known in Russian military history is the famous "cavalry maiden," Nadezhda Andreyevna Durova. The daughter of an army officer, she grew up on military posts and later enlisted under an assumed male identity. Beginning in 1806, she fought bravely in various battles, was commissioned as an officer, and played a role in the climactic defeat of Napoleon in Russia in 1812.

Marina Raskova, though, was about as far in her mindset from Nadezhda Durova as is possible among women warriors. She saw no reason why a woman should have to hide her identity and blend into a company of men. Nor, indeed, did she see why women warriors could not be organized and go into battle in the company of other women. Marina Raskova's idea of creating formal combat units comprised of women was unique to its time, although it was not entirely without precedent.

Throughout military history, mainly in premodern times, one can find examples of armies organizing specific units in which large numbers of women served routinely in combat. Ancient history—liberally seasoned with ancient folklore, of course—tells of tribes of warrior women. Notable are the Amazons, who lived in Scythia, roughly the area north and east of the Black Sea. Amazons are mentioned in the fifth century B.C. by the historian Herodotus and later by the biographers of Alexander the Great, among many others. Though the Amazons are often considered to have been mythical, David Anthony writes in his 2007 book *The Horse, the Wheel, and Language* that one in five of the graves of warriors found in the swath of Russia and Ukraine north of the Black Sea contains the remains of an armed woman.

In 1542, the Spanish explorer and conquistador Francisco de Orellana encountered a tribe of warrior women in South America, and the river where this happened became known as the "Amazon" because of them. Ancient Norse sagas, such as the Völsunga and Hervarar, speak of contingents of women warriors known as "shieldmaidens," and there are some written accounts by outsiders, circa the tenth century, which describe such women being seen in battle.

In the late Middle Ages and thereafter, there were even a few orders of women knights in Europe, although in most cases they seem to have been given their titles as honorary ranks, rather than for serving as warriors in battle. However, in about 1149, Ramon Berenguer, Count of Barcelona, established the *Orden de la Hacha* (Order of the Hatchet), which was specifically comprised of *cavalleras* (female knights) who had fought to save the city of Tortosa from attack by the Moors.

The seventeenth-century English historian Elias Ashmole, who created the Ashmolean Museum at the University of Oxford through the donation of his manuscript collection, specifically mentions the women who became knights. "The example is of the Noble Women of Tortosa in Aragon, and recorded by Josef Micheli Marquez," Ashmole writes in his 1672 *The Institution, Laws, and Ceremony of the Most Noble Order of the Garter*. "[Marquez] plainly calls them *Cavalleros* or Knights, or may I not rather say *Cavalleras*, seeing I observe the words *Equitissae* and *Militissae* (formed from the Latin *Equites* [the Roman equestrian warrior] and *Milites*) heretofore applied to Women."

By the nineteenth century and well into the twentieth, though, women in the uniformed military service of most nations were formally relegated to serving only in medical units. Notable among the exceptions were the Russian all-women "Battalions of Death" of 1917. While such an appellation conjures images from a "B-Movie" sexploitation film, the reality was more mundane. These units, some of which were simply called "Woman's Battalions," were created by the short-lived Russian Provisional Government, which was briefly in place between the fall of Tsar Nicholas II and the Bolshevik Revolution, at which time they were disbanded. It was at a time when the Provisional Government hoped to rally support for a continuation of the fight against the Germans in World War I. The 1st Russian Women's Battalion of Death saw limited action against the enemy in July 1917, but was badly defeated.

During World War II, women continued to serve in large numbers in medical detachments on all sides, but for the first time, most of the principal nations at war also created nonmedical women's units. In the United States, the largest such organization was in the U.S. Army's Women's Army Auxiliary Corps (WAAC). Formed in 1942, it became the Women's Army Corps (WAC) the following year. The roughly 150,000 "WACs" served at home as well as overseas in every theater of operations where the U.S. Army was active in jobs ranging from communications and clerical, to intelligence and logistics. Another 18,000 women served in the analogous U.S. Marine Corps Women's Reserve (USMCWR). The U.S. Navy initially called their women's unit the Women Accepted for Volunteer Emergency Service (WAVE), but when it became the U.S. Naval Reserve (Women's Reserve), the women continued to refer to themselves by the appealing earlier acronym, WAVEs.

Also with a memorable acronym, the closest American equivalent to the units imagined by Marina Raskova was the Women Airforce Service Pilots (WASP). These women pilots were specifically tasked with delivering U.S. Army Air Forces aircraft from factories to air bases from which they would be flown overseas to operational units by male pilots. In the course of this, the women flew—albeit never in combat—nearly every type of combat aircraft used by the USAAF during World War II, from fighters to heavy bombers.

In the United Kingdom, the units which were the rough analog of these American organizations were British Army's Auxiliary Territorial Service (ATS), a successor to the British Women's Auxiliary Army Corps (WAAC) of World War I; the Women's Royal Naval Service (WRNS), better known as the "Wrens;" and the Royal Air Force's Women's Auxiliary Air Force (WAAF), which were a ground support organization rather than pilots like the WASPs. As with the American women's groups—but unlike Marina Raskova's Soviet regiments—none of the British units was organized in such a way as to permit the women to be anywhere close to combat.

In the wake of the victory they helped to hasten, the contribution to the war effort by women in uniform was not overlooked so much as overshadowed by the great events of an enormous global undertaking. In the United States, the WACs and WAVEs were not disbanded, but the WASPs were, and their official records remained under wraps for nearly four decades. After World War II, there was a much larger proportion of uniformed women in the world's armed forces than before the war, but the idea of women in combat roles was not considered by most major countries for half a century.

In the Soviet Union, with the end of the Great Patriotic War, the vast majority of women in uniform were demobilized, and those few who remained were withdrawn from combat units. The three all-women aviation regiments pioneered by Marina Raskova were disbanded, never to be reconstituted. A handful of women continued as military pilots, integrated into all-male units, or assigned as test pilots. As in the West, women pilots found it hard to obtain work as pilots with nonmilitary organizations, such as the state airline, Aeroflot.

The fact that there had been Soviet women in combat, and that there had been all-women aviation regiments, received little attention after the war, even at home. The accounts of what the aviators had accomplished lived on in a few wartime accounts which had been published in newspapers from *Pravda* to *The New York Times*, in the incomplete scraps of records which survived the wartime censor's scissors to be filed away in the Tsentral'nyi Arkhiv Ministerstva Oborony (TsAMO), the Central Archive of the Soviet Ministry of Defense, and in memories of those who had been there.

In the West, what these Soviet women had done remained virtually unknown as the few published accounts were overshadowed and forgotten. The United States, the United Kingdom, France, and other Western countries had each been thoroughly involved in World War II themselves, and in postwar published narratives, there was naturally more interest in the wartime experiences of one's own country than in what may have happened in the Soviet Union. This was also the period of the Cold War, and a daunting curtain of secrecy hung along a line parallel with the Iron Curtain. If something was being ignored in the institutional memory within the Soviet Union, there was little chance that it would be noticed abroad.

Beginning in the 1960s, though, there were a handful of periodical articles, such as in the aviation journal *Aviatsiya i Kosmonavtika* (*Aviation and Cosmonautics*), which reached the West, and *Soviet Life*, the magazine specifically published in the Soviet Union for Western audiences. In 1962, the Moscow publishing house Molodaya Gvardiya published *V Nebe Frontovom* (*In the Sky Above the Front*), an anthology of oral history accounts by the women aviators themselves, which was edited by Militsa Aleksandrovna Kazarinova, who had served as chief of staff in one of Marina Raskova's regiments. A revised and expanded edition of the book was published in Moscow in 1971, and an English language edition, edited and translated by Dr. Kazimiera Jean Cottam, was published in 1998 under the title *Women in Air War*.

By the late 1970s, the story of one of Marina Raskova's three regiments began to garner particular interest. The women of the 46th Guards Night Bomber Aviation Regiment (*Gvardeiskii Nochnoi Bombardirovochnyi Aviatsionnyi Polk*, NBAP) had operated rickety Po-2 biplanes, flying over German lines at night, and the Germans called these women *Nachthexen*, meaning "Night Witches." The colorful name resonated with many who might have had only a passing interest in the Soviet aspect of World War II.

In 1981, the Night Witches were both the subject and the title of a book by BBC reporter Bruce Myles, as well as of a Soviet documentary film by Yevgheniya Andreyevna Zhigulenko, who herself had been a pilot in the regiment. Though the Myles book has been widely referenced, it also has been criticized by those familiar with the subject for mixing up facts and getting the names of many of the interviewees wrong. While it presents a number of events in incorrect sequence, it does provide an insight into the mood of the times.

Even as late as the 1980s, facts from the annals of Soviet history, especially with regard to military history, were hard to come by, often remaining closely guarded state secrets. Even Soviet historians with special access knew that they must tread lightly. Dmitri Volkogonov, a wartime Red Army officer who later headed the Institute of Military History at the Soviet Defense Ministry and who was a biographer of Josef Stalin, lost his job in 1991, fired by Mikhail Gorbachev for revealing the details from documents which had been deemed secret by Stalin half a century earlier.

When the Soviet Union came to an end and freer access to the archives became possible, it was merely freer access to an information labyrinth. Much of the detailed information related to the Great Patriotic War is incomplete because of erratic record keeping at the time, which is justifiably explained both by wartime urgency and by the fear of revealing too much in documents that might be compromised. Then, too, as with archives anywhere in the world, minutia is often discarded over time simply because a particular bureaucrat makes a spontaneous decision that it is not worth saving.

There is also a darker side, however. While the various archives groan under the weight of the paperwork created during the Soviet period, many documents never reached these archives or were removed at various times through the years by those who did not want embarrassing or inconvenient data available for posterity.

Especially with documents related to the three decades of Stalin's rule, the archives were like a box of jigsaw puzzle pieces, in which many are missing. Documents from this era, like many of the bureaucrats who created them, were periodically, thoroughly, and permanently purged.

Apropos of Soviet pilots and air operations during the Great Patriotic War, the scholarship of aviation historians such as Hans Seidl, Tomas Polak, and Christopher Shores has added greatly to the body of information available about a long-ago and erratically chronicled time.

The fall of the Soviet Union also provided a unique window of access to first-hand accounts that enrich books about Soviet women aviators produced in the 1990s. Anne Noggle, author of *For God, Country, and the Thrill of It: Women Airforce Service Pilots in World War II* and herself a former World War II WASP, took a unique interest in the Soviet women combat pilots and made several trips to the Soviet Union in the early 1990s to interview them for her book, *A Dance With Death*. Reina Pennington, a historian and former U.S. Air Force intelligence officer, also interviewed a number of the women pilots in the decade following the collapse of the Soviet Union for her excellent book *Wings, Women & War*.

Universally present in the oral histories is the women's determination to succeed, their pride in themselves and their comrades—and their love and admiration for Marina Raskova. To say that they held her in high esteem is a gross understatement. To say that they regarded her as mother figure only begins to describe the way that she was perceived by the women under her command.

"The noblest youths," wrote the great first-century Roman military historian Publius Cornelius Tacitus, "were not ashamed to be numbered among the faithful companies of celebrated leaders, to whom they devoted their arms and service. A noble emulation prevailed among the leaders to acquire the greatest number of bold companions."

So it was with Marina Raskova and the young women who actively sought to be numbered among those selected for her three regiments.

Just as she inspired them, she had a unique talent for recognizing and nurturing the great, innate potential within the young women of her regiments. Among them, few showed greater potential, nor realized it to a greater degree in so short a time, than Lilya Litvyak.

When Marina Raskova's piercing gray eyes fell upon Lilya, her mind imagined a fighter pilot. She saw in Lilya not simply a great aviator, but a woman who had the makings of an audacious warrior who could do battle, one on one, with opposing fighter pilots—and win.

To become a fighter pilot, one must be more than merely the operator of a flying machine, but a pilot for whom that flying machine is an extension of one's self. The line between human and machine blurs and fades. To become a fighter pilot, one must be able to loop, roll, and race through the sky as though the aircraft is not a machine at all, but part of the body of an acrobat. Marina saw this in Lilya.

The successful fighter pilot is a successful hunter, a successful killer. Indeed, one's success as a fighter pilot is marked by having achieved aerial victories, or "kills." Those who have achieved five or more aerial victories are honored with the title, "ace."

Beyond being a good hunter, a good fighter pilot never forgets that he or she is also the hunted, the object of other hunters. A fighter pilot who does not remember this won't survive long enough to become an ace.

Lilya Litvyak became a fighter pilot, and in time—actually a very short time—she became recognized as a very good fighter pilot. In turn, she came to be welcomed into a club into which no other woman had yet to be admitted. She became an ace.

The term was coined in World War I, which began in 1914 when aircraft were flimsy machines used primarily for observation. Soon however, observer pilots started to carry handguns to fire at other observer pilots and steel darts to drop on troops on the ground. The airplane gave birth to the warplane.

Fighter pilots became the knights of the air. They were, quite literally, a breed apart, fighting their battles high above the mud and muck of the battlefield, fighting one another one to one, like the knights of the medieval tournament. Just as a special folklore surrounded the knights of the Middle Ages and a code of chivalry defined knighthood and contained a special vocabulary, so it was with the knights of the air.

The use of the word "ace" to describe a victorious knight of the air originated in the French media, where the term *l'as* had been used to describe singularly triumphant sports stars. The first aviator known to have achieved an aerial victory over another was the French daredevil aeronaut turned military pilot Roland Garros, who achieved his victory on April 1, 1915. The first pilot to be referred to as l'as for downing five airplanes was probably Adolphe Pegoud, although Garros may have been responsible for downing five airplanes earlier than Pegoud.

In 1915, being an ace was truly a feat of skill. Aiming a gun at a moving airplane from moving airplane is not easy—then or now. Over time, aviation technology on both sides gave the knights of the air some very potent warhorses, and their victories provided the most—and arguably the only—truly heroic headlines of World War I. The aces became the great heroes of World War I, and because they were ripe for being transformed from the real to the mythic, their names were the true analogs of Sir Lancelot and Sir Galahad. Frenchmen such as Georges Guynemer and René Fonck, Englishmen such as Mick Mannock, and Canadians such as Billy Bishop were anointed by their media as the greatest names of their era.

While these names are no longer the household words they once were, we can say with little fear of contradiction, that the most recognized name of a warrior—on or above the battlefield—of World War I, is also that of the war's top-scoring ace. Baron Manfred Albrecht Freiherr von Richthofen, best known as the "Red Baron," became the archetypical knight of the air. He was a young and handsome nobleman who was also extraordinarily skilled in the deadly art of aerial warfare. The Red Baron scored eighty "kills" before his death in 1918 in the skies over Vaux sur Somme in France. By comparison, Aleksandr Alexandrovich Kozakov, Russia's leading ace, scored twenty, and Eddie Rickenbacker, the American "Ace of Aces," had twenty-six victories.

There were no women aces in World War I, and indeed, no women fighter pilots. To the sensibilities of the time, the notion of a woman as a "knight of the air" or as a knight of any realm was an anachronism. However, just as a select woman warrior in the Middle Ages could have been a *cavallera* to her counterpart male *cavallero*, or an *equitissa* to a male *equite*, Marina Raskova assured that in the Great Patriotic War, there would be women fighter pilots.

Marina may have made it possible, but she only opened the door for her *equitissae*. What they did with the open door was up to them.

To be a fighter pilot was to step into a unique world. As this author wrote in the recent book *Aces High* the dual biography of Dick Bong and Tommy McGuire, America's top aces of World War II, fighter pilots were "a breed apart from the others who fought the war, because they fought alone. They flew in the company of others, but when the bullets flew they were alone, facing another lone enemy in a contest that was likely a duel from which only one would emerge."

Lilya Litvyak emerged from enough of those duels to call herself an ace, and to call herself an ace twice over. This is her story, the story of a young woman barely old enough not to be called a schoolgirl, who rose from obscurity to accept the challenge of her times to become a warrior.

There is no better way to conclude this introduction to the life and turbulent times of an exceptional woman warrior than with a paraphrased excerpt from a work by one of her most celebrated countrymen, the great Russian novelist Count Leo Nikolayevich Tolstoy.

This selection, from *The Cossacks, Sevastopol, the Invaders and Other Stories*, is as Tolstoy wrote it, but with the gender-specific words changed. That done, few descriptions better characterize the young women aviators of Lilya Litvyak's generation:

Tomorrow, today, it may be, each one of these women will go cheerfully and proudly to meet her death, and she will die with firmness and composure; but the one consolation of life in these conditions, which terrify even the coldest imagination in the absence of all that is human, and the hopelessness of any escape from them—the one consolation is forgetfulness, the annihilation of consciousness.

At the bottom of the soul of each lies that noble spark, which makes of her a hero; but this spark wearies of burning clearly—when the fateful moment comes it flashes up into a flame, and illuminates great deeds.

# Prologue

The white cumulus billows against a deep blue sky. The landscape alternates between small, cultivated fields and open meadows, and the slightly rolling hills are ablaze with multicolored wild flowers. The country here could easily be mistaken for many places across the United States, from Missouri to South Dakota in the Midwest, or somewhere along the Deschutes River in north central Oregon.

A meandering family of streams flows gently through the woods in the broad ravine that clings to the eastern outskirts the village of Dmytrivka. The woods are cool and inviting, and the slowly gurgling waters seem to be in no particular hurry to join those of countless sister streams across this vast watershed that feeds the great Volga River.

It is a peaceful summer day in 1979 in the rolling rural countryside in the Shakhtarskyy region at the eastern edge of the Donetsk Oblast, at the eastern edge of Ukraine. It seems a million miles from Moscow, where Soviet Premier Leonid Brezhnev and Alexei Kosygin, the Chairman of the Council of Ministers, are fiddling with the Soviet Union's Tenth Five-Year Plan in the midst of a period of economic stagnation. The Plan is set to expire in 1980, which is still a year away, but already, the Eleventh is on the drawing boards. They are also beginning to plot their ill-considered invasion of Afghanistan, which will get underway by the end of the year. But out here in eastern Ukraine, everything is as peaceful as it has been for decades.

However, there are still people living around here who remember different times—very different times. They remember 1941. It was in September, even before the leaves on these trees had fully acquiesced to change their cloaks from summer green to autumn gold, that the invaders came. They came amid the grinding noise of tanks and the snarl of aircraft engines in the sky. They swept through Dmytrivka, and eastward for more than a hundred miles.

They came as soldiers in feldgrau uniforms and stayed on as *Einsatzgruppen*, the vicious cadres in uniforms of SS black, who were charged with remaking the Ukraine. The plan, as articulated by their Führer in Berlin, was to sweep away the Slavic people, whom the man in Berlin considered to be less than human, to replace them with German colonists, and remake Ukraine as the breadbasket—and the coal mine—of his Third Reich.

In 1941, Dmytrivka, also called Dmytriyevka, also seemed a million miles from Moscow, where Josef Stalin and his coterie of commissars were more preoccupied with the survival of Moscow, itself then being besieged by the German armies, and of the Soviet Union itself.

In December that year, as in Decembers before and since, the snow began to come to stay, and it grew cold. In the north, the Germans continued to move, albeit at a much slowed pace, toward Moscow. In the Ukraine, however, the Red Army counterattacked, and by the first week of December, Dmytrivka had the dubious distinction of being on the front lines of a static battlefront. In July 1942, once again, the great tide of war swept over and consumed Dmytrivka, bringing it again under the banner of the crooked cross. And so it would remain until the great Soviet offensives of early 1943 restored its unenviable status as a frontline place raked continuously by the guns and bombs of both sides.

For two years, from the autumn of 1941 through that of 1943, it was rarely possible to stand in the muddy streets of Dmytrivka, or in the muddy furrows on the surrounding hills, and not be able to hear the sounds of war, nor see the black columns of smoke rising in the near distance.

Each year, the streams meandering though the woods, and the great Volga itself, deposit layers of sediment in their respective flood plains, which can be viewed in cross-section to understand the passing of seasons and years. So it was with the terrain on the hills and in the fields surrounding Dmytrivka during the war. Each time an army swept through, from the east or from the west, it deposited a layer consisting of the detritus of war: shell casings, unexploded ordnance, wrecked machinery, downed aircraft, and human bodies.

In the exigencies of war, it is not uncommon throughout history that fallen soldiers would be buried where they fell. Sometimes they were buried singly and reverently in well-marked graves. Sometimes, it would be necessary to bury the dead anonymously, in the company of others, in mass graves.

After September 1943, the German invaders were finally swept out of the Shakhtarskyy region and out of the Donetsk Oblast. Eventually, they were swept beyond the northern and western borders of Ukraine and back to where they came. It was now possible, as it still is to this day, to stand on the streets and the hills and in the fields and gaze upon a limitless landscape of wildflowers, or a limitless blanket of snow, and hear only the sounds of the birds and the wind.

Yet beneath the snow, beneath the flowers, and beneath the rich black earth which made Adolf Hitler covet Ukraine, there lay in the successive layers of 1941, 1942, and 1943, all the artifacts of those battles which comprised the bloodiest war in human history.

Gradually, over time, the layers of shells—live, dud, and expended—were mostly peeled back and taken away by disposal experts. The burned-out hulks of abandoned tanks were dragged off as scrap metal, and the crumpled remains of downed airplanes were picked up.

So, too, were the human bodies exhumed from where they lay, and efforts were made to use dental records to identify the dead. As was the case on countless battlefields across the world, most of the unknowns who were taken from unmarked graves in later years remained unknown.

By 1979, more than three decades of winter snow and spring thaw had come and gone in eastern Ukraine since it was raked by war. Most of the rusty machinery was long since gone, and most of the mass graves had been located and marked as such. Of course, just as artifacts are still found at battlefields dating from antiquity, it can safely be said that some of the artifacts left in the layers of Ukrainian earth marking the years of the Great Patriotic War will continue to turn up; all of them will never be found.

On a warm summer day in 1979, though, a particular grave was found.

Looking back on this day, as more decades have come and gone, and the mists of myths drift into the legends, there are stories. Some say that the body was found accidently by children playing. Other stories say that it was found by people who had deliberately sought this particular grave for all those decades. Some say that it was near a piece of twisted metal barely visible above a sea of wildflowers, and some say that a name had been written on the fragment of what looked like a propeller.

All the stories converge on the identity of this small, definitely female, body.

Lidiya Vladimirovna Litvyak had last been seen in the skies over the Shakhtarskyy region of the Donetsk Oblast in eastern Ukraine on August 1, 1943. She had been seen last in the clouds, and in battle.

During summer afternoons, great mountains of cumulus boil up from the vast plains of Russia and the Ukraine, and it was within those clouds that Lilya was last seen. Her comrades saw her battling a Messerschmitt, and then they didn't. Suddenly there was a glimpse of her aircraft, then another. And then she was gone.

She vanished as though into thin air.

Beneath Lilya and her comrades that day was the great, titanic push by the Red Army, which would eject the invaders from this part of Ukraine. Lilya had fallen into a battlefield. Whatever was to happen in later years in the field where she fell, it is well known that those thirty-six years began with a week of massive of death and destruction.

The body was recovered, identified as that of Lilya Litvyak. Perhaps it is Lilya, and perhaps it is not, but it remains identified as such.

The important thing about the discovery of the remains of the small woman with the gold filling in her teeth is that after thirty-six years, Lilya is no longer officially listed as "missing in action."

*Chapter 1*

# BORN INTO A SEASON OF DARKNESS AND PROMISES

The little girl whose parents named Lidiya but called Lilya or Lil'ka was born into a chaotic epoch, and into a land racked by violence, war, revolution, and famine. It was a time of immense upheaval in which an established order, entrenched for three centuries, was overthrown by forces that were unique to history in the scale of what they did and what they brought into being.

Also born into this turbulent time was Aleksandr Solzhenitsyn, the renowned chronicler of this period in Russian history. Recalling that it was also a season of grand promises, he wrote of his and Lilya's generation that "we marched in the ranks of those born the year[s] the Revolution took place, and because we were the same age as the Revolution, the brightest of futures lay ahead."

Within the darkness, there were promises.

The Russian Empire that had been ruled by the Tsars of the Romanov Dynasty since 1613 crumbled, fragmented, and finally coalesced into an entity unlike any that had existed on such a scale before. It was that place that nationalist Vasily Shulgin would call "a form of state with no name."

It all began early in 1917, and when it ended nearly six years later when Lilya was barely a year old, the vast empire was unrecognizable as the state into which her parents had been born.

After humiliating defeats by the Germans in World War I and a general economic collapse, Tsar Nicholas II abdicated in March 1917. In November of that year, the ensuing provisional government was itself overthrown by a band of determined revolutionaries called Bolsheviks, in the tidal wave of the October Revolution (so named because Russia still used the old style Julian calendar until 1918). By the color of the Bolshevik banner, it was a red tide. Though they quickly renamed themselves the Communist Party, the name "Bolshevik" lingered for some time, especially in Western media. Their other, obvious nickname, "Reds," lingered even longer.

The message of the Bolsheviks, gleaned from *The Communist Manifesto* of Karl Marx, resonated with the proletariat, the working class. They were the workers and peasants who had been most abused under the Tsarist system and who would fight the hardest to put the Bolsheviks into power. "Workers of the world unite," Marx said. "You have nothing to lose but your chains."

Under the red banner of the Bolsheviks, a proletariat with nothing to lose toppled an oligarchy with everything to lose.

However, just as there had been an almost universal desire within the Russian Empire to be rid of the Tsar, there was no universal fondness for the Bolsheviks. Almost immediately after the Bolshevik Red Army seized power in 1917, they were challenged on all sides by a host of anti-Red factions—from capitalists to former monarchists to fellow revolutionaries—who coalesced under the banner of the "White Army," plunging the former Russian Empire into yet another round of bloodshed, a bitter and bloody civil war.

# BORN INTO A SEASON OF DARKNESS AND PROMISES

On December 30, 1922, as the Red Army was wrapping up its victory over the disunified Whites, the "state with no name" was named. The Communists called their new empire the Soyuz Sovetskikh Sotsialisticheskikh Respublik (SSSR), or in the Cyrillic alphabet, CCCP, meaning the Union of Soviet Socialist Republics (USSR). The "republics" were the former dominions of the Tsar, which were not liberated but merely folded into a new empire. The largest of the dominions, Russia itself, became the Russian Soviet Federative Socialist Republic (RSFSR).

Through all of this Revolution and Civil War, the crumbling, fragmenting and coalescing was generously marinated in oceans of mostly Russian blood. As military historian Grigoriy Krivosheyev writes in *Soviet Casualties and Combat Losses in the Twentieth Century*, there were 6.1 million Russian casualties in World War I (1914–17), and almost 2.7 million in the Civil War that followed the Revolution. This is not to mention those who died in the Revolution itself, or millions more who died of disease, starvation, and wholesale murder.

As millions died during those six years, so too were millions born. In this generation, along with Lilya Vladimirovna Litvyak and Aleksandr Isayevich Solzhenitsyn, were the millions who would grow up to be the young people who would make up the nineteen through twenty-four age group in 1941, the year that the Soviet Union entered the Great Patriotic War.

They were a generation born into chaos but who grew up with the promise that the brightest of futures lay ahead. They were promised that when the Tsar, the old nobility, and the landed gentry had been overthrown, and the chains of oppression had been cast off, a new world would emerge and that it would be a paradise for the workers and peasants.

Vladimir Litvyak and Anna Vasil'yevna Kunavin were in their late teens when the Revolution shook their homeland, and they believed in the promises. As indentured peasants working for a Russian nobleman on his farm about 50 miles northwest of the center of Moscow, they and their families were ready for anything that represented a change.

For most peasants living the lives of medieval serfs, the promises of the Revolution were like shafts of brilliant light illuminating the future. The future parents of Lilya Litvyak saw this light, and they believed.

For a moment, it seemed to be a dream come true, a dream that had been dreamed by drawing room and coffee shop revolutionaries since well before Karl Marx published *The Communist Manifesto* in 1848—but this dream come true was literally a dream, and only a dream. The promise into which Aleksandr and Lilya and the millions of others were born was an illusion. It was more like one of the stories in the tradition of Russian fairy tales than something that the Reds would be able to deliver.

To begin with, the Bolshevik leadership consisted mainly of men who were not, nor ever had been, either workers or peasants. They had no idea what it was like to toil in field or factory, or to work at a trade.

Their leader was a charismatic professional revolutionary named Vladimir Ilyich Ulyanov, who had changed his name to "Lenin" in 1902. He had grown up a member of the privileged middle class, his father an educator who had risen to a prominent place in the Tsar's bureaucracy. Lenin himself earned a law degree rather than pursuing a trade, and was a member of the well-to-do class of campus revolutionaries whose concern for the workers and peasants was an abstraction, pursued initially almost as a hobby.

Lenin and the Bolsheviks were men who were long on theoretical abstractions and short on practical experience. When they won their Revolution and were faced with having to put their abstractions into practice, they turned to the Marxist dogma that had provided the theoretical underpinnings of the Revolution.

Even as the Civil War was still raging, the Bolsheviks imposed a sweeping regime of nationalization and state control called "War Communism." Under War Communism, private property and private enterprise were banned and all industry was nationalized. Those who had supported the Revolution's aims of seizing the vast estates of the landed gentry were surprised to find that the state seized everything—including the surpluses from the peasants.

In explaining this, Lenin said that "the confiscation of surpluses from the peasants was a measure with which we were saddled by the imperative conditions of war-time," suggesting that it was imposed as a wartime expediency. Fellow revolutionary and party elitist Nikolai Bukharin clarified this by remarking that "we conceived War Communism as the universal, so to say 'normal' form of the economic policy of the victorious proletariat and not as being related to the war, that is, conforming to a definite state of the Civil War."

Vladimir and Anna had nothing, much less anything to confiscate. They had nothing to lose but their chains, and the Bolsheviks had made good on that promise.

The more substantial promises were harder to fulfill. For the peasants in the field, War Communism didn't work. It was like trying to turn a fairy tale into reality. Agricultural production imploded to 60 percent of prewar levels, producing a famine in which as many as 10 million people died. Having liberated the rural peasants from their virtual enslavement by the Tsarist landowners, the Bolsheviks quickly made steps to reenslave them by confiscating their produce.

Beginning in 1918, Solzhenitsyn writes, "the countryside, which had already been strained to the utmost limits, gave up its harvest year after year without compensation. This led to peasant revolts and, in the upshot, suppression of the revolts and new arrests."

Author and humanist Vladimir Galaktionovich Korolenko watched this happen and observed that "the hardest-working sector of the nation was positively uprooted." A longtime critic of the Tsars, a disillusioned Korolenko had turned the animosity of his pen to the Bolsheviks amid the postrevolutionary repressions.

That to which Korolenko and Solzhenitsyn refer was a series of revolts by the peasantry against the Bolsheviks, notably those that unfolded in the Tambov region south of Moscow in 1920 and 1921. These were brutally suppressed by a Red Army contingent under Mikhail Nikolayevich Tukhachevsky, who utilized poison gas against the peasants.

As Solzhenitsyn writes, "throughout the province concentration camps were set up for the families of peasants who had taken part in the revolts. Tracts of open field were enclosed with barbed wire strung on posts, and for three weeks every family of a suspected rebel was confined there. If within that time the man of the family did not turn up to buy his family's way out with his own head, they sent the family into exile."

As his source, Solzhenitsyn cites Tukhachevsky's own article, "Borba s Kontrrevolyutsionnymi Vostaniyami" ("The Struggle Against Counterrevolutionary Revolts"), in the summer 1926 issue of *Voina i Revolyutsiya* (*War and Revolution*).

While things were bad in the countryside, they soon grew even worse in the cities. For the workers in the factories, War Communism didn't work. Industrial output fell to just 20 percent of prewar levels, overall factory production to 10 percent, and coal production to barely 3 percent. The urban working class who had supported the Revolution's promise of a workers' paradise were surprised when the state announced that strikers would be shot.

Forced labor sounded more like the feudalism that had allegedly been overthrown than paradise.

An exodus of urbanites suddenly abandoned the cities to find employment in the economically devastated countryside. The population of Moscow had increased from around a million at the turn of the century to nearly 2 million on the eve of World War I, but declined by half during the Civil War.

In the turbulent aftermath of overturning the Tsar, things grew only worse. In *A Tale of Two Cities*, Charles Dickens writes of the period following the French Revolution that "It was the best of times, it was the worst of times … it was the Season of Light, it was the Season of Darkness."

For Russia after her Revolution, it was simply the worst of times.

Of Russia's season of darkness, historian and longtime Soviet insider Dmitri Volkogonov reminds us that the words "dislocation, desolation, starvation," do not do justice to "the degree of the shock, the deformation and the shattered state of society that existed at the beginning of the 1920s. Russia was a vast revolutionary island in a sea of hostile states. The country was convulsed as whole provinces and districts openly rebelled against or passively resisted the new order. The revolution had won, it had survived and consolidated the power of the Soviets, but the new regime could still do almost nothing for the workers and peasants."

Vladimir Litvyak and Anna Vasil'yevna Kunavin were married in 1918, their peasant wedding a bright moment within the Season of Darkness. No matter how dismal things were during the convulsions and famine of the Civil War years, the young couple maintained optimism about their future. They had grown up as virtual slaves, and now they were free.

Loosed from their bonds to the rural earth, they relocated to Moscow. With the old landlords suddenly gone and peasants denied ownership of the soil they once had tilled, there was nothing for them in the place where they had been born. They saw only promise in the great city.

Vladimir and Anna were lucky. They found themselves in the right place at the right time. Their arrival in Moscow just as a million citizens were abandoning the city actually worked to their advantage. Thanks to the declining urban population, they were able to find both employment and housing. They procured a tiny apartment, and Vladimir took a part time factory job. To help make ends meet, he worked nights as a railway clerk. Anna worked on and off in a retail shop in Moscow.

Finally, on March 21, 1921, when Anna was about three months pregnant with Lilya, Soviet leaders finally retreated from the failure of their earlier interpretation of pure Marxism. Lenin unveiled the *Novaya Ekonomicheskaya Politika* or New Economic Policy (NEP). While government would still retain ownership of banks and major industries, as well as foreign trade, the NEP opened the door a crack to allow limited private ownership of small businesses.

On the first day of 1922, when the Soviets also introduced a new, more stable currency, Vladimir and Anna were among those who lined up to trade 10,000 of their 1919 rubles for each of the new ones.

Foreign investment was now encouraged, a circumstance which greatly affected the aviation industry, a component of Soviet commerce that would play a role in Lilya's later life.

Having essentially ground to a halt during the Civil War and its aftermath, Soviet aviation received a jumpstart in 1923 when the German firm owned by Hugo Junkers cut a deal with the Soviet government to open a factory at Fili, near Moscow, to produce three hundred aircraft annually. Though this project never fulfilled its potential, it did bring advanced aviation technology into the Soviet Union.

In turn, the familiar German company BMW began manufacturing aircraft engines in the Soviet Union in 1924, and Germans were imported to help train Soviet military aviators. As with the Junkers operation, the Soviet skilled labor working in these ventures became part of a new generation of Soviet aviation innovation.

As Lilya was opening her eyes to the world, the Soviet economy, under the NEP, slowly retreated from the precipice of disaster as the men within the new Bolshevik oligarchy maneuvered among themselves for control of the Soviet state.

Emerging as the most powerful of Lenin's cohorts were two men who, like Lenin, were professional revolutionaries rather than workers or peasants. Also like Lenin, neither of them used the name with which he had been born. Lev Davidovich Bronshtein was a Ukrainian with a fiery and eloquent tongue who changed his name to "Leon Trotsky." The other man was a moody Georgian who had been born Ioseb (Josef) Besarionis Dze Jughashvili (in Russian, Iosif Vissarionovich Dzhugashvili). He changed his surname to "Stalin," because it is the Russian word for "steel." He wanted to be known— in Russian, tellingly, not in his native Georgian—as the "Man of Steel."

The internal struggle to succeed Lenin began sooner than anyone had expected. In 1922, Lenin was on top of the world politically, but he was fighting a losing battle against a revolution inside his own body. Two strokes suffered in 1922 left him haggard and partially paralyzed. A third in March 1923 left him a mute invalid.

Lenin had envisioned a power-sharing arrangement among his successors, but each star in the galaxy of would-be red Tsars imagined himself as the one. Trotsky and Stalin became the leading contenders, and the most bitter of rivals in their contention for the top job.

In January 1924, when Lilya Litvyak was just two and a half, Lenin died and Stalin made his move. Among all the men in the upper echelons of the Bolshevik oligarchy, Stalin was the most single-mindedly assiduous about consolidating his power. Long before Trotsky was finally forced into permanent foreign exile in 1929, Stalin's face became that of the party and of the Soviet Union.

Lilya took her first steps in Moscow, the epicenter of climactic moments in the Revolution and the seat of power, both for the Tsars and for the new Soviet rulers who succeeded them. Around the time that Lilya was taking those first steps, she and her young family moved to the apartment house at Number 88 Novoslobodskaya Street, about a mile west of the Kremlin, where she would grow up.

The narrow world of Lilya Litvyak and her younger brother, Yuriy, was sheltered from the madness of the Civil War and its disastrous economic aftermath. The shooting that reverberated in these streets during the Revolution had long since died away. The little girl with the big ribbon in her blonde hair, such as was the favored style for young Russian girls, looked out her window at an outside world which at least appeared peaceful.

In the comfort of their home, Lilya's first daydreams took shape to the sweet sound of her mother's voice. Lilya's *mamochka* sang her the songs and spun the fairy tales that had comforted her in her own childhood. These now served as the first building blocks of Lilya's imagination.

When Anna Vasil'yevna was a little girl, she heard from her own mother the stories such as that of "Vasilisa the Beautiful," and she shared these tales with little Lilya. Vasilisa was a self-confident girl who faced and overcame serial adversity and triumphed. Ingenious and resourceful, she was unafraid to face the darkest shadows that lurked in a cruel world. In the legend of a mythical heroine, there is an allegory for the heroine that Lilya would become.

As the story goes, Vasilisa was barely eight years old when her mother died. Her father, a merchant, married a woman (coincidentally named Lilya) with two daughters.

As with the stepmother and stepsisters in tales such as *Cinderella* with which we in the West are more familiar, Vasilisa's new family members were spiteful and mean to her, in part because she was unrelated, but mainly because she was beautiful, and the jealous stepsisters were not. All the while, though, Vasilisa had been comforted by a small wooden doll that had been given to her by her late mother.

Aleksandr Afanasyev, the nineteenth-century folklorist who became the Russian equivalent of the Brothers Grimm for his eight-volume anthology *Narodnye Russkie Skazki* (*Russian Fairy Tales*), interpreted the symbolism as peasants having created tales personifying nature. Storms and dark clouds were represented by the wicked stepmother and stepsisters, while Vasilisa herself was the brightness of sunlight.

One day, when Vasilisa's father failed to return from a long trip, the stepmother sold the family home and took everyone to live in a shack in a dark forest. The stepmother then extinguished all the fires and candles, and sent Vasilisa to obtain fire from the home of an old woman named Baba Yaga, an old woman sometimes portrayed as a witch, who is a recurring archetype in so much of Slavic folklore.

Guided by her doll, Vasilisa went into the dark woods, where she was passed by two horsemen, one dressed in white and one dressed in red. As night fell, a black rider passed her just as she reached a house surrounded by human skeletons. This was the home of Baba Yaga.

When Vasilisa asked for the fire, the old woman demanded that the girl complete a series of household chores under threat of being eaten. Aided by the magical doll who cleaned while Vasilisa cooked, the tasks were completed from top to bottom. Vasilisa said her prayers and went to sleep, but more chores were assigned the following day, and again they were satisfactorily completed.

When the girl asked the old woman about the three horsemen whom she was seeing each day, Baba Yaga explained that the white rider personified dawn, the red man the sun, and the black rider was the night.

Finally, when Baba Yaga asked by what magic Vasilisa had accomplished all the tasks, the girl answered that "my mother's blessing helped me," by which she meant the doll that her mother had given her. The witch replied that "I want no blessed daughters near me! Your mother's blessing hurts my very bones!"

Angry with competition from the sacred insinuation of the blessing, she sent Vasilisa away, giving her a human skull with fire glowing magically in its eye sockets.

When Vasilisa returned to her stepmother's house, she found her and the two stepsisters sitting in the darkness, for no light would burn there since Vasilisa had gone away. Frightened by the skull, they ran away, but the skull pursued them, its burning, vindictive eyes locked upon them until they caught fire and burned to ash.

Vasilisa buried the skull, and accompanied by her doll, she returned to her original home, where she was reunited with her father. In a later story, Vasilisa became a weaver, impressed the Tsar, and married him.

In the version Anna Vasil'yevna told to Lilya, there was no Tsar.

Like the Bolsheviks, Baba Yaga made promises but demanded servitude. After all was said and done, though, it was the perseverance and bravery of the young heroine herself that ultimately prevailed.

## Chapter 2

# GROWING UP WITH THE MAN IN RED

In the wake of the country's Civil War, the symbolism of the red and white horsemen in the story of Vasilisa had to have had conspicuous meaning, at least for the mothers telling the stories. Anna Vasil'yevna, being the wife of a good Bolshevik man, surely would have noticed this. The horseman in black could be interpreted any number of ways, but to paraphrase Aleksandr Solzhenitsyn, the man in red was the son who could always be counted upon to brighten that brightest of futures which lay ahead.

For Lilya Litvyak, growing up amid the red banners and the monumental posters, there was no doubt as to the identity of the man in red who would brighten the future. His was the face which shone down like the sun from those monumental posters: Josef Stalin.

Listening to the old stories, updated in their telling by a politically aware mother, was part of Lilya's childhood. It was an integral part of life for a generation growing up in a world in which everything was being updated for them by the politically aware—and this included what children such as Lilya would learn in school.

By the time Lilya started school, the Soviet education system had more or less recovered from a disastrous cycle of misguided social experimentation that had wreaked the same level of havoc as War Communism had on the Soviet economy. Before that, however, the education system had collapsed along with everything else that the Tsars had built. During the Revolution and Civil War, the schools, like all Tsarist institutions, had simply ceased to function.

In his 1933 book *Russia USSR: A Complete Handbook*, William Farquhar Payson reported that in 1914, on the eve of World War I, 91 percent of Russian children were attending school. After the Revolution, school attendance dropped to 62 percent in 1918 and 49 percent in 1919.

Recognizing this as a serious problem, Lenin initiated his Likbez program in December 1919. Short for *Likvidatsiya Bezgramotnosti* (Liquidation of Illiteracy), Likbez was aimed more at illiterate adults up to age thirty-five, but it also paid lip service to school-age children. Eventually the project was successful, but in 1920, its first year, adult literacy actually fell from 49 percent to a pitiful 25 percent. By comparison, according to the National Center for Education Statistics, adult literacy in the United States stood at 92 percent in 1910 and 94 percent in 1920, and 97 and 98 percent respectively for nonforeign-born Americans. According to the economic historian Dr. Roger Schofield, as cited by Gregory Clark of the University of California, the literacy rates in the United Kingdom were on par with those in the United States.

Literacy rates did not finally surpass the last year of Tsarist rule for a decade. In Imperial Russia, literacy had increased from 28.4 percent in 1897 to 56 percent in 1916. Sheila Fitzpatrick, citing census data in her book *Stalin's Peasants*, writes that it was only in 1926 that the literacy rate was finally back up to 56.6 percent. Meanwhile, Peter Kenez, writing in *The Birth of the Propaganda State*, puts the 1926 figure at only 51 percent.

He also points out that Likbez was dogged by budget constraints, and that its portion of the total education budget fell from 2.8 percent in 1924–25 to 1.6 percent in 1927–28.

The Bolsheviks created their People's Commissariat for Education almost as an afterthought, attaching it to their Commissariat of Culture. The well-educated son of an educator, Lenin perhaps took education for granted.

To oversee education in the Soviet Union, the Bolsheviks chose Anatoly Lunacharsky, who was given the bombastic, and almost humorous, title of "Commissar of Enlightenment (Narkompros)." Lunacharsky was a journalist and art critic, not an educator, although he had taught briefly at a school for socialist workers on the Italian resort island of Capri before moving to Paris, where he had organized a brandy and biscuits salon for intellectual revolutionaries, which he called the "Circle of Proletarian Culture."

Lunacharsky's primary qualification for official office seems to have been that he knew the prolific author Alexei Maximovich Peshkov, aka Maxim Gorky, who helped found the Socialist Realism literary style and who was the favorite author of the Soviet elite. The fact that the commissariat accomplished anything at all with regard to education was thanks to Lunacharsky's deputy commissar, Nadezhda Krupskaya, the wife of Vladimir Lenin, who had actually been active in the education field before becoming a revolutionary.

Commissariats were the equivalent of ministries in European governments or cabinet departments in the United States, but in the Soviet government, the term "commissar" was used instead of "minister" because Leon Trotsky thought that the latter term sounded too "bourgeois." Instead of a "cabinet," the Soviet Union had a Council of People's Commissars, or Soviet Narodnykh Kommissarov, which was called "Sovnarkom" for short. The term "ministry" was not adopted by the Soviet government until 1946.

The schools to which students returned after the long years of war and Revolution were now called Uniform Labor Schools. There were no more private schools or specialized schools, only the homogeny of the standardized state schools.

Of course, there were no more religious schools, either. Just as the Bolsheviks eliminated rival political parties, they greatly curtailed religious activities. There could be no other ideology than that of the Bolsheviks to distract the loyalties of the Soviet people. The Russian Orthodox Church survived, but just barely, and without authorization for schools.

The curriculum at the Uniform Labor Schools had been heavily overhauled to "decontaminate" it of Tsarist influences. Under the system established in 1923, even the old bourgeois subjects of reading, writing, and arithmetic were discarded, along with history, geography, and science. These were superseded by such complex integrated subjects as "the life and labor of the family in village and town," which was taught to eight-year-olds, or "scientific organization of labor," the course of study at age fourteen.

This impractical abandonment of basic education ran into problems that might well have been predicted, such as children not learning to read, nor able to do basic arithmetic. In turn, this led to the abandonment of the experiment itself by 1928. Just as the Soviet state had superseded the strict measures of the War Communism for the more pragmatic New Economic Policy in 1921, the state now retreated from their abortive experiment in education. By the time Lilya Litvyak entered school in 1929 at the age of eight, the Soviet curriculum had readopted reading, writing, and arithmetic as credible subjects.

School attendance was now theoretically compulsory, with a primary section for ages eight through thirteen, and a secondary section for ages fourteen through seventeen. However, the number of schools for the upper section was limited, especially outside the cities, so it would be a number of years before students older than thirteen were certain of completing the required course of study.

Students who made it through a full seven years had the option of going on to a *professionalno-tehnicheskoye uchilishche* (professional technical school) or a *technicum* (vocational school), where they would be trained for technical and low-level managerial jobs. If a student made it through nine years of schooling, he or she would then be eligible to attend a university.

According to the statistical journal *Narodnoe Obrazovanie, Nauka i Nul'tura v SSSR* (*Soviet Public Education, Science and Culture*), there were 8 million children in primary schools in 1929 when Lilya first went to class, and 3 million in secondary schools.

And then there were afterschool activities.

When she turned seven, Lilya became an *Oktyabryata* (Little Oktoberist), the first step in a young person's career in the Soviet equivalent of scouting.

Scouting had started in Russia in 1909, not long after Robert Baden-Powell founded the Boy Scouts in England, and the first Girl Scouts organization had been formed in Russia in 1910. But because the Russian scouting movement was tainted by the enthusiastic support of Tsar Nicholas II, and because many scoutmasters had sided with the Whites during the Civil War, the Bolsheviks eliminated the scouting movement altogether.

However, while scouting was eliminated for younger children, a Communist youth organization for people in their mid to late teens was formed in 1918. Called the *Kommunisticheskii Soyuz Molodyozhi* (Communist Union of Youth), it was universally known as the "Komsomol." While it was basically a political organization, the Komsomol was also seen as a means of diverting teenagers from the pitfalls of "hooliganism," and involvement in such harmful vices as smoking and drinking—and religion.

The absence of a program analogous to scouting for younger children was noted by Nadezhda Krupskaya at the Commissariat of Education. She recognized the value of creating a Communist children's organization based structurally on scouting, and advocated this in her 1922 essay titled "Russian Union of the Communist Youth and Boy-Scoutism."

In May 1922, the *Vsesoyuznaya Pionerskaya Organizatsiya* (All-Union Pioneer Organization) was created. Children from the age of ten to fifteen were eligible to become Young Pioneers. Unlike scouting, the program was to be co-ed, but aside from this, there were many similarities to scouting, from uniforms and special songs to sports and summer camps.

Children from ages seven to nine were eligible for the precursor to the Young Pioneers, and became Little Oktoberists, so named because when the program began, the first to join had been born in the same year as the October Revolution.

Having become a Little Oktoberist in 1928, Lilya was part of a small cell of five children. Under the watchful eye of a Young Pioneer, the children played and sang, danced traditional dances, learned to share in a communal way, and aspired to become Young Pioneers, just as the Young Pioneers would later aspire to become Komsomolyets and Komsomolkas.

Meanwhile, the consolidation of complete Soviet state control over education under the commissariat for education was a microcosm of what was being planned for all facets of the Soviet economy and Soviet society as Lilya was entering school.

The NEP had done what Lenin needed it to do: It had forestalled the collapse of the Soviet state even before it was officially declared. However, the NEP had not done what Stalin wanted to be done within the Soviet state. The empire the Reds had inherited from the Tsars was arguably the most backward major country in the world. Stalin's vision was to reshape the Soviet Union into a world economic power, a robust showcase of Marxist theory transformed into shining reality—and he wanted to do this as rapidly as possible.

In October 1928, shortly after Lilya became an Oktyabryata, Stalin unveiled the First Five Year Plan, a scheme designed to redirect the entire Soviet economy toward the rapid industrialization of what had heretofore been an agrarian economy.

The NEP had seen its day, Stalin decided. His Five Year Plan could succeed only by bringing the economy fully under strict state control. While the focus was on heavy industry, building giant factories, and goals such as doubling steel production, the Five Year Plan had tangible results, which Lilya and her family noticed close to home. The merchant at the corner store where Lilya's mother now worked was now merely another underpaid employee of the government. And he was not alone. Others were soon finding themselves under the thumb of the government as well.

As historian Sheila Fitzpatrick writes, Stalin's objective "was to lay the economic foundations for socialism by rooting out private enterprise and using state planning to promote rapid economic development. In the towns, private trade and private businesses were closed down. The state took over distribution as part of a new system of centralized state economic planning that was vastly ambitious but poorly thought out. Planning was seen in heroic terms as the conquest of hitherto uncontrollable economic forces."

As for the ultimate result of the Five Year Plan, it did eventually increase Soviet industrial output. However, it decimated the already struggling Soviet agricultural economy, creating vast food shortages. Soviet leaders, most of whom had never even been to a farm, much less worked on one, could not resist the urge to control the whole agricultural infrastructure of the world's largest country as a single unified entity.

The Five Year Plan had called for all of the farmland of the Soviet Union to be brought under centralized government control. The farms were all to be consolidated as *sovkhozy* (Soviet state farms) or *kolkhozy* (collective farms).

In order to collectivize Soviet agriculture, and indeed to bring the economy as a whole under his control, Stalin had circumvented an entire class of people, the middle-class farmers, who were called *kulaks*. He also skirted the way of doing business for both the kulaks and those to whom they sold their produce.

Back in 1906, Pyotr Stolypin, the prime minister under Tsar Nicholas II had begun a program of private ownership of farms by former serfs, with an eye toward creating a system of family farms such as had existed in the United States since before it became the United States. When the Tsar was overthrown, the Bolsheviks fixated upon these individual farmers, the kulaks, who were now being derided as "rich peasants."

With the nobility and the big landowners having been overthrown, the Bolsheviks needed an enemy upon which to focus the wrath of the proletariat. If the paradise of the workers and peasants was slow to materialize, it had to be someone's fault. That someone was the kulak.

In his 1918 missive *Comrade Workers, Forward to the Last, Decisive Fight!* Vladimir Lenin had referred to kulaks as "bloodsuckers, vampires, plunderers of the people and profiteers, who fatten on famine."

Stalin would be even less charitable in his attitude toward these middle-class entrepreneurs.

Solzhenitsyn explains cynically that "in Russian, a *kulak* is a miserly, dishonest rural trader who grows rich not by his own labor but through someone else's, through usury and operating as a middleman. In every locality even before the Revolution such kulaks could be numbered on one's fingers. And the Revolution totally destroyed their basis of activity. Subsequently, after 1917, by a transfer of meaning, the name kulak began to be applied (in official and propaganda literature, whence it moved into general usage) to all those who in any way hired workers, even if it was only when they were temporarily short of working hands in their own families."

For the Bolsheviks, the kulaks, or anyone identified as such, were an obstacle that was wrapped in an opportunity. Just as the Revolution had fixated on the notion of overthrowing the rich landowner, the rich banker, or whomever, the kulaks could now be manufactured into convenient targets against whom the state could direct the wrath of the masses as they mobilized the population to support the new concept of the Five Year Plan.

Just as tales like that of Vasilisa needed a wicked stepmother as a villain, Stalin need a bugaboo, a villain to frighten his people into action. If the kulaks had never existed, the Soviet state would have found someone else to use as a lightning rod.

"Dekulakization" became a priority for Stalin, and under the Five Year Plan, the clock was turned back to the days of serfdom.

Lilya Litvyak grew up hearing her parents mention kulaks, but by the time that she was old enough to comprehend who these "criminals" were, they had largely been eradicated from Soviet society.

To eradicate such problems in Soviet society, the man in red revealed his darker side. To force compliance with the decrees required for implementation of the Five Year Plan, Stalin had the able, though terrifying, support of the dreaded Soviet secret police. As early as 1917, Lenin had realized the necessity of having a contingent of enforcers at his beck and call, and he had created the *Chrezvychaynaya Komissiya*, the Extraordinary Commission for Combatting Counter-revolution and Sabotage), a state secret police force. Known by the acronym Cheka, this precursor to the dreaded KGB was headed by the sadistic aristocrat turned communist, Felix Edmundovich Dzerzhinsky, whom Bolshevik revolutionary and future editor-in-chief of *Pravda*, Nikolai Bukharin, called "the proletarian Jacobin."

Bolshevik theorist and Lenin supplicant Karl Radek later observed that "our enemies invented an entire legend about the all-seeing eye of the Cheka, the all-hearing ears of the Cheka and the ubiquitous Dzerzhinsky. They depicted the Cheka as an enormous army, covering the whole country and penetrating its own camp with its tentacles [which it was]. They did not understand the source of Dzerzhinsky's strength. It derived from the strength of the Bolshevik party, namely the total trust of the working masses and the poor."

Total fear was more like it.

In 1922, the Lenin-era Cheka became the Russian State Political Directorate or *Gosudarstvennoye Politicheskoye Upravlenie* (GPU), which in turn became the USSR-wide Joint State Political Directorate or *Ob'edinennoe Gosudarstvennoe Politicheskoe Upravlenie* (OGPU) in 1923. In the Russian SFSR, there was then also the People's Commissariat for Internal Affairs, or *Narodnyy Komissariat Vnutrennikh Del* (NKVD). When it later became the USSR-wide NKVD, the OGPU was subsumed into it. After World War II, this same apparatus went through a series of incarnations before becoming the infamous Committee for State Security or *Komitet Gosudarstvennoy Bezopasnosti* (KGB) in 1954.

In turn, the GPU and NKVD would operate under the legal imprimatur of the Penal Code of the Russian SFSR, most notably the odious Article 58, which went on the books in February 1927. From section 58-1, which dealt with "traitors," to section 58-14, which defined "counter-revolutionary saboteurs," it allowed for the arrest and imprisonment of anyone perceived as a threat to the state. Several sections, including 58-14, mentioned the crime of *vreditel'stvo*, which is usually translated as "wrecking" or "undermining." It was vague enough to allow later prosecutors wide latitude of interpretation.

Of particular note was section 58-10, which addressed "Anti-Soviet Agitation." Defined as "propaganda and agitation that called to overturn or undermining of the Soviet power," it could be used, and often was used, against virtually anyone for saying virtually anything negative about the state.

On the streets of Moscow, they marched in triumph, the men in red, the men carrying the red banners. However, far beneath those cobbled streets, in the prison cells in the sub-subbasements of the Cheka/OGP/NKVD headquarters on Lubyanka Square—too far down to hear the cheering—rotted the poor soulless creatures for whom the sun shone no more.

Section 10 also was used against the source of propaganda most feared by the Soviet state: religion. Though religious schools had been forbidden since the Revolution, anyone who instructed children in the practice of a faith tradition after 1927 was breaking the law. As Solzhenitsyn points out, people were not arrested and imprisoned for the actual practice of their faith, but for openly declaring their convictions. The latter included bringing up their children in their religion.

"In the twenties the religious education of children was classified as a political crime under Article 58-10 of the Code—in other words, counterrevolutionary propaganda!" Solzhenitsyn wrote. "True, one was still permitted to renounce one's religion at one's trial; it didn't often happen but it nonetheless did happen that the father would renounce his religion and remain at home to raise the children while the mother went to [prison]. Throughout all those years women manifested great firmness in their faith."

In telling Lilya the story of Vasilisa, Anna Vasil'yevna would have omitted the part about the heroine saying her prayers.

"My mother's blessing helped me," Vasilisa told Baba Yaga.

"I want no blessed daughters near me!" screamed the Soviet state as the face of Baba Yaga. "Your mother's blessing hurts my very bones!"

"You can pray freely," Russian poet Tanya Khodkevich wrote of life in Article 58 Russia, "but just so God alone can hear." Her words have been widely quoted in recent years, but at the time, they earned their author a ten-year prison sentence.

After 1930, prison sentences were carried out by a sister agency to the GPU/NKVD, the *Glavnoye Upravlyeniye ispravityel'no-trudovih Lagyeryey i Koloniy* (Chief Administration of Corrective Labor Camps and Colonies), which ran a system of more than four hundred forced labor camps across the breadth of the Soviet Union. The agency's acronym, "Gulag," came to be the euphemism for the camps themselves.

Article 58, and the enforcers who enforced it, would cast a dark shadow across life in the Soviet Union for more than half a century, but during the first ten years after it was promulgated in 1927, one at least knew what not to say or do in order to stay out of trouble. Later, it became more vague, and anyone could be imprisoned for doing or saying just about anything.

Initially, however, life under the Five Year Plan was focused on more mundane, day-to-day activities, such as putting bread on the table and finding a place to live.

Vladimir and Ann Vasil'yevna had been lucky. When they moved to Moscow, it was at a time when the population was going through an unprecedented period of downsizing. Plenty of apartments were available. However, as conditions in the countryside deteriorated, the tidal wave that had once flowed out of Moscow now flowed back in to take advantage of jobs created by the rapid industrialization called for under the Five Year Plan.

As Lilya and her family traveled about Moscow in the late 1920s, they witnessed big changes to the skyline. The rapid industrialization of the Five Year Plan demanded not simply the construction of enormous factories, but because enormous factories required a sizable workforce, the Five Year Plan demanded the rapid construction of housing on an equally massive scale, a process that would not catch up with demand for more than a generation.

There had been around a million people in Moscow when the Civil War came to an end in 1922, but in 1926, when Lilya was five, it was back over its prewar levels at 2 million, and on the path to double again to 4 million by the late 1930s.

Meanwhile, all-new industrial cities were being built all across the Soviet Union, characterized by long, repetitive rows of huge, featureless apartment blocks. Among the vast industrial cities created out of whole cloth during this period was Magnitogorsk, which came to symbolize the soulless company towns of the Soviet Union. Magnitogorsk, 800 miles east of Moscow, was created as the home of the largest iron and steel works in the Soviet Union. The name, which literally translated as the "Magnetic Mountain City," was derived from the city's proximity to Magnitnaya Mountain, an edifice that is, through geological anomaly, almost pure iron ore. The Five Year Plan turned it from a small village to an overnight metropolis of 90,000 in 1931, and a city of 146,000 by 1939, where grim superblock apartment houses were a stark monument to Stalinist planning.

Because a keystone precept of Communist doctrine was communalism, this was a guiding element in the design of these buildings. For many people, the idea of communal living conjures congenial images of college life, but in the Soviet paradigm, apartment houses for families in places such as Magnitogorsk were built with communal bathrooms and toilets and without kitchens because it was assumed that everyone would dine communally in cafeterias.

Lilya and her family were lucky to live in Moscow in an older apartment house rather than in one of the streamlined superblocks. In new cities such as Magnitogorsk, people had no choice. At least Lilya's family shared a communal bathroom with fewer people than in the new model highrise apartments that were going up under the red banner of the Five Year Plan. In many cases, from Magnitogorsk to the Moscow suburbs, people had to leave their apartment house to bathe at a public bathhouse.

In some places, even communal toilets were an unfulfilled dream. In its September 6, 1937, issue, *Kommuna*, the newspaper in Voronezh, reported that new apartment blocks for laborers were still being constructed with neither running water nor sewer connections. One would think that the author of such an article would have been arrested under Article 58 for Anti-Soviet Agitation, but such architectural omissions were so common that the government-run media mentioned it as a matter of course, and apparently did not notice the irony.

Documents in the *Gosudarstvennyi Arkhiv Rossiiskoi Federatsii* (GARF, the Central State Archive of the Russian Republic, formerly the Central State Archive of the RSFSR) confirm that as late as 1933, the Ukrainian industrial city of Dnepropetrovsk (population 180,000) had water rationing and no sewers, and that residential areas lacked electricity despite the city's proximity to the Dnieper hydroelectric complex.

In the official history of Stalingrad, published in 1968, M. A. Vodolagin admits that the city named for Stalin himself had no comprehensive sewer system as late as 1938. In Moscow in the early 1930s, a third of the population still lived in buildings with no running water or sewers.

Even as workers toiled on the vast hydroelectric projects damming Russia's great rivers and putting their power into electricity, they waited for years to have their own apartments connected to the power grid.

Not all the workers who flocked to the new industrial cities were citizens of the Soviet Union. Because there was a shortage of specialized personnel, many skilled and educated westerners were enticed to come. Some were adventure seekers, while others were idealistic individuals who had read—and believed—the stories of how the Bolsheviks were creating a workers' paradise on a massive scale. When they arrived, they found something quite different. As Zara Witkin wrote in her memoir, *An American Engineer in Stalin's Russia*, "the physical aspect of the cities is dreadful … Stench, filth, dilapidation batter the sense[s] at every turn."

Despite the building boom, apartment house overcrowding was endemic, as people crammed into existing housing stock that had been designed before the Revolution for far fewer people. Vladimir and Anna were lucky they had found their apartment on Novoslobodskaya Street when they did.

Had the Litvyaks been in the market in 1930, they would have been sharing their two rooms with more than just their two children. Many people, even in Moscow and Leningrad, lived in rooms within communal apartments, called *kommunalka*.

Paola Messana writes in her book *Soviet Communal Living* that during the 1920s, the Soviet state would deliberately place several families into the same apartment, making certain that they were from different socioeconomic or ethnic backgrounds. Officially, this was done to equalize class distinctions, but many historians concur that it was also to keep people on edge, encouraging them to spy on their neighbors and report Article 58 transgressions to the authorities.

As Timothy Colton writes in *Moscow: Governing the Socialist Metropolis*, the average living space was only 60 square feet (5.5 square meters) per person, and this declined after 1930. In Magnitogorsk, it was less than 32 square feet. Documents from the Central State Archive cited by Sheila Fitzpatrick mention a Moscow family of six living in a windowless, 65-square-foot closet beneath a staircase.

Another such document from GARF cited by Fitzpatrick tells of family of four living in a 450-square-foot room within a kommunalka in Moscow. "For all these years our room has been the apple of discord for all residents of our apartment," the wife, a teacher, complained, describing harassment from jealous neighbors. When these neighbors denounced them to authorities, the husband was arrested and sentenced to eight years for counterrevolutionary agitation. The rest of the family was evicted.

In Svetlana Boym's book *Common Places*, she uses a particular kommunalka as an illustration of life in the Soviet Union. Commenting on Boym's tales, Sheila Fitzpatrick writes that the kommunalka "is the ruin of the communal utopia and a unique institution of Soviet daily life; a model Soviet home and a breeding ground for grassroots informants. Here, privacy is forbidden; here the inhabitants defiantly treasure their bits of 'domestic trash,' targets of ideological campaigns for the transformation (*perestroika*) of everyday life."

A Soviet government pamphlet dating from 1935 described the pitfalls of kommunalka life, from rampant theft to "the infliction of beatings (in particular of women and children)," which are not unlike those encountered in American housing projects or British "estates" in more recent years. One can imagine that things were really bad when the government housing authority itself had to officially condemn hoodlums for "organizing regular drinking parties accompanied by noise, quarrels, and cursing" in the kommunalka. Noteworthy in the government's "official" list is the transgression of using "threats to get even by use of one's official or Party position."

In his satirical short story, "*Nervnye liudi*" ("Nervous People"), contained in his anthology of stories of Soviet life in the 1920s, the writer Mikhail Zoshchenko describes a fight that takes place inside his kommunalka.

"Not long ago in our kommunalka there was a fight. And not just any fight, but a full-out battle," Zoshchenko wrote. "Of course in their hearts the fight was virtuous. The invalid Gavrilov nearly got his head chopped off. The main reason—folks are very nervous. Erupt over trivialities. Lose control. And fight dirty, like in a fog. Of course they say that after a civil war the people are always jittery. That may be so, but ideology won't heal Gavrilov's head any faster … our tiny kitchen is narrow. Unsuitable for fighting. Tight. All around are pans and kerosene cooking stoves. Nowhere to turn. And in it twelve people are crammed. If, for example, you wish to strike the face of one, you hit three. And of course, one bumps into things, falls over. If the one-legged invalid had three legs he couldn't keep his balance here."

The catalyst for the fight had been a brush owned by a man named Ivan Kobylin, whose words further describe Soviet urban existence during the 1920s: "I work like a driven elephant for 32 rubles and a few kopecks in the [state-owned butcher store], and smile," Kobylin fumes when someone in the kommunalka is found with his brush. "[I] smile at customers and weigh their sausage. By my labored coins I buy my own brushes, and there's no way in hell I'm letting some stranger use my brushes."

Though his stories lampooned everyday life under the Soviet system, and he was under constant pressure to conform, Zoshchenko managed to skate around the edges of official sanction by not directly condemning the government.

Being the daughter of a woman who worked in a state-owned retail shop, Lilya Litvyak was in a position to understand. At least, though, given that the Litvyaks did not have to share their tiny apartment on Novoslobodskaya Street with anyone else, she and her family were spared the worst horrors of kommunalka life. Her family did share a bathroom with others, but not their sleeping quarters.

However, the reality of Mikhail Zoshchenko's world was not far from Lilya's doorstep, and indeed, it no doubt existed in the same apartment building. She certainly had classmates who lived in crowded circumstances. She had visited their kommunalka, and she knew their stories.

The fact that conditions were so bad gave rise to despair among the old, and among the frustrated workers such as Kobylin. However, to the young, there was still an optimism that the brightest of futures lay ahead.

Indeed, the collective father of the Soviet people had told them so.

*Chapter 3*

# MOTHER AND FATHER

Just as Lilya Litvyak had a mother, Anna Vasil'yevna, a woman who had endured the intimate pain of childbirth for her, so too did she have an allegorical mother who had endured centuries of pain to nurture a whole people.

All Russians, going back for as long as anyone can remember, have had one common mother: *Rossiya-Matushka* (Mother Russia), the personification of the land, has been integral to her children's sense of place and identity for generations, and this idea, born independently of the Tsars, did not die with the last of the Tsars.

Even after the Bolsheviks seized power and executed Nicholas II and his extended family, Mother Russia lived on. The Bolsheviks killed so many people, and so many traditions associated with the Tsar, but Rossiya-Matushka would not die. The only thing that they could do was to concede to her presence, and to subsume her into Red mythology.

By the time Lilya Litvyak started school and became aware of Russia as her mother, this universal mother had become *Rodina-Mat*, or Mother

Motherland—because she now represented not just Russia, but all of the non-Russian corners of the new Soviet Union. The "mother" could no longer be merely that of Russia, but had to fill that role for a greater Motherland which encompassed Armenians, Azerbaijanis, Byelorussians, Chechens, Cossacks, Georgians, Kazakhs, Kirghizians, Moldavians, Tajiks, Turkmens, Ukrainians, Uzbeks, and many others.

The notion of the land as a matriarch, thoroughly ingrained in the Russian psyche, was especially true for those urban Russians who harbored a romantically abstract picture of the pureness of the countryside and its people. This is a recurring theme in Russian literature. For example, in his classic 1833 novel *Yevgeny Onegin*, Aleksandr Pushkin contrasts the cold insincerity of urban high society with the warm openness and vitality of rural life.

Dmitri Volkogonov writes that "Almost all of us Russians have our roots in the peasantry. When sunny childhood memories come to mind, you feel yourself back in the village, with the smell of melting snow, the robins perched on the fence, the ice darkening on the stream, the thin, rust-brown line of the Sayan Mountains to the south, the squeak of sleigh-runners along the village street. And the faces of those long departed."

Just as Russians had long had a mother, and the Soviet Union now had its Rodina, the Soviet Union and its people also now had a common father: Josef Stalin. He was the personification of the man in red from the old folk tale. Indeed, like the red man, he was also often referred to as the "sun."

By the time Lilya was in school, and as she was beginning to learn the songs about her Motherland, she was also conscious of the ubiquitous image of the father figure. His picture was on the wall of her classroom—along with Lenin's, of course—and it was hard to miss his austere visage in signs and posters on the street. Stalin would be a dominant, and dominating, presence throughout Lilya's entire lifetime.

Iosif Vissarionovich Dzhugashvili, who changed his name to "Stalin," so that he could be called the "Man of Steel," had defeated or marginalized all of his would-be rivals, and was now the face of the Soviet Union. Historian and author Karsten Brüggemann reminds us that in Soviet culture, "one of the most prominent narratives was the 'great Soviet family' with Stalin as the Father, the country (*Rodina-Mat*) as mother and the people as their children."

By the late 1920s, this idea was an inescapable reality wherever Lilya and her family looked. The sense of identity with which Lilya's generation grew up was of their being part of the great family headed by both the Father and Motherland.

As an icon, Josef Stalin replaced the Tsar, but he stood even taller and assumed a mythos much greater symbolically than any Tsar had ever possessed. Few, if anyone, ever considered the Tsar to be a father of the equivalent eminence of Mother Russia.

Stalin was an unlikely man to emerge as ruler of the successor state to the Russian Empire, and even more unlikely to be considered as a worthy consort to Mother Russia. He was not even a Russian, but a Georgian, even if he had chosen a Russian word as his new name.

He grew up in Georgia at a time when it was ruled mainly by street gangs, and his early life alternated between petty crime and religious school. He had considered the Russian Orthodox priesthood, but never seriously considered his father's profession as a cobbler. Dmitri Volkogonov, his biographer, wrote that from the early 1920s, "the party and the country were to be ruled by a man who had no skills or profession, unless being a half-baked priest can be considered a profession."

Stalin showed an early interest in revolution, but in those days, this flowed more from his fascination with violence and mayhem than with ideology. His role in revolutionary circles was confined more to stealing money for the groups with which he was affiliated, than nuancing their doctrine. Volkogonov notes that "before the Revolution, Stalin was possibly better known to various branches of the police department than he was to other revolutionaries."

His biographer goes on to say that Stalin "had no qualifications or skills, he had virtually never done a day's work. Stalin, unlike [fellow Bolshevik leader Lazar] Kaganovich, could not even mend a pair of boots. The space on police forms for 'skill or profession' would either be left blank or filled in as 'clerk.' When he had to complete registration for party congresses and conferences, Stalin was uncomfortable answering questions about the nature of his occupation and his social origin … As a professional revolutionary, Stalin knew less about the life of a worker, peasant or office worker than he did about that of a prisoner or exile."

Having never actually held a job, he was as improbable as the ruler of the "workers' paradise," as he was to be the Father figure of the Soviet people.

As a public speaker, Stalin was awkward and dull. He paled by comparison to the honey-tongued eloquence of his bitterest rival, Leon Trotsky. As Volkogonov writes, "whenever he had to visit a workshop or factory, an army unit or a street meeting, Stalin felt an anxiety which, it is true, he learned in time to conceal. Unlike other revolutionaries, he never felt drawn into the thick of the masses, he did not enjoy and was anyway not good, at speaking in front of large crowds."

However, when it came to backroom political choreography, Stalin outmaneuvered Trotsky and the others with uncommon skill and bulldog tenacity. Stalin made up for his shortcomings through single-minded stubbornness. He was a determined man with an extraordinary memory for facts and details. In his dealings within the complex web of politics in the upper reaches of the Communist Party, Stalin was intuitively brilliant. He was, according to Volkogonov, "a master at passing off his mistakes, oversights and crimes as achievements, successes, farsightedness, wisdom and constant concern for the people."

Through the years, he gradually eliminated his adversaries, from the most prominent to the merely benign. It was as though he believed that his own stature could be elevated only by removing possible comparisons. As his rivals were gradually eradicated, he would see that history was carefully rewritten to erase them from the past as well as from the present.

Stalin's biographer observes that "At first, the real heroes of the Revolution were subjected to 'silence,' 'historical purging' and 're-editing.' In 1937–39 they were done away with physically. By the 1940s, you could count the active leaders of the revolution on the fingers of one hand. Only those who had helped to create the new October biography of the leader remained. The fewer the number of October veterans, the more inflated Stalin's role became."

Just as he had uncanny ability to manipulate his opponents, Stalin was unexpressive and impossible to read. He betrayed no emotions, perhaps because he was incapable of experiencing emotions.

"He knew how to hide his feelings," Volkogonov tells. "Very few people ever saw him angry. He was capable of making the harshest decisions with complete composure. In time, his entourage would take this as a sign of his great wisdom and perspicacity."

Aside from his first wife, Ekaterina "Kato" Svanidze, who died in 1907, Stalin showed little interest in his own family. Stalin later said that, aside from his own mother, Kato was the only person he had ever loved. He had a son named Yakov by her, for whom he had little, if any, affection.

His second wife, Nadezhda Sergeevna Alliluyeva, was twenty-eight years younger than Stalin, and barely seven years older than her stepson. Stalin married her in 1919 in the midst of the Civil War, and they had two children. Vasily Iosifovich Dzhugashvili was born in 1921, only five months before Lilya Litvyak. Like Lilya, he later trained as a pilot, but served mainly as a staff officer in the Great Patriotic War.

Stalin's only daughter, Svetlana Iosifovna Alliluyeva was born in 1926, six years before her mother's death. Officially, Nadezhda Alliluyeva died from "illness," albeit with a pistol at her side. It is now widely assumed that she shot herself after an argument with Stalin.

As is often the case with public figures, Stalin was an absent father, allowing his children to grow up with nannies. They were brought to him on the occasional weekends, and Svetlana was used for the sporadic photo op.

Yakov, who was considered a weakling by his father, was the object of frequent ridicule, which drove him to a failed attempt to blow his brains out. When Stalin saw him after this ultimate articulation of their absolute estrangement, he greeted Yakov with a sarcastic "Ha! You missed!"

Most people who seem cold and heartless have a soft side, a streak of humanity. This was not true of Stalin. "Pity was unknown to him, as was filial love or the love of a father for his children and grandchildren," Volkogonov writes. "Of the latter, he saw his daughter Svetlana's children and those of his son and first-born, Yakov, only a few times. His private life was completely fenced off. He had nothing but work. People liked this, they thought he was businesslike, a man who knew his duty, a man without sentimentality."

Of some people it is said that the more you see of them, the more you like them. With Stalin, it was the opposite. Stalin almost never appeared in public outside official circles in Moscow, yet became widely adored. Few of his 147 million subjects (by the 1926 census) ever saw him in the flesh, yet his popularity mushroomed. In the immense billboards he was a monumentally large. In person, he stood just 5 feet 4 inches. He was like a Wizard of Oz in a red, not emerald, city.

"Stalin made it a rule not to come into direct contact with the masses," Volkogonov writes. "With rare exceptions, he never visited a factory or collective farm, never travelled to any of the republics, or to the front during the war. His voice would resound from time to time from the pinnacle of the pyramid, while the millions listened in holy terror at its foot. He turned his remoteness into an attribute of the cult. The more enigmatic and secretive the leader, the more he provides fuel for legends about himself."

Having fought a Revolution ostensibly on behalf of the workers and peasants was one thing. To have to actually be around them was quite another for the Man of Steel.

Stalin's rare appearances created a mythic, rock-star-like, atmosphere. "The applause came like machine-gun fire," read a March 1, 1927, article in the newspaper *Rabochaya Moskva* about an manifestation the previous night. "The man wearing soldier's khaki and worn-down boots, a pipe in his hand, stopped at the curtain. Long live Stalin! Long live the [Central Committee!] Notes are passed to Stalin. Twirling his black moustache, he studies them diligently. The hall falls silent and Stalin, General Secretary of the party and the man after whom the workshops have been named, begins his conversation with the workers."

This imposing personification of the man in red, the mythic father whom average people never saw, became immensely popular. Indeed, by the time of the Five Year Plan, he was a cult figure, the center of a personality cult that was carefully crafted by the short man who longed to be larger than life.

As his popularity grew, Volkogonov writes, "Stalin decided it would be politic to reduce the frequency of [his public] appearances: the less he appeared, the more significant the appearances would become, and his seclusion would enhance the official legends, myths and embellished clichés about him."

The less he appeared, the larger he loomed. They called him "Father," of course, but the Soviet media and the Soviet people also came to call him the "wise leader," the "great helmsman," the "immortal genius." And they did call him the "sun," because his omnipresent image shone down on an empire which spanned a dozen time zones.

Early in 1937, Lion Feuchtwanger, the German novelist and playwright, visited Moscow. An armchair revolutionary and Soviet sympathizer, he went there predisposed with a fondness for the Soviet system. In his book *Moscow 1937: My Visit Described for My Friends*, he regards the Soviet Union as a Marxist theme park, noting in particular its central theme: Stalin.

"The worship and boundless cult with which the population surrounds Stalin is the first thing that strikes the foreigner visiting the Soviet Union," an awed Feuchtwanger reports. "On every corner, at every crossroads, in appropriate and inappropriate places alike, one sees gigantic busts and portraits of Stalin. The speeches one hears, not only the political ones, but even on any scientific or artistic subject, are peppered with glorification of Stalin, and at times this deification takes on tasteless forms."

Flowing from this idolatry, though more officially bureaucratic than spontaneously organic, a dizzying number of things and places, from schools to natural features, were named for him. So, too, were a dozen Soviet cities. There were Stalinogorsk in Russia, Imeni Stalina in Armenia, Staliniri in his native Georgia, and the capital of Tajikstan (now Dushanbe) was renamed as Stalinabad. There was a Stalino in Ukraine and another in Azerbaijan.

Most memorable to history was the former Russian city of Tsaritsyn, which was seized by the Bolsheviks during the Revolution and successfully defended by them against the Whites in the Civil War. Because of the role played by Stalin himself during this defense, the city became Stalingrad—the city of Stalin—in 1925. This place would become a critical nexus in the later life of Lilya Litvyak.

The crafting of the Stalin cult succeeded like no other in modern times. In Germany, they cheered for Hitler, but in the Soviet Union, they came literally to idolize Stalin. The Russian folklore familiar to the generations preceding that of Lilya Litvyak's was literally superseded by the canons of the Father's cult. As Frank Miller writes in *Folklore for Stalin: Russian Folklore and Pseudofolklore of the Stalin Era*, he was "the hero Joseph—Our Light—Vissarionovich."

Granted an audience with the man himself, the starry-eyed Feuchtwanger could not help mentioning this. He reports that Stalin merely grinned and shrugged, modestly remarking that "the workers and peasants are too busy with other matters to cultivate good taste."

In reporting Stalin's faux modesty, Feuchtwanger was merely playing into the carefully crafted illusion that the idolized leader was an unpretentious man. Volkogonov reminds us that "Occasionally Stalin would indicate to the party and the people that he was against all the glorification and idolatry [but this] was calculated in fact to enhance the glorification of Stalin, not to stop it. Who would now be able to say that he was not modest?"

Indeed, the idolatry was real, and for many, it actually seemed to have been genuine. Lion Feuchtwanger went away with the impression that the Soviet people, or at least a large number of them, perceived Stalin as a sort of beneficent deity.

Feuchtwanger extrapolates that "worship of the leader had grown organically with the success of economic construction. The people were grateful to Stalin for their bread and meat, for the order in their lives, for their education and for creating their army which secured this new well-being. The people have to have someone to whom to express their gratitude for the undoubted improvement in their living conditions, and for this purpose they do not select an abstract concept, such as abstract 'communism', but a real man, Stalin."

The message was that the beneficence of Stalin the Father was the reason that lives were getting better. Parents taught their children to believe that "if it were not for Stalin, we wouldn't be an industrial power, we wouldn't have a roof over our heads and a guaranteed crust of bread."

Indeed, Lilya Litvyak's generation was growing up with a fundamental belief that everything their great leader did was both vitally important and insightful. From earliest childhood, Lilya and her classmates were being told that "Stalin is thinking about us ... Stalin is thinking about every one of us."

Lilya and her friends learned this as Little Oktoberists, as they sang his praises along with those of their all-union Rodina. They sang them in school, and they sang them around the campfires at Young Pioneer Camp.

In 1931, half-way through the Father's First Five Year Plan, Lilya turned ten and at last became eligible to become a Young Pioneer. She and her Young Pioneer group met for an hour after school, learning to strive for excellence in school, in sports, and in being good Communist role models in life. Since the meetings were after school, it was a seamless transition. Everyone did it.

The experience of the Pioneer meetings was not something children dreaded, but something they looked forward to. Just as many afterschool activities are seen as opportunities to be with friends in an atmosphere more relaxed than the classroom, such was the case at a Pioneer meeting. The chance to go away to Pioneer Camp for a week or so was the highlight every child's summer. Most people who were there recall them as a Western child recalls scout camp—as fun.

For Lilya and her friends, the Young Pioneer years were filled with sports, singing, folk dances, and camaraderie. The songs were designed to celebrate Father Stalin, but because he was seen only in a stylized way, he remained a mythical character, like those in the Russian fairy tales which Anna Vasil'yevna told Lilya when she was a little girl.

"There are many songs in which the singing masses are playing the roles of thankful, loving children," Karsten Brüggemann writes. "The 'enthusiastic love' of [the] singing Pioneer camp is devoted to the country and the Father who is the only source of life, authority and wisdom; they are obliged to serve him. And love is only given to true Soviet citizens who are ready for any sacrifice. This world is full of young and never ageing people, where every sphere of human activity is infantilised, even love itself. People have to be thankful for their life in Stalin's own country, an honor that anybody can be rewarded with if he's got a clear conscience. But for the sake of the myth he has to be ready to sacrifice his soul."

Lilya and her friends had learned the Pioneer slogan, "the public above the personal," long before they turned ten years old. It expressed the ideal of the Soviet state, the ideal with which they grew up, that is to suppress the individuality of one's identity to the ideal of being part of that body of children of the Father and the Mother. It was the ideal that would mobilize them for war as young adults.

The celebration of this ideal is illustrated by the great engineering projects of the Five Year Plan. These ranged from the steel works at Magnitogorsk to the great hydroelectric projects constructed to bend the nature of the Soviet rivers, notably the Dnieper, to the Father's will. Perhaps the best example is "The Canal Named Stalin."

When Lilya was in her fourth year of school, a topic of classroom discussion—and civic pride—was the construction of a great ship canal that was being cut across northwestern Russia, allowing ocean-going ship traffic to penetrate 140 miles from Leningrad to the interior of Russia. The *Belomorsko-Baltiyskiy Kanal* (White Sea-Baltic Sea Canal) was better known as the "Stalin Canal," as it was believed to have been impossible without the omnipotent vision of the Father.

It was an enormous undertaking, and a much-touted example of Soviet engineering and construction might. Finally opened in August 1933, it was paradoxically also a monument to forced labor. As such, it was the grave of as many as 100,000 workers, many of whom were conscripted "enemies of the people" who were killed in accidents due to unsafe working conditions, or simply worked to death as convict laborers. Most of those who broke their backs or lost their lives for the Stalin Canal were too old to have ever been offered a chance to have been Young Pioneers, but they became shining examples of placing "the public above the personal"—whether they liked it or not.

Meanwhile, no less a literary figure that Maxim Gorky was commissioned to serve as general editor of a massive, six hundred-page laudatory book called *Kanal Imeni Stalina* (*The Canal Named Stalin*), which was released in time for presentation at the Seventeenth Party Congress in 1934. Gorky headed up a brigade of more than a hundred writers that included Mikhail Zoshchenko and Aleksei Tolstoy (a descendant of novelist Leo Tolstoy). Semyon Grigoryevich Firin the construction manager was also credited as a contributor.

Far from hiding the use of slave labor, Gorky's book celebrated the use of *zekas* (short for *zakliuchyonnyi*, meaning "inmates") on the project, seeing it as an exemplary means of reeducating "enemies of the people into their friends." It was, Gorky and his team insisted, "a uniquely successful effort at the mass transformation of former enemies of the proletariat and Soviet society into qualified representatives of the working class and even into enthusiasts of nationally significant labor … Engineers, academics, teachers and thousands of other intellectuals were thus changed into comrades-in-arms of the proletariat."

Waxing poetically, Gorky, or someone in on his team, added that "it is immeasurably more difficult to rework human raw material, than it is wood, stone or metal."

Finally, the authors gave credit to Father Stalin himself, citing the man whose inspiration was the catalyst and namesake for the project. "The Canal Named Stalin," they gushed, would not have been possible without the "brilliantly organized will, the penetrating mind of a great theorist, the courage of a talented leader, the intuition of a genuine revolutionary who has a subtle understanding of the qualities of others and who, while cultivating the best of these qualities, struggles pitilessly against those qualities which would prevent them developing to their maximum limit."

Indeed, without Stalin, there would have been no "enemies" to turn into zekas.

It is unlikely that Lilya ever saw the book, but she certainly knew about the reworkings of both stone and flesh it celebrated. From the perspective of a Young Pioneer, however, it still seemed a very noble undertaking.

Closer to home—perhaps a little too close for the Soviet state to celebrate slave labor, although not too close to use it when needed—another project of which Lilya was very aware was the Moscow Metro.

As the showplace city of the Soviet Union, Moscow needed a showpiece transportation system as an accessory to Stalin's desire to make it a world-class city. Berlin, Boston, London, New York, Paris, and even Budapest, had electric subways by 1904, and they were proudly touted as the last word in urban transportation. By this reasoning, the Central Committee of the Communist Party of the Soviet Union decided in June 1931 that Moscow must have a subway second to none, and its completion was to be the centerpiece of the Second Five Year Plan (1933–37).

Lilya was aware of the Moscow Metro because it was hard to miss seeing the construction equipment and the disruption to the city streets.

Meanwhile, her father, who had started out working nights as a railway clerk, was now an upwardly mobile bureaucrat in the People's Commissariat Transport, and the Moscow Metro was their biggest project. Indeed, it was so big as to consume around a fifth of the commissariat's entire budget. Heading the project, and also serving as Commissar of Transport after 1935, was Lazar Kaganovich. As the ruthless enforcer of collectivization under the First Five Year Plan, he became known as the "Iron Commissar," in part for his single-minded determination to get the Metro project completed.

It took four years to build the first line, the Sokolnicheskaya Line, which ran for 11 kilometers (not quite 7 miles) and connected thirteen stations across the center of the city, from Sokolniki to Park Kultury. In an article in the January 2003 issue of *Modern Language Review* titled "Archeological

Fantasies: Constructing History on the Moscow Metro," architectural historian Mike O'Mahoney writes that "a specialist workforce had been drawn from many different regions, including miners from the Ukrainian and Siberian coal fields and construction workers from the iron and steel mills of Magnitogorsk, the Dnieper hydroelectric power station, and the Turkestan-Siberian railway."

When the Metro opened to the public on May 15, 1935, Lilya and her classmates were let out of school en masse to attend the parade. Dressed in their Young Pioneer uniforms, of course, they were also part of an immense sing-along led by more than two thousand people identified as construction workers. Reportedly, twenty-five thousand copies of the sheet music for "Songs of the Joyous Metro Conquerors" were distributed that day, and a quarter of a million people rode its sparkling new coaches on the first day.

According to the diary of Aleksandr Semyonovich "Alyosha" Svanidze, who was Stalin's brother-in-law as well as deputy chairman of the Soviet State Bank, the Man of Steel himself had taken a private midnight Metro ride on April 29 before the official opening. Having fought a Revolution ostensibly on behalf of the workers and peasants was one thing. To have to actually be in a subway car with them was quite another.

Within a few days, a thirteen-year-old Lilya Litvyak and several of her teenaged friends had paid 50 kopecks to take their own first rides on the showplace city's showplace train. The girls had never seen anything like the architectural splendor of the Moscow Metro. The stations were like palaces, fitted with marble columns and gleaming with chandeliers. O'Mahoney calls it "one of the most spectacular achievements of the early Stalinist era."

There would eventually be a Metro stop at the head of Lilya's street, Novoslobodskaya Street, but it was not opened until 1952.

In a 2000 article in *Technology and Culture* titled "A Metro on the Mount: The Underground as a Church of Soviet Civilization," Andrew Jenks suggests that the Metro stations were part of a self-deification effort by Stalin himself, who imagined himself as a "sun god." In *The Journal of*

*Decorative and Propaganda Arts* in 2002, John Bowlt concurs, writing that the brilliance of the lighting was designed to make each station seem like an "artificial underground sun." The title of Bowlt's article, "Stalin as Isis and Ra: Socialist Realism and the Art of Design," speaks volumes.

The Metro was a monument to Stalin's desire to transform the Soviet Union into a state the rest of the world would take seriously. Just as the rapid construction of gargantuan steel mills, great canals, and vast hydroelectric projects was intended to transform the country industrially, the Metro was intended to dazzle not only visitors from abroad, but especially the Muscovites themselves.

For Lilya Litvyak's generation, who knew nothing—at least, not yet—of the Father's brooding, sinister side, the Metro offered tangible proof that Stalin really was working wonders to ensure a brilliant future for his children.

There is perhaps no better illustration of this positive mood than in the songs that everyone knew and sang around the Young Pioneer campfires each summer. One of the most popular camp songs was written in 1922 by Aleksandr Zharov, with music by Sergei Dyoshkin. It is variously called the "Young Pioneer Anthem" or "Young Pioneer March," but is perhaps best remembered by those of Lilya's generation as "Higher Rises Our Campfire." Roughly translated, it begins with the verse:

> *Fires in the blue night,*
> *Rise to our cheers!*
> *We're children of workers,*
> *We're young Pioneers.*
> *Near is the era*
> *Of bright, happy years.*

*Chapter 4*

# BRIGHT, HAPPY YEARS

In a rare personal appearance on the first day of December in 1935, Stalin told a hand-picked assembly of harvesting machine operators that "Everybody now says that the material situation of the toilers has considerably improved, that life has become better, more cheerful."

Naturally, "everybody" would say that to the Father. To say otherwise would have been dangerous.

Though it may have been more by offhand accident than by design, seldom had the "brilliant Father" been more brilliant. The ineloquent Stalin had inadvertently crafted a statement that his propagandists quickly paraphrased as a hugely significant slogan. Eventually it even became the title of a pop song.

As she made her way to school that winter, a fourteen-year-old Lilya Litvyak had become used to seeing the ubiquitous posters plastered on walls across Moscow that read "Life has become better, comrades; life has become more cheerful."

During the course of the next few years, Lilya would see the slogan repeated continuously in newspapers, on billboards, and on broadsides in Metro stations. It became a fixture of Soviet internal propaganda, and the promise by which the Soviet people looked ahead to their future.

Throughout the pain and sacrifice of the First Five Year Plan, the young people of Lilya Litvyak's generation continued to believe in the eventual coming of the bright, happy years that had been promised in the songs they sang at Young Pioneer Camp. As we have noted, Aleksandr Solzhenitsyn wryly summarized the optimistic mood of their generation, a youthful, not yet cynical generation, who believed that "because we were the same age as the Revolution, the brightest of futures lay ahead."

The First Five Year Plan had achieved much—at least toward the goal of rapid industrialization—through its great and Herculean industrial projects. Therefore, the Second Five Year Plan was beginning to roll with great enthusiasm and confidence by 1932, even before the First officially ended in 1933.

The Moscow Metro was the glittering highlight reported to the outside world by Western journalists, but there also were other examples that Soviet propagandists and press release writers could—and did—cite.

They, as well as Soviet supporters in the Western media, routinely mentioned the hundreds of brand-new cities, cultural palaces, factories, hospitals, laboratories, rest homes, roads, and schools being built under the Five Year Plans. These were the big things of which the people could take abstract pride, but the state was now turning to changes that made life better and more cheerful on a practical, personal level—even if you still had to leave your newly constructed apartment house to take a bath.

At the beginning of 1935, the Soviet state officially terminated bread rationing, mainly in an effort to bring an end to the bread lines that had been a way of life for more than a decade. Lilya and her family had seen this happen and were reminded of it every day when they passed the shops where the bread lines had once been. How could this not make a person more cheerful?

By the time that Lilya was entering her teen years and the Soviet Union was entering the early years of its Second Five Year Plan, there was an increasing emphasis on consumer goods within the planned economy. Not only was there bread without the lines, there was an increasing variety of food and apparel goods in the shops, at least in Moscow and other major cities. An article in the *Vecherniaia Moskva*, Moscow's evening paper, on October 4, 1934, announced that a shop on Gorky Street was now open, selling fresh fish, cheese, more than a hundred kinds of pastries and sweets, and many varieties of previously unavailable sausages.

Consumer goods made for more upbeat internal public relations, and their availability made a good impression on foreign visitors who came to experience the "artificial suns" in the Moscow Metro. People may have been crammed into communal apartments from Moscow to Magnitogorsk, but at least they could buy bread and sausage without standing in line.

In his 1946 book *The Great Retreat: The Growth and Decline of Communism in Russia*, Nicholas Sergeyevitch Timasheff, a Russian sociologist living in New York since 1920, wrote that the emphasis on consumer goods was merely a ploy. Stalin and his henchmen deliberately "retreated from socialist values" during the 1930s solely for the propaganda value.

Timasheff asserted that the lifting of bread rationing was done to convey the impression that the era of privation had given way to a new era of plenty. If it was merely a ploy, it seemed to have worked. Not only did it now appear that things were getting better, but the people also believed that Stalin himself was the architect of their bounty.

From another perspective, Julie Hessler wrote in *Culture of Shortages: A Social History of Soviet Trade, 1917–1953* that to answer a growing demand for consumer goods, "state and cooperative shops relied on a burgeoning class of clerical employees, whose wages, demographics, and workplace ethics elicited frequent interventions from above. The prewar Stalin period was the turning point: between the late 1920s and the early 1940s a new sectoral hierarchy was consolidated, in which retailing and public catering came to anchor the bottom end of the wage scale."

Of course, that burgeoning class of clerical employees included the young bureaucrat from the Commissariat of Transportation, Vladimir Litvyak. He and his wife, who worked in retail, were part of the target audience of the new Soviet consumer culture. They and their two children may have lived in a cramped two rooms, but it was now possible to put fresh fish and cheese on the table in the tiny apartment on Novoslobodskaya Street.

Meanwhile, Anastas Mikoyan, who had been the Commissar for External and Internal Trade since 1926, was himself a big proponent of consumer goods. Mikoyan was especially inspired in this direction after making a three-month tour of the United States during the early 1930s. Even in the midst of the Great Depression, Americans seemed awash in "things." On his visit, he was introduced to the canning of farm produce and was taken on a shopping expedition to Macy's in New York City.

He returned to the Soviet Union fired up about everything from hot dogs to ice cream, which he described as "very tasty and nutritious" in a comment published in the Novgorod newspaper *Gorkovskaia Kommuna* in April 1938.

Mikoyan was particularly excited about the fact that mechanized food processing could make such things as ice cream available to "the masses." He saw American-style mechanization as a means of providing everyone with simple luxuries once enjoyed only by the Tsarist elite.

Another of the food products Mikoyan found in the United States was tomato ketchup. In her book *Everyday Stalinism*, Sheila Fitzpatrick mentions an advertisement in which she even detected possible evidence of an importation of "American copywriting conventions." In the ad, the Soviet copywriters explained that "In America a bottle of ketchup stands on every restaurant table and in the pantry of every housewife. Ketchup is the best, sharp, aromatic relish for meat, fish, vegetables and other dishes ... Ask for ketchup from the factories of Chief Canned Goods Trust in the stores of Union Canned Goods Distribution syndicate and other food stores."

The fun-loving Mikoyan lamented the fact that the Soviet Union lagged behind European countries as a wine-producing nation. In a

*Gorkovskaia Kommuna* article in July 1936, he quipped that "Champagne is a symbol of material well-being, a symbol of prosperity … What kind of happy life can we have if there's not enough good beer and good liqueurs?"

People may have been crammed into communal apartments from Moscow to Magnitogorsk, but at least they would now know that Mikoyan wanted them to have good liqueurs to break the monotony of a vodka diet.

It was not only in the fancy shops in Moscow, but in simple farmers' markets where the impression of a growing abundance was conveyed to the Soviet people. After trying for years to stamp them out, the state also allowed the existence of *kolkhozes*, or "collective" farmers' markets, recognizing this age-old practice as an expedient means of getting produce to consumers, especially in cities.

From the nice stores on Gorky Street to the kolkhozes in small towns, the economy was starting to look a lot like a free market environment. Therefore, the state felt compelled to assure its subjects that the trend was not in the direction of latent capitalism. The official decree of May 20, 1932, which permitted the kolkhozes insisted that they were not an example of private enterprise, and local enforcement officials were ordered not to "allow the opening of stores and booths by private traders and in every way to root out resellers and speculators trying to make a profit at the expense of workers and peasants."

Of course, there was latent capitalism in the Soviet Union, though the high-end merchants were not turning their profits at the expense of workers and peasants. The workers and peasants would have had to get into the best shops in order for that to happen, which they could not.

The Soviet Union had possessed a privileged oligarchy from its very inception, and this oligarchy came to relish its privilege when it came to retail. Under the promise of the Revolution and the Five Year Plan, everyone in Soviet society was theoretically equal, but everyone, including young Lilya, knew this was not true. As George Orwell writes in *Animal Farm*, his satirical parody of the Soviet Union, "some are more equal than others." The latter naturally included the new oligarchy, the high party and government officials. Naturally, the higher they were in the organization chart, the "more equal" they were.

Those more equal than others were granted a "proletarian preference" that gave them priority on hard-to-obtain services, from housing allocations to school admissions, as well as the availability of consumer goods at exclusive state stores. Such goods reached the privileged through a complex network of "closed distributors" who provided them for members of a particular commissariat or state enterprise, and not to the general public or to members of other enterprises. These arrangements were common throughout the Soviet Union and were particularly useful to the "more equal" class during times of shortages, especially of food.

Jockeying for rare consumer goods became a way of life for Lilya's parents. Given that the streets were filled with a burgeoning consumer class, they were not particularly "more equal" than the average Muscovite. Of course, for people who had grown up as serfs, bound to a medieval form of servitude, even the promise of special consumer goods was better than their circumstances had been during the days before the men in red had sent the Tsarist nobility packing.

In Moscow under the Five Year Plans, the elite always had access to a good shopping experience. There were even special shops—state-owned, of course—at which foreigners and Soviet citizens with hard currency, gold, or jewels could buy goods. These *Torgovlia S Inostrantsami* (*Torgsin*) stores were established in 1931 by the order of Vyacheslav Molotov, the future commissar of foreign affairs, when he was chairman of the Council of People's Commissars (*Sovnarkom*). As Sheila Fitzpatrick writes, "Torgsin prices were not high (both Soviet 'commercial' prices and prices at the kolkhoz market were higher), but for Soviet citizens, Torgsin was a very costly place to shop because you had to sacrifice the remnants of the family silver or your grandfather's gold watch, or even your own wedding ring."

In her book *Gold for Industrialization*, Elena Osokina writes that Torgsin stores were an important source of gold and hard currency, which was used by the Soviet state to finance the Five Year Plan industrialization projects.

Of course, Vladimir and Anna Litvyak had come to Moscow with nothing. They had no gold to begin with.

As much as Lilya and her friends were now able to enjoy ketchup and ice cream—when they could find it—the more high-end consumer goods remained beyond reach, as they would for decades. Julie Hessler points out that trade exhibitions were organized in major cities across the breadth of the Soviet Union that teased would-be Soviet consumers with things such as cameras, kitchen appliances, and cars—none of which they could ever actually own. One peeved citizen put it succinctly when he complained at a trade fair "That's all very well, but [these things] aren't in the stores and you won't find them."

He was right.

When the October 4, 1934, article in the *Vecherniaia Moskva* trumpeted news from Gorky Street of the shop with a hundred kinds of pastries and sweets, and previously unavailable sausages, there was no mention of how much was available, nor of how long these things were in stock. Indeed, there was no predictability to availability.

Lavish displays such as that described in *Vecherniaia Moskva* alternated erratically with severe shortages caused by inefficient production and distribution of food. During the winter of 1934, the British journalist and author Malcolm Muggeridge visited Moscow. In his 1934 satirical novel *Winter in Moscow*, he describes a bizarre scene at the exactly the same Gorky Street store, where people stood "in wistful groups looking at tempting pyramids of fruit; at boots and fur coats tastefully displayed; at butter and white bread and other delicacies that are for them unobtainable."

In her book *Popular Opinion in Stalin's Russia*, Sarah Davies quotes a Leningrad worker who grumbled in 1935 that "I can't afford to buy food in the commercial shops, everything is expensive, and so you walk and wander around like a deathly shade, and get very thin and weak."

Father Stalin had told his children that "life has become better … life has become more cheerful," and except for unfulfilled promises of cameras and cars, it generally seemed as though that was true. Almost no Soviet citizens other than Mikoyan and his entourage had ever shopped at Macy's so their only point of reference was their recent past, and by that measure, things really did appear to be getting better.

So what if you could not buy kitchen appliances? At least you had bread and ice cream. Even if the people couldn't get sausages and fruit, nor the good liqueurs that Mikoyan wanted them to have, at least they no longer had to endure bread lines.

However, the suspension of bread rationing only disguised an inconvenient fact that Soviet grain harvests in the early 1930s were actually worse than they had been in the 1920s. There was actually less grain in 1935 than there had been earlier.

A contemporary Western perspective on Soviet consumer culture comes from British-born Ivy Low, a young and impressionable coffee house intellectual who married a young Russian expatriate Marxist named Maksim Litvinov. Having grown up sheltered in an upper-class Victorian home, she was impatient for excitement, and had become enthralled with the student's eye view of Marxism as the solution to the world's injustice and inequality.

Having married Litvinov in 1914 when he was in London, she traveled to the Soviet Union with him in the 1920s, anticipating it to be the workers' paradise promised by Lenin's colorful rhetoric.

In her memoirs, Ivy complained that in England, "things" mattered more than "ideas." She expressed excitement at the prospect of going to a place where she believed that ideas mattered throughout society as they did only in the off-campus salons in England. Like so many, she imagined the Soviet Union to be a kind of Marxist intellectual theme park.

However, in the Soviet Union, she found not a paradise, but an epidemic of shortages. As her eyes opened to unanticipated reality, she admitted that "when I walked about the streets of Moscow peering into ground-floor windows I saw the things of Moscow huggermuggering in all the corners and realized that they had never been so important."

That insight is crucial for understanding everyday Soviet life the Litvyaks experienced under the Five Year Plans. "Things" mattered enormously in the Soviet Union for the simple reason that they were so hard to get. Things became a bright ray of happiness—when you could get them.

As it turned out, Ivy had little to worry about personally. She had married well, and to a man who was "more equal than others." Her husband would later play a key role in the post-Revolution Soviet government, and their lives would be more equal than those of most people, including those of Vladimir and Anna. Indeed, Maksim and Ivy spent much of their time outside the Soviet Union, as he served as a roving ambassador and later as ambassador to the United States.

The propaganda narrative with which the Soviet state marketed the Second Five Year Plan was about making the Soviet people feel good about themselves, their country, and their fellow countrymen. The notion of "life getting better" was only one part of this theme. As during the First Five Year Plan, there was also great pride to be derived from heroic sacrifice and heroic accomplishments.

Nowhere did these ideals come together more beautifully for Stalin's propaganda machine than in the person of Alexei Stakhanov. He was not a revolutionary, nor a bureaucrat, nor a Party leader. Stakhanov was a simple man, a worker who became, quite simply, the quintessential Soviet man. Lilya knew all about him because his picture was on her classroom wall.

He was one of those men about whom it could be said that if he had not existed, the administrators of the Second Five Year Plan would have had to invent him. And, to a certain extent, that's just what they did.

In 1935, Stakhanov was a twenty-nine-year-old jackhammer operator working in a Ukrainian coal mine when he was singled out for greatness. On the last day of August, he single-handedly dug a record 112 tons of coal in less than six hours, exceeding his quota fourteen-fold. Three weeks later, he topped his record with 250 tons in a single shift.

It might have been obvious at the time, and it would eventually be officially revealed, that this was a specially planned and prepared exercise, with a number of support workers in place. Nevertheless, Stakhanov quickly became an example of the kind of person in whom all Soviet workers could take great pride. Indeed, as had been the plan all along, he literally became the poster child for the Second Five Year Plan. His face appeared not only on posters, but in newspapers and magazines in the Soviet Union and around the world.

The state propaganda machine, which had not so much created Stakhanov as facilitated his signature accomplishments, did create an entity called the "Stakhanovite Movement." When the poster child graced the cover of *Time* magazine on December 16, 1935, the caption called him, not simply by his name, but "Stakhanovism's Great Stakhanov." The lowly worker could now aspire to become an "ism."

As Sheila Fitzpatrick writes, it was the beginning of "the heroic age, launching the country on a make-or-break effort to transform itself. A heroic age called forth heroic personalities and feats, and gloried in them."

Quoting Gorky, she goes on to say that "free from the burden of serf consciousness inculcated through past exploitation and deprivation, the contemporary hero—'man of the new humanity'—is 'big, daring, strong.' He pits the force of human will against the forces of nature in a 'grandiose and tragic' struggle. His mission is not only to understand the world but also to master it!"

The Stakhanovite Movement was merely one element in the fabrication of an alternate folklore. As Frank Miller wrote in 1990, in his *Folklore for Stalin: Russian Folklore and Pseudofolklore of the Stalin Era*, "folklorists and writers collaborated with performers of traditional folklore to produce pseudofolklore in which the motifs and poetic devices of traditional folklore were applied to contemporary subjects."

Stakhanovism became a hallmark of the Second Five Year Plan, and an organized propaganda campaign by which all workers could mark their own accomplishments. Indeed, schoolchildren such as Lilya Litvyak were told in the classrooms that they should, like Stakhanov, aspire to great achievements. Anyone who beat his or her quota in the field, factory, or classroom was eligible to be feted as a "Stakhanovite." The Stakhanovite Movement was an example of propaganda that worked, as throughout the land, production increased as people strove to be called a Stakhanovite, or a hero of socialist labor.

At the end of 1938, the Presidium of the Supreme Soviet even decreed the official title of "Hero of Socialist Labor" and began decorating those workers who embodied the power and magnificence of the state. The poster children could now be recognized by their red-ribboned, gold-starred medals. Strangely, Stakhanov himself did not receive his Hero of Socialist Labor medal for thirty-two years.

As Sheila Fitzpatrick writes, "It was indeed an age of achievement, but it was also an age of extraordinary boosterism, boasting, and exaggeration of what had been achieved. Statistical handbooks were published, often in foreign languages as well as Russian, to document these achievements."

A great many statistics were being quoted in the Soviet media and in the sympathetic Western press to support the scale of those achievements. While statistics published during the 1930s were naturally subject to exaggeration, even the *Narodnoye Khozyastvo SSSR za 70 Let: Yubileynyy Statisticheskiy Yezhegodnik* (*The Economy of the USSR During the Last 70 Years: Anniversary Statistical Yearbook*), published in 1987, paints a picture of substantial accomplishment a half century earlier, pointing out that by 1935 the average gross output from heavy industry exceeded the 1914 level by 5.6 times. As Volkogonov admits, "Having lived through the industrial breakdown caused by the First World War and Civil War, the people could not but be amazed at the huge energy and creative drive unleashed by the October Revolution."

When it came to industrialization, the foremost goal of the Five Year Plans were working, the planning had succeeded.

It was an age of heroic slogans.

Just as the Father's words became the phrases on the posters, so, too, did words attributed to the "workers" themselves. There was nothing more Stakhanovite than the slogan "We can do a lot! Let's complete the Five Year Plan in four!"

It was an age of heroic songs.

Not just the Young Pioneers, Komsomolyets, and Komsomolkas had their songs, but the whole Soviet popular music industry was geared to support the propaganda machine. In the United States, it was an era of great popular standards. Duke Ellington had Swing Era hits with "It Don't Mean a Thing (If It Ain't Got That Swing)" and "Sophisticated Lady," while George and Ira Gershwin's "Summertime" appeared in 1935, and Richard Rodgers and Lorenz Hart's "My Funny Valentine" came two years later.

In the Soviet Union, the songs which Lilya Litvyak would have heard on the radio as a young teenager included Sergei Tretyakov's "Granddaddy Sebastian Went Godless" in 1934, or "The Stakhanov Movement Explained," penned by Yury Zhukov and Roza Izmailova, which was on the charts in 1936.

One of the most popular songs of Lilya's teenage years was the "March of the Happy-Go-Lucky Guys" (also called "The Merry Youth March"), written in 1934 by Vasily Lebedev-Kumach and Isaac Dunaevsky. They sang it at Young Pioneer Camp and hummed it in the hallways of their schools.

In the song, the merry fellows express the mood of the day, that "When our country commands that we be heroes/then anyone can become a hero … A song helps us building and living/Like a friend/it calls and leads us forth."

The songs and slogans were doing their job. Utopianism, like Stakhanovism, was alive and well, especially among that generation who had been born into the Revolution. They had grown up believing in what Aleksandr Zinovyev, who was only a year younger than Lilya, described as the "Svetloe Budushchee" or the "Radiant Future."

Though Zinovyev published his book by this name in 1978 as a satire, the concept was very much a part of Soviet internal propaganda in the 1930s, and it was widely believed. At least, Lilya's generation reasoned, things could get no worse.

Indeed, for the young members of the Soviet youth groups, the task of building the radiant future, or "building socialism," was life's great adventure.

Raisa Orlova, an author and literary critic who was a member of Lilya's generation, wrote in her memoirs that "I had an unshakable faith that my existence between these old walls was merely a preparation for life. Life, properly speaking, would begin in a new and sparkling white house. There I would do exercises in the morning, there the ideal order would exist, there all my heroic achievements would commence. The majority of my contemporaries … shared the same kind of rough, provisional, slapdash way of life. Faster, faster toward the great goal, and there everything would begin in a genuine sense. It was both possible and necessary to alter everything: the streets, the houses, the cities, the social order, human souls. And it was not all that difficult: first the unselfish enthusiasts would outline the plan on paper; then they would tear down the old (saying all the while, 'You can't make an omelette without breaking eggs!'); then the ground would be cleared of the rubble and the edifice of the socialist phalanx would be erected in the space that had been cleared."

Another girl of Lilya Litvyak's generation who wrote of these times was Nina Kosterina. While Nina never wrote her memoirs, she did leave a personal journal, which provides an insight into those years. Born on April 8, 1921, Nina was just four months older than Lilya, and like Lilya, she grew up in Moscow. The two girls were in the same year at school, and both attended at many of the same public events in Moscow during the late 1930s. For a few years, their lives were intertwined.

Hidden for two decades, Nina's journal was serialized in the Soviet monthly literary magazine *Novy Mir* (*New World*) in the early 1960s, and was translated into English by Mirra Ginsberg for publication in the West in 1968.

Nina gives us a personal, youthful perspective on the greater reality of Soviet life in the 1930s. She speaks of the pastries that her grandmother bakes for "the holidays," the annual commemorations of the October Revolution. She mentions the massive May Day celebrations in Red Square, and how the children danced and shouted as their leaders stood high atop the Kremlin Wall looking down upon them. Two among those tens of thousands of anonymous specks swirling about below Josef Stalin were Nina and Lilya.

For them, as they were among those gathering around the Young Pioneer campfire, the early years of the Second Five Year Plan actually were, in the words of the song, "bright, happy years."

The two girls were fourteen years old as the year 1936 began, and the focus of their attention was not on the availability of kitchen appliances, but on the things such as schoolwork. Nina mentions the time that spring that she became so absorbed in reading Victor Hugo's *The Man Who Laughs* that she forgot to study for a physics test.

Lilya and Nina were also preoccupied with their final exams, coming in June, and with the important transition from seventh year to eighth year.

It was also a time of the transition from the sorts of traditional dancing that they had done all their young lives, to dancing with boys. Nina mentions that she "loved to dance," but it was in early 1936 that she first "ventured to dance with boys." She writes that "a shiver ran through me" when a boy named Alik put his arm around her waist, and that when he lifted her into the air, "my heart stopped, I could not catch my breath and my cheeks flamed." It was that same night that she was first kissed by a boy, and she adds that she kissed Alik back.

Lilya is also remembered for having enjoyed dancing, and for having been one of the girls whom they boys desired to kiss.

As they were turning from fourteen to fifteen, Lilya and Nina were also excited about making the big step from their lives as Young Pioneers to membership in the Komsomol. As the youth auxiliary of the Communist Party of the Soviet Union, it was the next step in the series of organizations they had joined since their parents had first enrolled them as Little Oktoberists. Like the first kiss shared with a boy, the Komsomol was another milestone on their pathways to adulthood.

Though Komsomol membership was expected, even assumed, one still had to apply: membership was seen as a privilege, not a right. One was expected to do well in school and in sports, as well as to be willing to become involved in volunteerism. Most of all, one was expected to aspire to being a good citizen of the Soviet state and an exemplary member of the Communist Party.

Nina recalls there being a great deal of anxiety associated with her application. Her father talked to her for two hours, briefing her on the questions that she would be asked.

"After the talk with him, I went to the District Committee of the Komsomol quite calmly. What a father I have!" Nina writes. "There were ten of us at the District Committee, and everybody was nervous. I did not like the District Committee office: dirty, with smudged, dingy walls, nowhere to sit down. It seemed to me that I was calm, but others said that I came out of the office white as chalk. They gave me a membership card, tiny-tiny, white."

From this, one can imagine Lilya Litvyak's own experience at the District Committee office. One can imagine how overcoming obstacles, both real and imagined, to become a Komsomolka was another proud milestone on their pathways to the radiant future.

As students going into their eighth year of school, both Lilya and Nina were aware of the journal of that radiant future. *Nashi Dostizheniia* (*Our Achievements*) was a popular magazine founded in 1929 by Maxim Gorky and published by the State Publishing House of the Soviet Union, Gosizdat, until 1937. Indeed, the girls were very aware of Gorky, who was arguably the most important literary figure alive as they were growing up. Nina mentions him frequently with a sort of pop star reverence, and recalls his work as being popular among young people.

Lilya and Nina grew up with Gorky, and when he died in June 1936, around the end of the school year, Nina confided in her diary that "Gorky's death was like a personal sorrow to me. We have his complete works. I've read many of them, and some stirred me so much that I could not sleep. And now, Gorky is gone ..."

Presented as a literary magazine, *Nashi Dostizheniia* was actually a utopian propaganda magazine created to celebrate the positive aspects of Stalinism the state wished to emphasize. In the premier issue, Gorky admitted that Stalinist times were not exactly the best of times. Nevertheless, he wrote that his magazine was necessary "to sharply differentiate our good from our bad ... That's why it's necessary to set apart the good, so that even those people who do not adequately understand the enormous significance of our labor and the greatness of our aims will see what we have already achieved and how we succeed in building the new life. We will learn from the good. Only upon it may we build our new morality, those rules of conduct which will further elevate and define our labor energy and will compel us to fully sense the joy of creative life."

Nina Kosterina writes of attending a large Komsomol event in September 1936 at which Nikolai Krylenko, the People's Commissar of Justice spoke. However, she was more enthusiastic in recalling that there was a concert, and that later, she and her friends danced to exhaustion. "We went home at two in the morning," she writes. "I was so happy and excited after the evening that a militiaman in the street asked, 'Why are you laughing so much?' And I said, laughing, 'I feel good, so I laugh!'"

As Father Stalin said, life was becoming more cheerful.

How long could this last?

Chapter 5

# BONFIRES OF PARANOIA

I n January 1937, Nina Kosterina's cat died. She and her sister emptied their life savings to come up with three rubles to buy medicine in a failed attempt to save their "darling kitten." In their world, it was an all-consuming tragedy, but in the overarching scheme of things, it was merely a microcosmic allegory for the dark shadow that was then beginning to fall across the people of the Soviet Union.

It was the shadow cast by their metaphorical Father, a flickering shadow illuminated not by the innocent campfires of Young Pioneer songs, but by the metaphorical bonfires of paranoia which blazed within his mind.

The arc of things growing ever more cheerful now turned downward at a steep, indeed precipitous, angle until it descended into the bonfire itself. The year 1937 marked the start of the massive hammer blow to Soviet society known as the Great Purge.

The importance of January 1937 as a turning point in the story of the Soviet people cannot be overemphasized. For both Nina Kosterina and

Lilya Litvyak, the darkness that began gathering that month would be extremely personal.

Back in 1932 and 1933, the transition from the First Five Year Plan to the Second had been marked by great enthusiasm. How could there not be enthusiasm? The goals of the First had largely been met in only four years.

Buoyed by this and the apparent rise in the standard of living, the Second began optimistically, but ended badly in 1937, with production goals unmet and a general downturn in the Soviet economy. One might say that it collided with the Great Purge and was thereby derailed like a speeding freight train. Things had suddenly stopped getting better.

The catalyst for the Great Purge, and for all of the misery that would accompany it—and flow from it—was Josef Stalin's singular obsession with one man. If Stalin had ever written a candid autobiography, which he almost certainly never would have done, he would have ranked as his biggest blunder his choice of deporting Leon Trotsky from the Soviet Union in 1929 rather than arresting and executing him. Having his archrival meddling from abroad nagged Stalin like an open sore for more than a decade, and he resolved not to make that same mistake with any other potential rival.

Through the years, Stalin had become more and more obsessed with the influence that Trotsky still held on others, and he gradually became more and more single-minded in his determination to eradicate them. If he could not get his hands around the throat of Trotsky, he could do so with the "Trotskyists." Real or imagined, they were essentially anyone inside the Communist Party ruling elite whom he perceived as his enemy.

Stalin and his fellow Bolsheviks had always been cognizant of the fact that their Revolution was as transformative to the course of world history as was the French Revolution, nearly 130 years earlier. Just as French revolutionaries used the term *ennemi du peuple* (enemy of the people) to describe counterrevolutionaries as harshly as possible, so too did the Bolsheviks. To be an enemy of the people, a *vrag naroda*, was an indefensible crime.

Said Maximilien Robespierre in December 1793, "The revolutionary government owes to the good citizen all the protection of the nation; it owes nothing to the Enemies of the People but death."

Said Vladimir Lenin in November 1917, "all leaders of the Constitutional Democratic Party, a party filled with enemies of the people, are hereby to be considered outlaws, and are to be arrested immediately and brought before the revolutionary court."

One is also reminded that in 1934, Maxim Gorky had remarked that the use of slave labor in the construction of the "Canal Named Stalin" had been an exercise in reeducating "enemies of the people into their friends."

Because in his greatness, Stalin had become synonymous with the state, and the Father consort to Mother Russia, to Rodina-Mat, Stalin considered the enemies of the people, his people, to be his enemies, his personal enemies.

The irony is that, by 1937, Stalin had no true rivals left within the Soviet Union. He had to look deep and grasp at straws to find even the most remotely serious enemies. As his biographer Dmitri Volkogonov writes, "an enemy was anyone who did not or might not share his outlook. No one in fact opposed Stalin's personal rule, but he sensed that many, especially the Lenin old guard, secretly did not approve of his brand of socialism. This was enough for him to arrive eventually at his terrible decision. With the help of his ideological apparatus, Stalin gradually created an atmosphere of suspicion in the country, preparing the people for the impending bloody purge."

First of prominence to fall had been Sergei Mironovich Kirov, the party boss in Leningrad. His assassination in December 1934 shocked a nation that would grow numb to such events by the end of the decade. Though Stalin almost certainly ordered the hit, he used it as an excuse to crack down on others. This reign of terror, which paled by comparison to what was to come in 1937, culminated with the August 1936 "show trials" of sixteen "Old Bolsheviks," including Grigory Yevseevich Zinoviev, the prominent long-time head of the Communist International, and Lev Borisovich Kamenev, who had been the acting Premier in Lenin's last year.

The full-scale war against the "enemies of the people" began on January 23, 1937.

As Lilya Litvyak and Nina Kosterina, two fifteen-year-old, eighth-year schoolgirls, made their way to their classes through drifting snowflakes that winter, they saw the headlines in the newspapers that screamed constantly about "enemies" and villains worse than enemies, including the "Lowest of the Low," "Spies and Murderers," "Traitors of the Motherland," and the "Trotskyist Gang of Capitalist Restorers."

The first trials of 1937 saw another seventeen "Trotskyists" in the dock. The Old Bolsheviks had learned to dread the Man of Steel.

"A feature of the trials was Stalin's desire not merely to destroy his opponents, real and imagined," Volkogonov points out, "but first to drag them through the mud of amorality, betrayal and treason. All the trials are an unprecedented example of self-abasement, self-slander, self-condemnation ... Promises of leniency, threats of repression against their families and systematic physical torture broke these people and forced them to play their humiliating parts."

This was often manifested in preposterous ways, as defendants readily perjured themselves to confess to being enemies of the people. In 1936, Kamenev had admitted that "we served Fascism. We organized counter-revolution against socialism." In 1937, long-time Central Committee member Georgy Pyatakov was coerced into "confessing" that he met secretly with Trotsky in Oslo in December 1935 to "receive terrorist instructions." Pyatakov had not actually been to Oslo, but he confessed in order that the court might treat him with leniency. He was executed.

Stalin's enforcer, his grand inquisitor, the man who rounded up the enemies of the people, was Nikolai Ivanovich Yezhov, who became People's Commissar for Internal Affairs and thereby head of the NKVD, in September 1936. Naturally, Article 58, with its immense vocabulary of vague crimes, from *vreditel'stvo* (wrecking) to Anti-Soviet Agitation, provided Yezhov with the validation he needed to make his arrests.

Sitting in judgment of those arrested by Yezhov was Stalin's merciless hand-picked jurist, Vasiliy Vasilievich Ulrikh, while Andrey Januaryevich

Vyshinsky served as the lead prosecutor, a role which he reprised for Stalin after World War II during the Nuremberg Trials. Volkogonov notes that Vyshinsky's "accusatory tirades ... literally paralysed his victims in the dock. Most of them could only find the words to agree with him in the end."

The trials dominated the headlines in newspapers from *Pravda* to *Vecherniaia Moskva*, and they were the talk of the town. Amazingly, public opinion was solidly on the side of the state prosecutors. People had been told for so long and with such conviction that Stalin and the state were without fault that they automatically assumed all the victims to be guilty. After all, they had read the charges in the newspapers, so they must be true. After all, *Pravda* means "truth."

As Dmitri Volkogonov points out, Stalin's "manipulation of public opinion created the phenomenon of unity around a false idea. Thus Stalin brainwashed the millions. The wreckers were seen as enemies by everyone, and it could not have been otherwise ... the overwhelming majority of Soviet citizens indisputably believed that it was [still, as late as the 1930s] a struggle to the death with people who still wanted to restore capitalism ... The nation was turned into a lynch-mob."

Instead of feeling anger at the accusers, many people turned on their own family members. One extreme case was that of Osip Pyatnitsky, a friend of Lenin who headed the *Otdel Mezhdonarodnoi Sviazi* (International Liaison Department, or OMS) of the Comintern.

When he was arrested in 1937, his wife, Yulia Pyatnitskaya-Sokolova, wrote "that's why he lived like that, so withdrawn and severe. Evidently it was a weight on his soul ... I would be capable of spitting in his face, giving him the name of a spy." She was later arrested herself. It was guilt by association.

On the average streets among the average people, even schoolgirls such as Lilya Litvyak and Nina Kosterina were aware of what was going on, and they were outraged at the "crimes" for which the defendants were promptly convicted.

On February 7, 1937, Nina confided in her diary that "the terrible trial is over. Of course, they will be shot. How could it have happened that old revolutionaries who had fought for decades for a people's government became enemies of the people?" She then turned to a narrative about school activities and volleyball.

That same evening, she attended a costume ball dedicated to Aleksandr Pushkin. Nina dressed as Masha, the captain's daughter, wearing a long orange dress with white lace around the throat and on the sleeves, and, of course, a mask. She recalled feeling "wonderful all evening," and that the costume was very good for dancing.

Life went on, at least for the moment.

More arrests and more trials came quickly on the heels of the executions. As February gave way to March, delegates at the Central Committee plenum heard further damning reports. Andrei Alexandrovich Zhdanov, the Central Committee secretary and a favorite of Stalin, set a chilling tone, telling the assembled membership that "while our people slumber and are only getting going, our enemies are already active." The enemies of the people were, he insisted, within the party itself, and that brutal measures were required as much in 1937 as they had been during the Civil War.

On March 21, Nina welcomed spring, writing that "the snow is melting, rivulets run down the street. It makes you want to run and jump, but the third quarter is just ending, and we have tests every day."

She mentioned that she had written a composition for her literature class on the topic of nineteenth-century critic Vissarion Belinsky's critique of Pushkin's novel *Yevgeny Onegin* as "an encyclopedia of Russian life."

She does not say exactly what she wrote, but it would have been an opportunity for a commentary on the events which were unfolding around her in Moscow at the time. Just as Stalin was murdering his old Bolshevik colleagues, Pushkin's hero killed Vladimir Lensky, his best friend, in a duel. While Onegin is forever haunted by the incident, and condemned to the pain of loneliness, Stalin felt no remorse and instead took comfort in his isolation.

As Volkogonov writes, "Stalin agreed to the extermination of people with a startling and chilling absence of feeling. Enormously long lists of individuals and groups were sent to him. [In researching the files in the

Soviet state archives] I found only one document in the Stalin archive which suggests a degree of mercy on his part." A. S. Kuklin, who was "suffering from a malignant esophageal tumor," was released to die at home.

As the snow was melting and running like a dirty river into the Moscow sewers, neither Lilya nor Nina had been touched personally by the growing tide of the Great Purge. It was still an abstraction, playing out in headlines and involving public figures they did not know. Lilya, Nina, and their classmates were looking forward to the upcoming school vacation and the exams which separated them from that moment of freedom.

"With the coming of spring, we have all gone a little mad," Nina writes happily. "The effect of spring. I bought myself a hat, inexpensive, but lovely. It will go beautifully with my red dress. I can't wait for May Day!"

However, the cold hand of reality was even then lurking outside her window like the inhuman alter ego of Yevgeny Onegin, who haunts the nightmares of his girlfriend, Tatyana Larina, in the form of a monstrous bear.

March 25, only four days after writing happily of the coming of spring, Nina's tone changed dramatically.

"Something frightful and incomprehensible has happened," she writes. "They arrested Uncle Misha, father's brother, and his wife, Anya. Irma, our little cousin, was sent to a children's home. They say that Uncle Misha was involved with some counterrevolutionary organization. What is going on? Uncle Misha, a member of the Party from the very first days of the Revolution—and suddenly an enemy of the people!"

In the beginning, there had been just the despicable sixteen of the 1936 trials, and then the seventeen scoundrels charged in January 1937. Faster almost than anyone noticed, there were eighteen more, and then another eighteen. For a while, there seemed to be villains everywhere, and then they were no longer obvious villains, but many whom you could never have imagined being on the lists of those arrested, tried, and convicted. You started seeing your neighbors being arrested, and then your friends, and finally yourself. Misha Kosterin was merely one of the many who could never have imagined he would be on Stalin's list. Yet, here he was, perhaps because he had known someone or perhaps merely because he had been seen speaking to someone who had spoken to someone who was an enemy of the people.

As Aleksandr Solzhenitsyn recalls, "Arrests rolled through the streets and apartment houses like an epidemic. Just as people transmit an epidemic infection from one to another without knowing it, by such innocent means as a handshake, a breath, handing someone something, so, too, they passed on the infection of inevitable arrest by a handshake, by a breath, by a chance meeting on the street. For if you are destined to confess tomorrow that you organized an underground group to poison the city's water supply, and if today I shake hands with you on the street, that means I, too, am doomed."

On April 17, nearly a month after her uncle's arrest, Nina Kosterina was in a gloomy mood, writing of a six-hour Komsomol meeting that lasted well into the night. "The subject on the agenda was Criticism and Self-criticism," she writes. "The director gave us a short report on Stalin's speech on this question. Then we began to offer criticism. The director got most of it. And for good reason. A stick-in-the-mud, not a director. I also spoke and attacked him. I said everything that had been on my mind for a long time-about the poor discipline, about our section leader, and about him personally. … I got my share of criticism too: they said that I've stopped paying attention to my schoolwork, that I don't come to political study sessions, and so on. They are right. I really haven't been doing anything lately. … I cannot stop thinking about my little orphaned cousins."

The lists of those thousands who were arrested and executed included not true enemies of the people, but people who were enemies only in Stalin's paranoid fantasy.

Volkogonov, who had unrivaled access to the lists in the secret Soviet archives, reports seeing the names of countless army men, Comintern personnel, cultural figures, regional party chiefs, scientists, and writers, many of whom had met or communicated with Stalin, "or who had once called him 'comrade.'"

Many later years later, the great Russian poet Yevgeny Aleksandrovich Yevtushenko, who had turned five during the Great Purge, wrote in his poem *Fears*:

*Fears are dying out in Russia*
*like the ghosts of bygone years,*
*and only like old women, here and there,*
*they still beg for alms on the steps of a church.*
*But I remember them in their strength and power*
*at the court of triumphing falsehood.*
*Like shadows, fears crept in everywhere,*
*and penetrated to every floor.*

As the months passed, Nina Kosterina wrote of more people swept up in Stalin's dragnet. The NKVD came knocking at the door of the superintendent at her building. His daughter wailed as he was hauled off.

The father of Nina's friend Stella was arrested, and another friend, Laura, lost both parents in an NKVD sweep. Nina argued at a Komsomol meeting in September that Laura should not be expelled from the organization for refusing to denounce her parents. Meanwhile, Nina did some soul searching and wondered what she would do if her own father "turns out to be a Trotskyite or an enemy of his country." Naïvely Nina writes, "I shall not be sorry for him!" Then she adds, "I wrote this, but (I confess) there is a nagging worm of doubt."

She did not have long to wonder. In December, she learned that her own father, who had been working in the Soviet Far East for the past year, had been expelled from the Party and fired from his job.

"I shall not go into details," Alexei Kosterin wrote in a letter home. "At your age much will still be unclear to you. But you must remember one thing: you will need a great deal of calm and endurance now. I do not know as yet how events will turn for me. But even in the worst case, you must be sure that your father was never a scoundrel or double-dealer, and has never blemished his name by anything dirty or base. And therefore be steadfast! Of course, these are difficult days, but we must not and should not lose courage. We shall live through and overcome all ordeals."

Meanwhile, it should be noted that the "difficult days" of which Kosterin spoke were unfolding against the backdrop of a suddenly worsening Soviet economy. Only two years before, Stalin had said that things were getting better, and for a while, thanks to artificial manipulation, they had been. Now, clearly, they were not.

While urbanites had been growing more cheerful over the past few years, out in the countryside, the weather had been uncooperative, and the harvest in the autumn of 1936, like that in 1935, had been a disappointment. Some called it a failure. By 1937, bread lines were appearing again.

The farther one traveled from the centers of population, the less bright seemed the future—and indeed the present as well. In rural areas, where 90 percent of 25 million small households had been collectivized by the mid-1930s, living standards had barely, if at all, improved since Tsarist times, and output remained weak. As the *1987 Anniversary Statistical Yearbook* reports, between 1909 and 1940, grain production rose by only 19 percent, meat production by 15 percent, and milk increased by just 14 percent. Wool production, meanwhile, fell by 20 percent.

According to letters in the Leningrad Communist Party Archives quoted by Sheila Fitzpatrick, urban bread shortages were reported in the Voronezh region as early as November 1936. In Vologda, a wife wrote to her husband that "Mama and I stood from four in the morning and didn't even get any black bread because they didn't bring any at all to the store and that happened in almost all the stores of the town."

The news was bad even from the collective farms themselves. "We stand in line for bread from 12 o'clock at night, and they only give one kilogram, even if you're dying of hunger," complained a woman at a kolkhoz in Yaroslavl Oblast, 160 miles northeast of Moscow. "We go hungry for two days ... there are awful scenes—people push, many people have been injured. Send us something, or we will die of hunger."

Fitzpatrick adds with a great deal of irony that this round of hunger and famine took hold in the autumn of 1937, "when the harvest was the best in the decade and there was plenty of food in the stores."

While the countryside was witnessing bread lines and shortages, in Moscow, the epidemic of trials and executions had created an atmosphere of gloom, not one of the promised cheerfulness. Fitzpatrick writes that "both educated and uneducated Russians were seeing signs that a time of national misfortune was at hand."

The Great Purge continued unabated into 1938. On March 12, 1938, *Pravda* reported state prosecutor Vyshinsky's closing remarks in the trial of Nikolai Bukharin, a former *Pravda* editor-in-chief, Comintern chairman who had once been one of Stalin's closest allies.

"The whole country, from the youngest to the oldest, are waiting for and demanding one thing: that the traitors and spies who sold out our motherland to the enemy be shot like vile dogs!" Vyshinsky emoted. "The people demand one thing: that the accursed vermin be squashed! Time will pass. The hated traitors' graves will become overgrown with weeds and thistles, covered with the eternal contempt of honest Soviet people, of the entire Soviet people, while over our happy land, bright and clear as ever, our sun will shine its rays. We, our people, will as before stride along our path now cleansed of the last trace of the scum and vileness of the past, led by our beloved leader and teacher, the great Stalin."

For young people such as Lilya Litvyak, Nina Kosterina, and their thousands of ninth-year classmates, the days were filled with school, with Komsomol meetings, and with friends. Against a backdrop of almost cataclysmic turmoil in society, the young people in school focused on their own microcosmic world, on the smaller, more focused picture, rather than the big picture. Nina writes of ups and downs with her best friend, Lena Gershman, and of falling in love with a boy named Grisha Grinblat. She speaks of the special place where they used to sit along the Moscow River, and how she laughed when he expressed concern that she might fall into the water.

As summer came, and with it the hope that her father might soon be coming home from the Far East, Nina took a job, along with fellow Komsomol members, as a counselor at a summer camp for Young Oktoberists and Pioneers. She soon had her hands full with an "unorganized, undisciplined mass of kids," and a camp director who was "an incompetent weakling."

"I knocked myself out working with the first group," she writes. "My unit had twenty Oktyabryata, most of them boys, regular demons. From one school they sent us the worst brats. … This whole first term was like an ugly nightmare. I was glad when I was sent to Moscow two days before closing of the term to collect the clothing of the second group."

However, when she got home, the first news she heard was that her father, who was supposed to be coming home at last from the Far East, had been arrested.

"My head reeled," she recalls. "I went frantic and wrote Lena such a raving letter that she burned it immediately. At home we all felt as though we were about to be overrun by some ruthless invader. I decided to return to camp, now with a definite aim: we needed money … I had twenty-five kids in my unit, and it was a pleasure to work with them. It was only this work and my children that saved me from black despair and total confusion over what had happened to my father."

Nina Kosterina and Lilya Litvyak now had one more thing in common.

Lilya's father was also a victim of Josef Stalin's Great Purge.

Vladimir Litvyak, who was reportedly now a deputy commissar in the Commissariat of Transportation, had, like so many other Party men, and government bureaucrats, fallen under the freight train of arrests and convictions. Like Alexei Kosterin, Litvyak had been posted "temporarily" to the Far East. He had apparently gone there to play a role in the Second Five Year Plan expansion of the railway network in that unimproved region of the Soviet Union.

Litvyak was among the "enemies" who were weeded out by Lazar Kaganovich, the infamous "Iron Commissar" who ruled the Commissariat of Transportation through most of the Great Purge. He was already notorious for his own vicious purges, especially in the hierarchy of Soviet state railroads. Kaganovich was, and remained, one of Stalin's closest associates and trusted henchmen.

The situation within the Iron Commissar's Commissariat was downright dangerous in those days. Years later, Ivan Vladimirovich Koralev, a well-known figure in the history of Soviet railways, spoke with Dmitri Volkogonov. He explained that in 1937, Kaganovich had assigned him as head of a state railway division based in Minsk.

"I arrived in Minsk and went to the administration office," Koralev said. "It was empty. There was no one to hand over the job to me. My predecessor, Rusakov, had been arrested and shot. I called for his deputies. There weren't any. They'd been arrested. I looked for anyone, but there was only a strange and terrible silence. It was if a tornado had passed through. I was amazed that the trains were still running and wondered if anyone was controlling this enormous operation. I went to the apartment of an acquaintance who worked in the railway administration. To my surprise I found him at home with his wife, who was in tears."

"'Why aren't you at work?' Koralev asked, before even greeting him.

"'I'm waiting,' the man replied. 'They said they'd come for me today. See, I've got some clean shirts packed. [Viktor] Nasedkin of the NKVD [Central Staff] is purging every second man. He's probably paralysing the railway.'"

Such was the world of the transportation bureaucracy under the Iron Commissar.

Koralev goes on to say that "Having got the picture and recovered my composure, I phoned Stalin in Moscow—after all, if the railway didn't work as it was supposed to, I'd be the next on the list. [Alexander Nikolaevich] Poskrebyshev [director of administration of the General Secretary of Central Committee of CPSU, and therefore a Stalin assistant] answered. I told him of the situation. Somehow the rampage was rapidly brought to a halt. Anyway, there was no one left to put in gaol."

Vladimir Litvyak was not so lucky. As Ivan Korolev's acquaintance had explained, Viktor Nasedkin of the NKVD was purging "every second man," just a random selection of people, purged for no cause other than that he was just the "second man." Vladimir had been a randomly chosen "second man." Before the railway rampage was halted, he joined the long line of the purged.

"Hundreds of thousands would be cut down as if by a terrible plague," Volkogonov laments of the devastation wrought by the Great Purge. "Large gaps would soon appear in the top ranks of the party, state and economic administration, in the professional army and the technical and creative intelligentsia, as well as in organizations in the republics and provinces."

Litvyak and Kosterin had not been alone.

Even men who had once been "more equal" found themselves as "second men." Between a half and three quarters of the members of the Supreme Soviet and the officer corps of the Soviet armed forces were arrested, then sent to Gulags or executed. The higher they were in the Party or government hierarchy, the harder they fell.

In a speech given on November 26, 1938, Commissar for Defense Marshal Kliment Yefremovich Voroshilov boasted that "In the course of purging the Red Army in 1937–1938, we got rid of more than 40,000 men."

He did add that in ten months in 1938, more than 100,000 new officers were created. It was the lack of experience among the latter which would greatly harm the Soviet Union in the coming war.

Among those officers who had been eliminated was Marshal Mikhail Tukhachevsky. The same man responsible for putting down the peasant rebellion in the Tambov region back in 1921, Tukhachevsky was also regarded as an astute tactician who had been working toward transforming the Soviet Union into a military superpower. His loss is seen by historians as having been a serious disaster for the Red Army and a contributing factor to the debacle that allowed that army to be decimated by the Germans in World War II.

Sheila Fitzpatrick reminds us that while history recalls the names of the prominent, high-ranking victims, "enemies of the people" might be found at every level of society. She writes that "Finger-pointing at 'self-criticism' meetings in offices and enterprises, public accusation in newspapers, and private denunciation by citizens were among the selection mechanisms. Chains of associations were also very important. The NKVD would pull in one person and interrogate him, asking him to name his criminal associates; when he finally broke down and named some names, they would be pulled in turn, and the process continued."

The lines which Nina Kosterina wrote in her diary in September 1938 spoke for her friends Stella and Laura, as well as for Lilya Litvyak and for countless other sons and daughters on men and women who had fought the Tsar in the Revolution and against the Whites in the Civil War.

"What an ominous darkness has shrouded my whole life. Father's arrest is such a blow that it bends my back," Nina sobs. "Until now I have always carried my head high and with honor, but now … The nightmare thought oppresses me day and night: is my father also an enemy? No, it cannot be, I don't believe it! It's all a terrible mistake … My father and Uncle Misha are supposedly enemies of the people. How can I, their daughter in flesh and blood, believe this?"

By the end of 1938, the steam was starting to seep out of the binge of purging. So many people had been arrested that there was virtually no one left to be purged. Even Stalin loyalists who had replaced the purged Trotskyists were now being purged.

"In a society with almost a million office-holders, ranging from powerful figures to petty, poverty-stricken officials out in the countryside, where does the boundary-line between 'them' and 'us' lie?" Sheila Fitzpatrick asks rhetorically. "Moreover, if 'they' are the people who have access to state power through office-holding, how can a terror like the Great Purges, in which office-holders were the primary victims, be understood in 'them' against 'us' terms?"

It was no longer a matter of "us" and "them," of Stalinists versus their enemies, but of Stalin versus the phantoms within his imagination.

Ironically, one of the last to go was Nikolai Yezhov himself.

When Stalin discovered that his sadistic enforcer was an alcoholic, he transferred him to the post of People's Commissar for Water Transport in April 1938. In January 1939, he was at Stalin's side for the fifteenth anniversary of Lenin's death, but two months later, he was arrested. He begged for mercy, but was shot.

Then he was "erased."

One of the most grisly, yet almost amusing, artifacts of this era in Soviet history is the retouched photograph. Stalin was often seen in published pictures among groups of henchmen. As a particular individual was discredited, the same photograph would be reissued for publication with that individual carefully airbrushed into oblivion. One of the more infamous of these, so well known that it even shows up today in Stalin's Wikipedia entry, features a grinning Yezhov to Stalin's left. The picture was later published with Yezhov having been literally erased.

The biggest enemy of them all, in Stalin's mind, Leon Trotsky, survived the Great Purge of 1937–38. By the time he was finally killed—butchered with an axe in his comfortable Mexico City hacienda in August 1940 by NKVD operative Ramón Mercader—Stalin was preoccupied by a far more serious list of concerns.

Paradoxically, throughout the Great Purge, Stalin had appeared to remain above the fray. People blamed the Kremlin bureaucrats, and they blamed themselves, but Stalin remained as the light, the red sun upon the horizon, the archetypical man in red who had represented the sun in the story of Vasilisa that everyone of Lilya's generation had heard as a child in the formative years of the Soviet Union.

As historian Roger Reese writes in his book *Why Stalin's Soldiers Fought*, "People certainly were aware of the repressive actions of the secret police, the abuses of power and privilege by party members and government officials, and the hardships of life brought on by the economic policies of the Communist Party; however, they did not generally ascribe them to some evil intent on the part of Stalin or see them as inherent to the economic and social systems. Instead, they saw them as abuses of the political system by unscrupulous people who were, in fact, sometimes punished for their misdeeds."

Vladimir Litvyak and Alexei Kosterin were just two men, two "second men," in the company of millions. There is no consensus on how many, or the total number of victims. Based on party statistics, local reports, court records, and various statements by Stalin and others, Volkogonov makes a "cautious estimate" that between 4.5 and 5.5 million people were arrested, of whom as many as 900,000 were executed. Also citing Soviet archives, Richard Pipes writes in *Communism: A History* that 1,548,366 persons were arrested in 1937 and 1938, and 681,692 were executed. Other estimates of the death toll by scholars of the period range from 1.2 million, by Michael Ellman, to more than 1.7 million, according to Robert Conquest.

Most victims who were not executed received sentences of ten years or more. In a document uncovered in the Soviet archives by Volkogonov and dated March 7, 1948, Sergei Nikiforovich Kruglov, the Soviet Minister of Internal Affairs, reported to Stalin that "on 1 January 1948 there were [still] 2,199,535 prisoners in camps and colonies" of the Gulag Archipelago.

Alexei Kosterin and Aleksandr Solzhenitsyn were among those in the Gulags, but they were the lucky ones.

Vladimir Litvyak had been executed. Lilya had lost her own father to Father Stalin's purges.

Decades later, even after the purges were finally admitted and denounced, it remained the official position of the Communist Party of the Soviet Union that they were directed only at high-ranking bureaucrats, rather than at the masses, and not at "every second man" as had occurred in the little empire of Lazar Kaganovich.

"They have kept on assuring us, and we have unwittingly fallen for it, that the history of 1937 and 1938 consisted chiefly of the arrests of the big Communists—and virtually no one else," Aleksandr Solzhenitsyn wrote in 1973. "But out of the millions arrested at that time, important Party and state officials could not possibly have represented more than 10 percent. Most of the relatives standing in line with food parcels outside the Leningrad prisons were lower-class women, the sort who sold milk."

Indeed, the Great Purge had touched many millions who were not among its direct victims.

"I am sunk in a deep, gnawing depression," Nina Kosterina wrote in 1938. "Everything is either repulsive or meaningless ... I feel as though a rope were tightening around my throat. Such despair comes over me that I have no strength to shake myself, to unbend my back and look people boldly in the eye ... To take a deep and joyous breath."

## Chapter 6

# HEROES IN THE SKY

I t is an endlessly evocative and intriguing irony that even in the
gnawing depression of the Soviet Union's most horrendous and
pervasive repression, the cult of Stalin as both Father and sun
remained alive and flourishing. He was still the red rider of legend and
folklore, a man whose brilliance shone in the sky, which was becoming
the playground of a new form of mythical hero.

The pain and suffering were not his fault, they reasoned. As those who
were there—from Nina Kosterina to Aleksandr Solzhenitsyn—remind us,
the pervasive belief was that either the people arrested really were guilty
or that, perhaps, certain innocent people had been swept up in a noble
effort to rid society of true enemies.

Lilya Litvyak could blame Kaganovich, the Iron Commissar, who
likely had been directly responsible for her father being hustled away by
NKVD thugs, but she probably would not have allowed herself to believe
that the man whose face radiated from her classroom wall was in any
way culpable.

Continuing at the same time as the unabated celebration of the Stalin cult was that of the Stakhanovites and those lucky workers who had the good fortune to wear the medals that proclaimed them as Heroes of Soviet Labor. Even as Stalin and his henchmen were purging Party officials and bureaucrats, they were elevating "regular folks" as heroic exemplars of the purist ideals of Socialism.

Among the heroes who especially caught the fancy of the great leader and his people during the 1930s were Soviet aviators.

After Charles Lindbergh's New York-to-Paris solo flight had become a global media sensation in 1927, there had been an enormous fascination in the West with record-breaking fliers. As he had with Soviet workers, Stalin became interested in seeing his Soviet airmen ranked second to none on the world stage.

With the leader having become a booster of Soviet aviation, the people now turned their faces skyward to this new breed of hero. Coincidentally, it was Lazar Kaganovich, of all people, who verbalized the notion that this new breed had been bred by the Father himself. An unabashed Man of Steel sycophant, the Iron Commissar said of Soviet aviation that it "is the highest expression of our achievements. Our aviation is a child of Stalinist industrialization; fliers are our proven *sokols* [falcons], raised lovingly and with care by Stalin."

As proclaimed in the Soviet media, the heroic aviators would not be "the peoples' falcons," nor even "Soviet Falcons," but Stalin's Falcons.

The media also referred to them by the term *bogatyr*, the name for "daring hero" long used in the classic, epic tales of Russian literature and folklore. Indeed, aviators easily symbolized the ideal of such an intrepid champion of man over nature. In his book *Technology and Society Under Lenin and Stalin*, Kendall Bailes writes that these bogatyrs became "prime exhibits of the 'new Soviet men,' whom the authorities wished to create."

Stalin, who was extremely apprehensive of a personality cult growing up around anyone other than himself, felt particularly unthreatened by aviators. They harbored no political ambitions, and their feats were of singular daring, unique to a specific field of endeavor. Their realm was among the clouds, not of the earth. The Soviet people could lift their eyes to see the skies filled with falcons—Stalin's falcons.

Soviet aviation had risen slowly from the ashes of the Revolution. The Tsar's Imperial Russian Air Force had been defeated by the Germans, and most of its better officers and pilots either joined the Whites or fled Russia entirely. In 1918, the Bolsheviks cobbled together an air force for the Civil War, calling it the *Raboche-Krest'yansky Krasny Flot* (RKKF), meaning the Workers' and Peasants' Red Air Fleet.

The RKKF had started out as little more than a random collection of World War I-era machines and pilots who chose to fly with the Reds rather than the Whites. In 1930, the RKKF was renamed as the *Voenno-Vozdushnye Sily* (VVS), literally the Military Air Force of the Soviet Union. It was by this name that the Soviet air arm would flourish, and the name by which it would be known when Lilya Litvyak joined it, and by which it would be known, even after the demise of the Soviet Union in 1991.

Also in the early 1930s, the Soviet Union, unlike other countries, created an independent service specifically devoted to air defense, the Soviet Air Defense Forces (*Protivo Vozdushnoy Oborony*, PVO). During the Great Patriotic War, the PVO came to constitute a second, smaller air force. This parallel air force included not just antiaircraft artillery units, but also interceptor aircraft. Though she started out in the VVS, it would be with the PVO that Lilya would first go into combat.

The VVS began to evolve into a major world air force after the Soviet Union began to develop an indigenous aircraft industry. Many, especially the influential military theorist Mikhail Frunze, argued in favor of developing a strong, home-grown arms and aircraft industry.

Before Stalin began to encourage such an industry, however, the Communists had recognized the need to cultivate a cadre of pilots. Indeed, the importance of the Soviet airman was a concept that predated Stalin's fixation on aviators in the 1930s.

The underlying strength of Soviet aviation was not in hardware or in the industrial base, but in its pilots—not simply the supermen of great achievements, but in the rank and file of competent aviators. While the

Soviet Union would have neither a world-class air force nor an aviation industry of any note until the 1930s, the state had taken a proactive step toward creating a large number of pilots in the 1920s.

When it was formed, the RKKF had been short of everything but zeal, and the Communist Party had recognized the potential of exploiting and focusing this enthusiasm. In 1923, it was the Party that established the *Obshchestvo Druzei Vozdushnogo Flota* (ODVF), or the Society of Friends of the Air Fleet.

As Von Hardesty writes in *Red Phoenix*, his history of Soviet aviation, "With more than five thousand branches and around one million members, ODVF became a nationwide repository of Soviet air consciousness. Participants donated a portion of their salary, usually a day's wage, for the building of aircraft. ODVF called upon the workers and peasants for hard work and personal sacrifice. It became a conduit to express Bolshevik enthusiasm for the benefits of modern technology. Slogans, hyperbolic language, and organized events to dramatize Soviet devotion to air power punctuated the life of ODVF."

In turn, the ODVF was soon merged with another paramilitary organization, the Society of the Friends of Chemical Defense, resulting in the group that was called the *Obschestvo Sodeistviya Aviatsii i Khimicheskomu Stroitel'stvu* (The Society for Assistance to the Aviation and Chemical Industry). Formed in January 1927, this entity, with its impossibly long-winded name, was known universally by the acronym *Osoaviakhim*.

The activities of the Osoaviakhim, which was not unlike the Komsomol in its organizational structure and its emphasis on young people, were many and varied, but the two most important were its preparation of youth for defense in time of war and its flight-training program. Indeed, if the strength of Soviet aviation was its pilots, the Osoaviakhim air clubs were destined to be the nucleus of the program that turned Soviet youths into Soviet pilots.

Far below, on the streets of Moscow, Young Pioneers—girls as well as boys—still too young for the Osoaviakhim, strained their necks skyward at the sound of aircraft engines and the sight of the growing number of airplanes. These machines, and the aviators who flew them, were like the Russian knights in the old stories they remembered as children. The bogatyrs in their flying steeds fueled the imaginations of impressionable, aviation-minded young people such as Lilya Litvyak.

One day in 1933, a bright, happy day before the Great Purge, as Lilya gazed upward, there was a sign in the sky that she could not ignore. They declared her twelfth birthday as Soviet Air Fleet Day!

For Lilya, it was an auspicious coincidence that General Yakov Ivanovich Alksnis, the commander of the VVS, picked August 18 as the official date for the annual event. As she visited the displays in Gorky Park that week and watched the airplanes flying from the Central Moscow Aerodrome to perform in the sky, it confirmed that she had to be be part of this.

There was much to celebrate on that summer day. Soviet aviation was finally recovering from a stumbling start technologically, and soon the skies above Lilya's home would be filled with inspiring, world-class machines.

On the technological side, the Soviet Union suffered in its earliest days from having lost some of the best aeronautical minds in Imperial Russia, notably Igor Sikorsky, who defected to the West during the Revolution. However, the Soviet aeronautical infrastructure was gradually rebuilt in the 1920s by men such as aviation pioneer Nikolai Yegorovich Zhukovsky, who formed the *Tsentralniy Aerogidrodinamicheskiy Institut* (TsAGI), or Central Aerohydrodynamic Institute, in Moscow.

One of the rising stars within the TsAGI was Andrei Nikolayevich Tupolev, who would be one of the Soviet Union's leading aircraft designers for decades. After designing several smaller single-engine aircraft, he moved up to larger and larger aircraft. He borrowed concepts, such as all-metal, corrugated skin monoplane designs, which had been pioneered in Germany by Hugo Junkers for his twin-engine ANT-4 (designated with his initials), which became a VVS bomber under the designation TB-1.

In the winter of 1934, the ANT-4 became a symbol of Soviet aviation ascendancy. One of these aircraft, piloted by Anatoly Liapidevsky, spearheaded the rescue of seamen stranded in the Arctic Ocean after the sinking of the Soviet merchant steamer *Chelyuskin*, lost while en route from Murmansk to Vladivostok.

In an earlier era, the Soviet polar explorer had reigned prominently as an archetypical bogatyr. Now, the Soviet media trumpeted the transition to a new era of Soviet airman as bogatyr. The pilots participating in the rescue became the first recipients of the recently created Hero of the Soviet Union medal, which would become the Soviet Union's highest decoration for bravery.

Though Andrei Tupolev would himself be a victim of the Great Purge in 1937 (imprisoned though not executed), he had caught Stalin's fancy and favor around 1930 with his large, multiengined designs such as the ANT-6 and the ANT-16. Meanwhile, it was decided in 1932 that the fortieth anniversary of the start of Maxim Gorky's literary career should be celebrated by the commissioning of the largest aircraft yet built in the Soviet Union. This aircraft, designated as ANT-20 and named, of course, *Maxim Gorky*, was first flown amid great fanfare in April 1934.

With a wingspan of more than 206 feet and measuring nearly 108 feet from nose to tail, Tupolev's *Maxim Gorky* was an ostentatious behemoth that was plushed out in over-the-top amenities in the same spirit as the palatial stations on the Moscow Metro. These included red carpeting, a buffet bar, a movie theater, and even a film-processing lab. The ANT-20's cabin had a sixteen-line internal telephone exchange at a time when such a thing was rare in Moscow apartment buildings.

The aircraft was an expression to the outside world of Soviet technological might, just as the immense steel mills of the First Five Year Plan were an expression of Soviet Industrial might.

Tupolev's organization was also instrumental in creating the medium by which Stalin's Falcons would achieve their greatest milestones in the 1930s, the ANT-25. With a wingspan of nearly 112 feet, the single-engine aircraft was designed specifically for long-range flights, and its official name was "RD," for *Rekord Dal'nost* (meaning Record Distance). First flown in June 1933, the RD was followed three months later by the RD-2 *Dubler* (RD Double) variant with an improved, geared M34R engine.

Mikhail Gromov, the first man to test fly the ANT-25/RD-2 in 1933, went on to fly it, along with A. I. Filin and I. T. Spirin, on an exhausting seventy-five-hour flight in September 1934. Their journey took them on a 7,712-mile closed-course from Moscow over Dnepropetrovsk to Kharkov.

With the world's headlines and imaginations being fueled by a series of spectacular Lindbergh-inspired trans-Atlantic, trans-Pacific, and around-the-world flights in the early 1930s, Stalin desired such a milestone for his own Falcons. The goal set for Soviet airmen would be to fly nonstop from the Soviet Union to the Western Hemisphere across the Atlantic Ocean. It was Sigizmund Levanevsky, one of the pilots from the Chelyuskin rescue mission, who proposed the novel approach of flying to North America across the North Pole instead of across the Atlantic.

When the first attempt, in August 1935, failed due to engine trouble, Levanevsky blamed Tupolev and the ANT-25. However, his copilot, an aeronautical engineer named Georgy Baydukov, disputed the assessment and offered to make a second attempt. Levanevsky was replaced by a highly regarded fighter pilot named Valery Chkalov. With Aleksandr Belyakov as a third crewmember, Baydukov and Chkalov made a July 1936 flight in the ANT-25 from Moscow to the Soviet Far East, covering 5,825 miles in 56 hours and 20 minutes and landing on an island in the Okhotsk Sea.

By the summer of 1937, even as the Great Purge was in full swing, the stage was set for a diversion of public attention to the greatest of Stalinist aviation spectaculars. On the mind of the Man of Steel, and deliberately designed for global headline grabbing, were not one but two transpolar flights to the United States.

On June 18, Chkalov, Belyakov, and Baydukov took off from Moscow and headed north across the pole toward San Francisco. They made it to Seattle after about sixty hours and continued south but ran short of fuel over Eugene, Oregon. They turned around and made a landing at the U.S.

Army's Pearson Field near Vancouver, Washington, across the Columbia River from Portland, Oregon. They had covered 5,670 miles in 63 hours and 25 minutes.

Less than a month later, on July 12, Mikhail Gromov, a veteran of the record 1934 flight, left Moscow with A. B. Yumashev and S. A. Danilin in a second ANT-25/RD-2. They crossed the pole and traveled as far south as a fog-bound San Diego before turning inland to find a place to land. They touched down in a cattle pasture near San Jacinto in California's Riverside County after a 6,306-mile, nearly 63-hour flight. In so doing, they set new nonstop world distance record that was officially validated by the Fédération Aéronautique Internationale, the international governing body for aeronautical world records since 1905.

They returned to Moscow and a well-choreographed heroes' welcome. Though the state media and the party leadership did their best to spin their accomplishments into an epic triumph, they need not to have bothered. The Soviet people readily embraced their bogatyrs, just as they would embrace and celebrate Alexei Stakhanov a year later.

A Moscow diarist named Sokolov wrote of the parade on July 26 that "Today they met the heroes of the flight across the North Pole—Chkalov, Baydukov, and Belyakov. The [reviewing] platforms and [Red] Square were crowded with people. They greeted the heroes very stormily. The whole of Tverskaia Street was also crowded. Their cars, driving to the Kremlin, drove along a living corridor."

If Lilya Litvyak was not there, she knew about it and had wanted to go.

As Sheila Fitzpatrick writes in *Everyday Stalinism*, "with record-breaking aviators dominating the headlines, and children all over the Soviet Union dreaming of becoming aviators, the names of Soviet record-breaking aviators ... were known to everybody in the Soviet Union (at least everyone who read the newspapers) ... and Stalin and other party members did their best to cash in on their popularity ... when they returned in triumph, Stalin and his colleagues were at the airport to embrace them. Stalin was represented as a Father to the aviators, some of whom actually called him 'Father.'"

Indeed, as Kendall Bailes points out in *Technology and Society*, Chkalov actually wrote a widely published tribute entitled "Our Father," in which he explicitly says that "[Stalin] is our Father." Bailes goes on to say that other accounts "credit Stalin with much of the initiative and planning of [important flights, including, but not limited to] listening carefully to the ideas of Soviet aviators and aviation planners, tracing [the pilots'] routes, determining who [would] fly, and ... giving the final permission."

It was a two-way street. The Father was also able to bask in the considerable reflected glory of his falcons. In a 1998 article in the *Journal of Contemporary History* titled "Valerii Chkalov: Soviet Pilot as New Soviet Man," Jay Bergman writes that the aviators were held by the Soviet public as being beyond heroes, beyond Lindbergh. They were a form of superman who transcended time as they transcended the spatial bonds of earth.

He characterizes the Soviet pilots as "ideological prototypes, precursors of the people who would inhabit the future, from whose achievements ... the Soviet people could develop a sense of what living under communism would be like."

## Chapter 7

# HEROINES IN THE SKY

For the girl whose birthday fell on Soviet Air Fleet Day—or vice versa, as she preferred—these were exciting times. In a 1968 article in the journal *Aviatsiya i Kosmonavtika* (*Aviation and Cosmonautics*) titled "*Vyletala Lilya v Boy*" ("Lily Flew Out to Fight"), S. Gribanov writes "The Thirties were a time of enthusiasm for flying, when Soviet pilots set records and covered themselves with glory ... and the little girl's bold urge to fly gradually grew more and more persistent. When Lilya turned fourteen [in August 1935], the mustachioed janitor at the flying club wouldn't even let her come near the club's building. How was she to make the old man realize that she couldn't imagine her future without flying, that going up into the sky was possibly her calling, her fate?"

Indeed, it was at age fourteen that Lilya received what Gribanov called "semi-official permission" to attend classes at the local Osoaviakhim flying club. She was too young to enroll, and because she was so small of stature, she looked even younger than her years. Nevertheless, she was already demonstrating the thirst for adventure and her determination to get what she wanted, which would be her trademark for the rest of her life.

At first, she did not tell her parents that she was haunting the flight line. Her mother was horrified when she found out, and she never stopped fearing for Lilya. In later years, though, her immense pride in her daughter emerged. According to what Anna Vasil'yevna told Gribanov in the 1960s, Lilya "passed her theoretical examination brilliantly, but was not yet permitted to fly ... However, Ulyanov, the instructor, would sometimes go up into the air with the bewitched Lil'ka."

At first, Lilya did not tell her parents when she finally took the controls of a Polikarpov U-2 biplane training aircraft.

One day in 1936, when she was fifteen years old and in her eighth year at school, Lilya was at the airfield where she had first experienced the thrill of flight and the feeling of her hand on the control stick. Ulyanov was there. He was waiting for various student pilots to return from practice circling or cross-country flights.

It was late in the day, and the skies were clear. According to the memory of Anna Vasil'yevna as related to Gribanov, Ulyanov turned to Lilya and told her to get into the rear cockpit of one of the Polikarpov biplanes. The rear cockpit was where the instructor usually sat. The student rode in the forward position, which is where Lilya always sat.

"Would you like to fly solo?" Ulyanov asked.

"Of course!" Lilya replied with a smile, as though she thought he was just kidding.

As Gribanov writes, "He went on to brief her for an umpteenth time about what she should do. After tightening her safety harness, he slapped the girl's shoulder in a friendly fashion."

"Well, let's go," he said, jumping off the wing.

As the Soviet journalist recalls, "Clouds floated in her eyes for a long, long time. But the bright passenger did not daydream while she was airborne; she soon learned how to control the aircraft and orientated herself well in the air."

Lilya Litvyak's first solo flight was "a unique and inexpressible sensation!"

Another young woman who soloed around the same time as Lilya, Nina Raspopova, later told Anne Noggle that she had already fallen in love with flying before she made her first solo flight. "Only a pilot can understand how it feels to be in the air without the instructor," she explained. "Only a pilot knows the whole scope of feelings and sensations you experience when face to face with the sky and aircraft! On my first solo flight I sang, cried, and sobbed with happiness. I couldn't believe I was manning the plane."

Lilya, Nina, and their fellow Osoaviakhim fledglings, male and female, logged their first hours primarily in the ubiquitous Polikarpov U-2 biplane, which first flew in 1927 and entered VVS service in 1929. The two-seat, open-cockpit U-2, designated with a "U" for *Uchebny*, meaning "trainer," was designed by Nikolai Polikarpov, who had worked for Igor Sikorsky before World War I and who stayed on to become one of the Soviet Union's important early aircraft designers.

A simple and durable little aircraft, the U-2 was a far cry from the enormous and complex Tupolev planes. While Tupolev's big aircraft were grabbing headlines, Polikarpov's planes were training pilots—by the thousands.

More than 40,000 examples of the U-2 (later redesignated as Po-2 in Polikarpov's honor) were built, more than any other Soviet aircraft, and they remained in production for more than a quarter century. The noted aviation historian Bill Gunston wrote in his book *Aircraft of the Soviet Union* that "Polikarpov created roughly 99 percent of Soviet trainer, fighter and reconnaissance aircraft up to 1941."

It can also be said that the U-2/Po-2 created a roughly equal proportion of the pilots in Lilya Litvyak's generation.

Meanwhile, as the obsession with Stalin's Falcons, the majestic bogatyrs of spectacular achievements, was creating a class of great male heroes of Soviet aviation, it was also in the process of creating female role models for girls such as Lilya.

Chkalov, Gromov, and the others had inspired "children all over the Soviet Union dreaming of becoming aviators," but it would be the arrival of the great women pilots that would be the inspiration of the generation of teenage girls at the Osoaviakhim flight schools. These girls would become the generation of women pilots who rose to prominence during the Great Patriotic War.

On the global aviation scene, there was a great deal of interest and headline ink devoted to the records being set by women pilots. Among them were Britain's Amy Johnson and the American pilot Ruth Nichols. The great Amelia Earhart became internationally famous in 1932 as the first woman to fly the Atlantic solo, and in 1935, as the first person to fly solo from Hawaii to the mainland. Her disappearance on an around-the-world flight in July 1937, the same month as Gromov's record flight, was one of the prominent news stories of the year and is still a widely discussed mystery.

In the Soviet Union, three women pilots would come to be elevated above all others in the official media. Valentina Grizodubova, Polina Osipenko, and Marina Raskova became widely celebrated household names within the Soviet Union and garnered headlines abroad as well.

Like Stalin's male falcons, with whom they shared popular notoriety, the women were all officers in the VVS. The former were both pilots, while Raskova had been trained initially as a navigator. She among them was a Russian. The others were Ukrainian, one a peasant girl, the other the daughter of a family who had been part of the pre-Revolution upper middle class.

Valentina Stepanovna Grizodubova was born in the city of Kharkov (Kharkiv in Ukrainian) in 1910, the daughter of a pilot and successful aircraft builder named Stepan Vasilyevich Grizodubov. Between 1910 and 1912, during the later years of the Tsar's rule, Grizodubov was known for having built a number of aircraft modeled after the biplanes of America's Wright brothers and France's Voisin brothers. By the age of fourteen, Valentina was an accomplished pianist, while her parallel interest in aviation led to her having soloed in a glider. She graduated from the technical institute in Kharkov and later taught at the advanced flying school in Tula.

Polina Denisovna Osipenko was born in 1907 in the village of Novospasovka—since renamed Osipenko in her honor—in the Zaporizhia Oblast in eastern Ukraine. Later nicknamed "Goldfinch," she graduated from the Kacha Aviation School in 1932. She served as a junior pilot and flight commander in VVS fighter aviation where she demonstrated skills that soon got her noticed by her senior officers. After a brief marriage to her childhood sweetheart, a pilot named Stepan Govyaz, ended in divorce, she married Aleksandr Osipenko, a fighter pilot who was one of the highest scoring aces flying with Soviet "volunteer" units during the Spanish Civil War. While Govyaz went to the Gulag during the Great Purge, never to return, Aleksandr Osipenko was a Party man who rose quickly to the rank of general and was in the upper command echelon of the PVO during and after World War II.

Marina Mikhailovna Malinina was born in Moscow in 1912, the daughter of a music teacher. A gifted musician in her own right, she had been an aspiring opera singer as a girl, but had abandoned music after the death of her father to train as a chemist. She was married for several years to an engineer named Sergei Raskov, and kept her married surname, Raskova, after their divorce.

Marina had no interest in becoming a pilot until after she left the Butyrsky Chemical Plant to go to work in the drafting department of the Nikolai Zhukovsky Air Force Engineering Academy in October 1931. She was later one of the first women on the faculty of this institution, which was located on Leningrad Prospekt, near Moscow's Central Airfield. In 1933, she joined the VVS, where she became the first female navigator in that service. In 1934, while she was teaching aerial navigation to VVS pilots, she trained to become a pilot at a Moscow air club.

Marina Raskova, Polina Osipenko, and Valentina Grizodubova made headlines at home and around the world. Even *The New York Times* had carried articles about the flights made by these women. On July 3, 1938, the paper made mention of a 1,498-mile flight from Sebastopol to Arkhangelsk in which Raskova and Osipenko crewed with Vera Lomako. In the piece, the *Times* gave them top billing over a male pilot, quite well-known in the

Soviet Union at the time, Vladimir Kokkinaki, who had made a 4,300-mile flight from Moscow to Vladivostok. The paper even misspelled his name. Such was the interest in a record-setting flight by women in an era when the world was still obsessed with Amelia Earhart.

The Sebastopol to Arkhangelsk flight set the stage for a major showpiece of Soviet aviation: a flight across the entire breadth of the Soviet Union by an all-women crew. Their aircraft was a variant of the Tupolev ANT-37, which was officially named *Rodina* (Motherland), a patriotic word, of course, and a description of the vast land that would unfold beneath their wings.

Like the ANT-25 of earlier record flights, the ANT-37 bore a Tupolev designation, though it was designed primarily by Pavel Sukhoi, who worked under Tupolev at the time. Later, Sukhoi headed his own design bureau, which became well known for its association with important jet fighters later in the century.

The ANT-37 had a very large wing, spanning almost 102 feet, specifically designed for long-distance flying. Unlike the ANT-25, for which a bomber variant was an afterthought, the ANT-37 was originally intended as a warplane, and it officially bore the VVS designation DB-2 (for *Dal'ny Bombardirovschik*, or long-range bomber). The type first flew in 1935, and several variants had been tested before Raskova, Osipenko, and Grizodubova were assigned to fly across the continent in the DB-2B model.

The plan was for the *Rodina* to fly from Moscow, across Siberia, to Komsomolsk, a city on the Amur River about 200 miles from the Pacific Ocean. It was a feat easier said than done, and which was expected to take around thirty hours. The official press release stated that Stalin himself was consulted on the route.

It was reported that both Polina Osipenko and Valentina Grizodubova had met with Stalin personally before the flight, and that he made "valuable practical suggestions." In fact, the Man of Steel knew little of useful importance about aviation technique. He was deathly afraid of flying and would not make an airplane flight until 1943—the one and only flight of his life. It was reported in the Soviet media that he did insist upon a radio station—probably no more than a radio beacon or a radio relay installation—being set up on the north side of Lake Baikal to facilitate communications.

In keeping with Stalin's desire for his record-setting flights to be spun as high-profile media events, the upcoming flight garnered a great deal of attention in the Soviet and European media.

Numerous dignitaries from the world of Soviet aviation visited the women at the airfield as preparations were being made for the flight. Among them was I. S. Levin, the manager of the aircraft factory in Irkutsk. An associate of aircraft designer Aleksandr Sergeyevich Yakovlev, Levin was to play a key role in Marina Raskova's professional career four years later when her VVS units were in need of fighters from Yakovlev's factories.

Early on the morning of September 24, 1938, the Soviet media gathered to watch the this *troika* (threesome) of women as they climbed into their aircraft. Pictures showed them swathed in cold weather gear. It was already winter in Siberia, and it would be very cold at the altitude they would be flying. Marina Raskova took her place as the navigator in the large glass nose of the aircraft, and the others strapped into the flight deck above and behind her. The gaggle of dignitaries who gathered to see them off included Mikhail Kaganovich, the brother of the Iron Commissar, who was himself the Commissar of Defense and Aviation Industry.

As was customary on intended distance record flights, officials from the Fédération Aéronautique Internationale sealed the fuel tanks to ensure that the aircraft did not land to refuel en route. Unfortunately, this took place before the tanks could be topped off after the engine run-ups that had taken place overnight. This oversight was the harbinger of an ominous confluence of glitches that unfolded as the *Rodina* winged its way eastward.

The weather grew steadily worse, and communications with the three women were lost before they even got close to Stalin's new Lake Baikal radio station. As the navigator, Marina Raskova faced a unique challenge. Few people had ever done what the troika was attempting, and navigational charts for this part of the Soviet Union were hit and miss when it came to specific details. Indeed, they were little better for their area of coverage than were the navigational charts used by the ocean-going navigators who visited the Americas in the sixteenth century.

For the most part, terrain and landmarks in the Soviet Far East had never been seen from the air. Marina was compelled to navigate with a compass and sextant, but the weather and cloud cover made it difficult to take sextant readings. When they managed to get above the clouds, the temperature plummeted. Ice built up on the *Rodina*'s wings, and it felt as though ice also was building up on hands that necessarily went gloveless when Marina was using her sextant.

Nevertheless, the women pressed on, and their young navigator kept the *Rodina* on course. They finally reached the airspace near Komsomolsk on the morning of September 25. However, a blanket of low clouds and continued poor visibility made it impossible to land. Had their fuel tanks been full on takeoff, they might have had more time to locate a clear runway, but the engines were starting to sputter.

The two pilots decided to look for any patch of level ground that might be visible through a break in the clouds on which to make an emergency landing. This put Marina Raskova at a serious disadvantage. Out in the nose of the aircraft, enclosed in the greenhouse-like glass room, the navigator's position was a wonderful place to be while flying on a sunny day, but in a crash landing, it was a deathtrap. There was absolutely no protection if the plane collided with a tree or came in too steeply. Because the ANT-37/DB-2B was designed with no passage between this position and the rest of the aircraft, the crash landing procedure called for the navigator to bail out. Marina had no choice.

Once she had ditched, Polina and Valentina picked what looked like a level place, throttled back, and hoped for the best. The good news was that it was a level spot. The bad news was that it was a muddy marsh. They survived the crash landing without the *Rodina* sinking in the muck, but they wound up having to get by mainly on chocolate bars in the remote taiga for eight days before they saw a rescue party.

In the meantime, they assumed that their comrade's parachute had come down near the crash site, but it hadn't.

In fact, Marina Raskova had come down quite far from the crash site, injuring her legs. Alone, barely able to move, and having lost the pack carrying her emergency rations, she was by far the worst off of the three. She would not be reunited with her crewmembers for ten days.

The loss of the *Rodina* became headline news in the Soviet Union and around the world. An enormous air search was launched as soon as the weather cleared, and motor launches cruised the numerous Amur tributaries that snake throughout the region, but there were millions of square miles to search.

At last, the hunt bore fruit. On October 3, the Associated Press carried the news that "three of fifty planes engaged in the search reported seeing a twin-engine plane with two persons signaling from the ground. Preparations were made immediately to send a parachute landing party, including a physician, as well as supplies of food, medicines, boots and hot drinks to be dropped by parachute."

Because the AP report was based on Soviet sources, these details were essentially identical to what seventeen-year-old Lilya Litvyak and her friends read in *Pravda* that day. On October 8, they read that Marina Raskova had been found, and that Stalin had sent his congratulations by telegram.

Lilya almost certainly attended the huge celebration in Red Square when the famous troika returned, triumphant, to Moscow. At the celebratory banquet, Raskova was seated next to Stalin himself, and the two struck up a lasting friendship.

Though the *Rodina* had ignobly crash-landed in the muck, the women had succeeded in setting their straight-line distance record of about 3,700 miles. They had covered more than 4,000 miles in their more than twenty-six hours aloft, but part of that distance had been consumed by circling in search of a place to land.

The trio became the first women to be decorated as Heroes of the Soviet Union, and the only women to receive this medal prior to the Great Patriotic

War. Their hardships and accomplishments were chronicled in an officially sanctioned book titled *The Heroic Flight of the Rodina*, and Marina Raskova wrote a book herself titled *Zapiski Shturmana* (*Notes of a Navigator*), which was published in Moscow in 1939. The three women officially joined the heretofore all-male pantheon of Soviet aviation bogatyrs.

As aviation heroines, all three remained on flight status. Polina Osipenko became a test pilot, but two years later, this cost her her life. On May 11, 1939 (some sources say May 10), she was killed in a crash, along with fighter pilot Anatoli Serov. Like Valery Chkalov, the superman of male falcons, who was killed on December 15, 1938, in the crash of the prototype Polikarpov I-180 fighter, Polina died young and violently, doing what had become the reason for her life as a heroine of the Soviet Union.

Aleksandr Osipenko, her second husband, took Polina's loss hard. Indeed, it has been said that he remained bitter about it for the rest of his life. A conspiracy theory lurks in some accounts of her life, whispering that her aircraft had been sabotaged, and that the aviator known as the Goldfinch had been deliberately murdered, although the exact motive remains murky.

Stalin's preoccupation with women in aviation is illustrated by the fact that, although Serov was a general and Polina was merely a captain, it was at her funeral and interment in the Kremlin wall that the Man of Steel actually acted as a pallbearer. His interest in the topic is further indicated by how, of all the junior officers in the VVS, Marina Raskova would continue to have his ear.

During the years following the flight of the *Rodina*, Marina became one of the most prominent figures in the heroic folklore that had grown up around Stalin's Falcons. A charismatic woman, she developed a great following among the young women who were learning to fly during the late 1930s. Many, like Lilya Litvyak, followed her career and even carried clippings of her exploits in their scrapbooks. She had become their role model, and when war came, she would be their leader.

*Chapter 8*

# FROM BEHIND DARK CLOUDS

D uring the 1930s, as the Osoaviakhim was training the thousands upon thousands of pilots who would become the backbone of the wartime VVS and PVO, the inevitability of a second world war was coming into sharper and sharper focus.

After World War I, a defeated and bitter Germany had seen its armed forces greatly restricted as a result of the Treaty of Versailles. However, this abruptly changed when Adolf Hitler's National Socialists came to power in 1934, and Hitler became *Führer und Reichskanzler* (leader and Reich Chancellor). He began rearming Germany, and tensions quickly increased between that nation and its wartime enemies, Britain and France.

Meanwhile, because the National Socialists were vehemently anti-Communist, Germany became a serious ideological antagonist to the Soviet Union. Indeed, the two nations were actually engaged in combat against one another between 1936 and 1939 as both of them sent elements of their armed forces, especially their air forces, to actively support opposing sides in the Spanish Civil War.

Hitler's animosity toward the Soviet Union and its people transcended his passionate hatred of Communism and Communists. It was personal. Though little was said about it in the 1930s, when it was merely theoretical, Hitler had written at length in his 1926 manifesto *Mein Kampf* (*My Struggle*) about the concept of *Lebensraum* (living space). Essentially, he imagined that Germany was running out of space and needed more land—land that was then part of the Soviet Union. As for the people who lived there—Russians, Byelorussians, and Ukrainians—they were mainly Slavic people, and in Hitler's mind, the Slavs were "subhuman."

As Hitler had written, the German policy toward the Slavs and their "Jewish-Bolshevik masters" should be to "either sterilize these racially foreign elements to ensure that [the German] people's blood is not continually adulterated or remove them altogether and make over to [the German] people the land thereby released."

The ticking of the time bomb of World War II began with Hitler's grab for the territory of Germany's closest neighbors. In March 1938, Hitler annexed Austria in a move that was called *Anschluss*, or "connection." This fulfilled the dreams of Germanic ethnocentrists in both countries who wished to see all German-speaking people united in a single Reich. There were also large numbers of ethnic Germans in Czechoslovakia, and Hitler next demanded that Czechoslovakia's German-speaking Sudetenland region also be folded into his Third Reich.

In September 1938, at the now infamous summit conference, Britain's Prime Minister Neville Chamberlain and France's President Edouard Daladier flew to Munich, the mother city of the Nazi Party, to meet with Adolf Hitler. The Führer told these gentlemen that the Sudetenland should properly be part of Germany, and he promised that this was the end of his territorial ambitions. Czechoslovakia naturally complained, but Chamberlain and Daladier ignored the Czechs and acceded to the Führer's demands. When Chamberlain arrived home, he happily announced that he had helped to negotiate "peace for our time."

Viewing these events from Moscow, Josef Stalin was deeply troubled. As Dmitri Volkogonov writes, it was crucially important to the Man of Steel "not to allow the imperialist states to form a bloc against the Soviet Union … Stalin was very worried about what was contained in the Munich deal, the Anglo-German declaration of non-aggression signed in September 1938 and the similar Franco-German agreement signed in December. These understandings in effect gave Hitler a free hand in the east and could form the basis of an anti-Soviet alliance. Stalin knew that if this happened it would be hard to imagine a worse position for the country."

In March 1939, Hitler decided that he wanted to possess the remainder of Czechoslovakia. The price tag for "peace for our time" had gone up. Chamberlain and Daladier were willing to go to almost any lengths to appease Adolf Hitler and avoid war. Like a terminal patient in a hospital bed, Czechoslovakia had no choice. The helpless country was chopped into bits. Slovakia was sliced off as a quasi-autonomous satellite of Germany, while the remainder of Czechoslovakia became the Reich Protectorate of Bohemia and Moravia.

"Stalin was ripe for a decision," Volkogonov writes. "He could either make a treaty with Britain and France, or a pact with Hitler or, least welcome, remain in isolation. The first option was the most desirable, as it would make the USSR part of an anti-Fascist coalition, having both enormous material potential and moral advantage. But lacking time, he could not wait any longer, especially as London and Paris were not keen on a rapprochement with the USSR. Stalin's mistake was to exaggerate the possibility that England and France would form a bloc with Nazi Germany."

Stalin feared war and wished to avoid or forestall a conflict with his foe, for which the Soviet Union was ill prepared. The Great Purge had dangerously gutted the Red Army officer corps, and elements of the Red Army were then tied down in border skirmishing with the Japanese army in Manchuria. With this in mind, he undertook negotiations with both sides. Even though they were his natural enemies, the Germans wound up giving Stalin a better deal than the Anglo-French negotiators.

On August 24, 1939, much to the surprise of international leaders and the global media, the world was stunned to learn that Nazi Germany and the Soviet Union had signed the Treaty of Non-Aggression.

Calling this move one of Stalin's biggest blunders, Volkogonov asserts that "an alliance with the Western democracies would have been immeasurably preferable. But neither Britain nor France was ready for such an alliance. From the point of view of state interest, the Soviet Union had no other acceptable choice. A refusal to take any step would hardly have stopped Germany ... Rejection of the pact could have led to the formation of a broad anti-Soviet alliance and threaten the very existence of socialism."

It was, according to Hitler's timetable, time for war.

A week later, on the morning of September 1, German bombs began falling on Poland, and German troops raced across the border. On September 3, Britain and France declared that a state of war between them and the Third Reich had existed for two days.

World War II had begun.

Not revealed until after the war was the fact that the nonaggression pact contained "secret protocols" by which Stalin would be Hitler's partner in dismembering Poland. "Following the unexpected agreement with Hitler, Stalin went still further," Volkogonov explains. "He agreed to a number of supplementary treaties, known as the 'secret protocols', which gave a distinctly negative character to an otherwise forced and perhaps necessary step. Stalin's understanding with Hitler over the fate of the Polish lands appears especially cynical, for it was tantamount to the liquidation of an independent state."

Most of western Poland disappeared into the Third Reich, while the parts of the old Tsarist empire that had been transformed into the eastern part of independent Poland were reincorporated—permanently—into the Soviet Union.

According to an account in *Pravda* on September 17, Molotov spoke to the Soviet people on the radio the day before, explaining that "no one knows the present whereabouts of the Polish government ... The Polish population has been abandoned to its fate by its unfortunate leaders ... The Soviet government regards it as its sacred duty to proffer help to its Ukrainian and Byelorussian brothers in Poland ... The Soviet government has instructed the Red Army command to order its troops to cross the border and to take under its protection the life and property of the population of the western Ukraine and western Byelorussia."

As though it had been Poland's fault that Poland had ceased to exist.

Meanwhile, the secret deal had also allowed Stalin to absorb into his Union of Soviet Socialist Republics Estonia, Latvia, and Lithuania, which were part of the Tsar's empire but had been independent since World War I.

Another of the "secret protocols" placed Finland in the Soviet sphere of influence. In 1939, Stalin sent the Red Army to occupy Finland, but the Soviets were stopped by the Finns in a series of bloody clashes that unfolded over the next several years. The reasons for the Soviet failures in this sideshow to World War II are generally attributed to Stalin's decimation of his officer corps and command staff during the Great Purge.

As far as the main thrust of the action in World War II, though, Stalin was now able to sit back as a mere spectator, while Germany's Wehrmacht swept westward, conquering most of Western Europe, from Norway to France, between April and June 1940.

Especially impressive—and horrifying—to all observers was the coordinated German air and ground offensive tactic, known as *Blitzkrieg* (lightning war). It was the most rapid and efficient mode of military attack the world had ever seen. The use of fast-moving tanks, mobile forces, dive-bombers, and paratroop units, all working together as one tight, well-disciplined force, stunned the world.

The success of the German air force, the Luftwaffe, was remarkable. From aircraft development to pilot training, the Luftwaffe was seen as the most effective air force in the world. Even after sparring to a draw with the British Royal Air Force in the Battle of Britain in the summer and early autumn of 1940, the Luftwaffe was seen by many air planners as a force second to none.

When considering his choice of a nonaggression pact partner, Stalin had to have been feeling rather smug after Hitler's successes in 1940. Nevertheless, through the lens of 20-20 hindsight, we can easily see that he should have known better. Indeed, as Volkogonov recalls, "There is evidence to suggest that Stalin was aware even before the war that he had made an error. In striving to avert or at least postpone war, he had crossed the last ideologically justified boundary, and this would have far-reaching consequences."

No one was more impressed with the German war machine than Adolf Hitler himself. His successes in the West only emboldened him to look east toward that which he still perceived—the nonaggression pact notwithstanding—as his most mortal enemy. The audacious German plan to invade the Soviet Union was hatched in the summer of 1940 at the time of the fall of France, and planning took place through the ensuing winter. Based on his own successes and the Red Army's failure in Finland, Hitler was optimistic, and he planned for a quick and decisive campaign.

As the Germans began moving immense quantities of troops and supplies eastward toward the Soviet border, Stalin continued to ignore a number of warning signs. Stalin's biographer writes that "In the last two months before the war, Stalin received several reports from a variety of intelligence, diplomatic and other sources, warning of Hitler's impending attack on the USSR. The British and US governments also sent warnings. In April 1941, [Winston] Churchill, who was now prime minister, sent a report that the Germans were moving large numbers of their forces to the east."

For most people in the Soviet Union, 1941 had unfolded much as any other. Bread lines persisted. Harvests were brought in from the fields. For young people who had completed much of their classroom career, it was time for practical fieldwork in their area of study. Coincidentally, Nina Kosterina and Lilya Litvyak, both now twenty-year-old geology students, were doing their fieldwork far from their homes in Moscow.

In the Soviet Union, the summer of 1941 began as had any other in recent memory. Children went away to Pioneer Camp, and their parents went about their business. The war was on everyone's mind, but it was still far away.

That summer, Nina Kosterina had fallen in love. "Life is good," she confided in her diary. "I love a fine, wonderful man. He is not only a man to me, not only a lover; he is also our friend, our brother, full of concern for us. He is loved and respected by every member of our geological party."

Lilya Litvyak, meanwhile, had returned from her geology fieldwork to her own first love, flying. After having been an instructor at the Kherson Flying School for a time, she had returned to Moscow. Though naturally shy, she had matured into a confident young woman. Her skills as a pilot didn't hurt.

Bruce Myles writes that a woman named Larissa Rasanova, whom he identifies as a fellow instructor pilot, later told him that "Lilya was one of these people who was good at everything she tried. And she was so popular with the boys. I think every man at the flying club was in love with her. Women being what they are, it didn't go down too well with everyone. But, surprisingly, there wasn't nearly as much jealousy as you might have expected of a girl as talented and good-looking as she was."

On the fourth Sunday of June, Nina was still in the field with her fellow geologists, and Lilya was at Klyazminskiy Airfield. Within a matter of hours, they each heard the distressing news that this would not be a summer like all the others after all.

In the predawn hours of that Sunday, June 22, the German Wehrmacht launched its invasion of the Soviet Union. The largest military action in world history, it was known as Operation Barbarossa, named for the twelfth-century German conqueror king and Holy Roman Emperor, Frederick I, who was called "Barbarossa" because of his red beard. The invasion achieved conquests Barbarossa himself could never have imagined—and a faster pace than almost anyone could have imagined.

More than 4 million Axis troops, most of them German, supported by 3,300 armored vehicles and a Luftwaffe contingent numbering around 4,000 aircraft spilled across the border. They consummated quick and decisive victories, pushing deep into the Soviet Union across an 1,800-mile front. According to Russian military historian Mikhail Meltyukhov, the Soviet armed forces then numbered 5.8 million, with 3.3 million being on the front facing Operation Barbarossa. Nevertheless, they literally collapsed under the weight of the invasion force.

The German strategic objectives were threefold. Army Group North was to drive on and capture Leningrad, while Army Group Center did the same with Moscow. The objective of Army Group South was to capture the rich agricultural regions of Ukraine and the city of Kiev, pressing eastward across the steppes toward the Volga River, while capturing the Soviet oil fields in the Caucasus.

The immediate German tactical objectives were to achieve air superiority over the entire front and to capture as many Red Army troops as possible by using fast mechanized forces to encircle them and trap them in pockets.

Citing sources in the German Bundesarchiv-Militararchiv at Freiburg and the Luftfahrtmuseum at Hannover-Laatzen, as well as the Soviet Record Archives and the TsAMO (*Tsentral'nyi Arkhiv Ministerstva Oborony*, the Central Archive of the Ministry of Defence), Christer Bergström puts the Luftwaffe strength on the front on June 22 at 4,389, and total VVS strength at 11,537 aircraft. Von Hardesty, in *Red Phoenix*, quotes VVS Marshal Konstantin Vershinin, who states that the totals were 4,950 and 10,980, respectively. Despite their numeric superiority, though, the Soviet airmen were hopelessly outclassed.

In accordance to the blitzkrieg battle doctrine, German air power was tasked with eliminating Soviet air power. On the first day, the Luftwaffe attacked sixty-six air bases containing three quarters of the VVS aircraft. The Germans claimed that they destroyed 1,811 aircraft that day, 80 percent on the ground.

In an official Soviet account by I. V. Timokhovoch, published in Moscow in 1976, the VVS acknowledged losing 1,136 aircraft on the first day, 70 percent of them on the ground. Most had been lined up wingtip to wingtip on their fields, sitting ducks. By the end of the first week, the Germans claimed 4,017 VVS aircraft, while admitting 150 losses. TsAMO records cited by Volkogonov indicate that the VVS had lost 96.4 percent of its prewar aircraft strength by the end of September.

By substantially eliminating the VVS fighter force as a threat, the Luftwaffe quickly captured and maintained air superiority over the battlefield. This permitted a focus on air-to-ground operations in support of ground forces who were blitzkrieging their way deep into the Soviet Union

Meanwhile, there was panic in the Kremlin, and according to some, no one was more weak-kneed than the Man of Steel himself.

"When, on the morning of 22 June, the question arose of who should tell the nation about the German attack, everyone naturally turned to Stalin," Volkogonov writes. "Almost without hesitating to reflect, he refused unequivocally. It has been generally accepted that Stalin acted in this way because, as [Anastas] Mikoyan, for example, recalled, he was in a depressed state and 'did not know what to say to the people, for he had after all taught them to think there would be no war, and that if it did start, then the enemy would be beaten on his own territory, and now he would have had to admit that we were suffering defeat in the first hours'."

It was Vyacheslav Molotov, the foreign commissar, not Stalin, who spoke to the nation by radio to urge people to resist the invaders.

However, Stalin's biographer does not believe he lost his nerve—at least on the first day. He writes that "I believe things were somewhat different. The matter of addressing the nation was decided early in the morning when no one in Moscow yet knew that 'we were suffering defeat'. Everyone knew there was going to be a war, yet it came so suddenly. Stalin did not have a clear idea of what was happening on the border. Most likely, he did not want to address the nation until he had clarified the situation. On the 22nd he received no news of victories and so was in a state of alarm and confusion, but he was confident that in two or three weeks he would repay Hitler for violating their agreement, and then he would appear before the nation."

Indeed, Stalin set about issuing orders, although he naïvely ignored tactical realities. Volkogonov notes that "still unaware of the scale of the catastrophe, [he] demanded that the military 'destroy the invading enemy with crushing blows' [and he commanded Marshal Semyon Timoshenko to direct] the forces to use all their strength and means to come down on the enemy's forces and destroy them where they have violated the Soviet border."

Volkogonov believes that it was only later that Stalin really fell into a state of depression. "The paralysing shock only struck him after four or five days, when he finally understood that the invasion was a mortal threat to him, and not only to the country," Volkogonov writes. "Toward the last days of June, the scale of the fatal threat finally sank in on Stalin and for a while he simply lost control of himself and went into deep psychological shock. Between 28 and 30 June, according to eyewitnesses, Stalin was so depressed and shaken that he ceased to be a leader."

Beneath the Kremlin walls, out on the cobbled streets of Moscow and the cities, and on the muddy, rutted main streets of villages and collective farms, there was a genuine and universal outrage at the German attack.

It was in *Pravda*, on June 23, the day after the attack, that they coined the term "Great Patriotic War." The phrase was first used in print as the headline an article by Yemelyan Yaroslavsky titled "*Velikaya Otechestvennaya Voyna Sovetskogo Naroda*" ("The Great Patriotic War of the Soviet People"). The reference was to the name "Patriotic War," by which Russians had long referred to the resistance to Napoleon's invasion of Russia in 1812. The term had also appeared in the press during World War I, but it never caught on in the popular imagination of the masses. In 1941, though, it became the rallying point of the Soviet people.

On June 23, Nina Kosterina wrote to a friend: "Do you remember, Nina Alexeyevna, how you secretly dreamed of experiencing great and stirring events, how you dreamed of storms and dangers? There you have it—war! A predatory black beast has suddenly swooped down from behind dark clouds on our homeland."

As in the old folk tales which Nina, Lilya, and all the others had heard from their mothers in childhood, the black riders on the black horses were at large in the land, in the Rodina, and for the time being, all the red men and all their red horses could not put things back together again.

## Chapter 9

# ENEMIES AT THE GATES

"When Barbarossa commences, the world will hold its breath," Hitler had confidently predicted. "We have only to kick in the door and the whole rotten structure will come crashing down."

For a while it looked as though he was right. Within a week, the German spearhead was a third of the way to Moscow and tens of thousands of Soviet troops had been captured. Unprepared and badly trained Red Army units crumbled and defensive positions collapsed. The German tactic of using fast-moving units to encircle Soviet units had worked splendidly. Entire divisions were swallowed up and taken captive.

By the first week of July 1941, the Wehrmacht had captured 400,000 Soviet troops. By the first week of August 1941, they had killed or captured more than 2 million. The three German army groups had pushed 400 miles into the Soviet Union across the entire front. Army Group Center had defeated the Red Army at Smolensk and was only 250 miles from Moscow. The area of the Soviet Union now occupied by Hitler's legions was more than double the size of Germany. They had conquered and occupied more territory faster than any army in history.

Hitler had every reason to believe that his armies were invincible, but his euphoria led him to make important tactical errors. In August, his armies might easily have captured Moscow, but against the advice of his field commanders, he diverted Army Group Center assets to other operations, thus breaking their remarkable momentum. Nearly a million Red Army troops were encircled and captured near Kiev in Ukraine, but the final push on Moscow, called Operation Typhoon, did not get underway until the first of October, more than two months after Smolensk had been captured.

From Moscow, there was an exodus, with many civilians being evacuated to the east, and still others drafted to go west to dig trenches for the Mozhaisk Line, which was being hurriedly constructed about 100 miles from the city to protect Moscow from the advancing Wehrmacht. It was during this period that a massive relocation of Soviet industry took place. Entire factories were disassembled and moved to beyond the Ural Mountains, 500 miles east of Moscow.

Nina Kosterina, who had been out of town with her geology team near Krutitska in Oryol Oblast, 220 miles to the east, finally returned to Moscow on October 24, badly shaken by her first impressions of seeing damage from Luftwaffe air raids. Her apartment was empty, but there was a letter from her mother saying that her office had been evacuated beyond the Urals, and that Nina should come east as well.

"The empty rooms depressed me," she wrote in her diary. "I tried to divert myself and fight off loneliness with my beloved books. Alas, the dead silence was unbearable. I passed my finger over the bureau—leaving a clear line in the dust … Outwardly, Moscow is the same, although the boarded-up windows in many houses jar the nerves. In some buildings, the doors and windows seem to have been forced out. A bomb struck the Moscow State University building; the heavy, massive shutters were blasted out; the sidewalk is covered with piles of glass and broken brick … How my heart aches for everything in Moscow … I walk through the streets and think with terror: another ton of explosives, and this magnificent building will disappear. Judging from the stories of eyewitnesses, many people have been killed in the raids. A few days ago a whole line before a store on Gorky Street was hit: people waited for raisins and got a bomb. They say the whole street was covered with bodies."

A week earlier, on October 13, as elements of the German 4th Panzer Army were moving to encircle the city, Stalin directed that the offices of the government and the Communist Party be evacuated to Kuibyshev (now Samara), 500 miles to the east. Hearing this, civilians began a mass exodus from the city, which barely avoided turning into chaos by Stalin's public announcement that he would remain in Moscow.

Now, even as Nina was passing her finger through the dust atop the bureau in her apartment, changes were in the wind. With October came the cold autumn rains, harbingers of winter snow. For three months, the Wehrmacht had the run of the steppes of the western Soviet Union, vast open plains across which tanks could dash and troops could march.

With the rains, the steppes, once flat and as easily traversed as a soccer pitch, were transformed into a limitless ocean of mud. The mechanized forces that had made the blitzkrieg possible ground nearly to a halt. Not only advancing troops, but the logistical network supporting them slowed to a crawl—when they could move at all.

By November, snowflakes were in the air. The mud and muck froze solid, as did the machinery that had been the Wehrmacht's great advantage in the summer. And so too did the German troops themselves, who had invaded the Soviet Union in the heat of summer and expected to end their campaign before gloves and winter coats were necessary.

Meanwhile, Red Army commanders had learned to anticipate German tactics and were now able to avoid the encirclements that had been so costly in the summer. Indeed, as the Wehrmacht struggled eastward in fits and starts, the Red Army was able to launch the occasional counterattack.

On November 7, the traditional date for the annual parade in Red Square celebrating the October Revolution, the German forces were within 100 miles from Moscow. Nevertheless, Stalin demonstrated that he had regained the icy composure he had lost in June, by ordering the parade to go forward.

Hitler had once promised that he would preside over the parade in Red Square on that day, but instead of the black riders on black horses, the Man of Steel looked down upon long lines of sober-faced men of his Red Army.

As a practical matter, it was foolhardy to stage a celebration when artillery duels were audible in the distance, but as a propaganda ploy, it did a great deal to encourage Muscovites and lift their spirits at a time when pessimism ruled the day. Stalin was a master of the propaganda ploy.

"And so, this is the day when Hitler promised to review his troops on Red Square," Nina Kosterina wrote with a certain smugness that had not been present in her diary entries of late. "But everything turned out somewhat differently. Yesterday Stalin addressed us. We all sat motionless by our [radio] receivers, listening to the leader's speech. And outside the windows, bombs were crashing—it was so extraordinary, so strange. Stalin's voice sounded calm, confident, without breaking for a moment. In the hall where he spoke, everyone shouted hurrah and greetings to him. Everything was the same as in the past, except for the booming artillery, which spoke of the extraordinary character of our time. Today as always, year in, year out, troops marched in parade across Red Square, planes flew, tanks rolled. Of course, I ran down to the center and watched the parade … In spite of everything, the streets are festive. The red flags flutter over doorways in the cold wind."

In his speech that day, the oration which so stirred the patriotism of Nina Kosterina, Lilya Litvyak, and countless others, the Man of Steel conjured up unspeakable horrors to frighten his people into action against the enemy.

"The German fascist invaders are plundering our country, destroying the cities and villages built by the labor of the workers, peasants, and intelligentsia," Stalin insisted. "The Hitler hordes are killing and violating the peaceful inhabitants of our country without sparing women, children or the aged."

Though he spun it to fit the Party narrative, Stalin was not exaggerating.

Stalin had rebounded from his moment of near panic and had become an angry and vengeful man, a man obsessed. His biographer, Dmitri Volkogonov, paints a picture of a madman, writing that "working sixteen to eighteen hours a day, going without sleep, he became still more harsh and intolerant and often vicious."

To his people, he radiated only calm confidence, but Stalin had now reverted to the persona of the paranoid monster who had emerged from his tormented inner being back in 1937. Back then, the foe had been imaginary enemies whom he had perceived to be lurking everywhere, even in the souls of those who were most loyal. In 1941, however, the enemy was real—and pouring into the Soviet Union by the millions. Yet Stalin still found his fears fixated upon his own subjects.

His new fixation targeted those beneath the red banner itself, indeed it was those least fortunate among them. Just as he despised and distrusted the Trotskyites among his own colleagues whom he had purged in 1937–38, Stalin despised and distrusted those who had surrendered to the Germans. By doing so, they had become traitors in his eyes.

When his own son, Yakov Dzhugashvili, was captured in July 1941, Stalin remained steadfast. The Man of Steel refused numerous offers by the Germans to repatriate Yakov in a prisoner swap. Dzhugashvili died in captivity in 1943. Some reports suggest that it was suicide.

It was well known that those who were captured in the great encirclements of the summer and early autumn, and who managed to get away, were not welcomed back. Rather, they were treated with suspicion, as were their families. Not only were such former Soviet POWs often sent to the Gulags, so too were those whose units had been encircled by the Germans but never captured and who had battled their way through German lines to get away.

Railing against the irrationality of their treatment, Aleksandr Solzhenitsyn writes that "instead of being given a brotherly embrace on their return, such as every other army in the world would have given them, instead of being given a chance to rest up, to visit their families, and then return to their units—they were held on suspicion, disarmed, deprived of all rights, and taken away in groups to identification points and screening centers where officers of the Special Branches started interrogating them, distrusting not only their every word but their very identity. Identification consisted of cross-questioning, confrontations, pitting the evidence of one against another."

They say that paranoia often flows from desperation, and these were, indeed, desperate times.

It was out of desperation that Stalin and his subordinates felt the necessity to switch from inspiration to coercion to get the troops to fight. The historian Roger Reese writes in his book *Why Stalin's Soldiers Fought* that "Stalin, hard-pressed by the string of major Nazi victories in the late summer and autumn of 1941 and again in the spring of 1942, veered sharply in the direction of coercion by issuing Order No. 270 in August 1941 and Order No. 227 in July 1942. As early as 17 July 1941, he had signed an order authorizing the Special Sections to shoot noncompliant men on the spot. Although the Red Army never abandoned efforts to motivate soldiers with positive approaches, coercion remained the most visible tool for the duration of the war. The following analysis considers how these ideas of morale and motivation affected compliance, how the military and Soviet state sought to manipulate them, and how successful they were."

Under Order 270, anyone who was captured or surrendered would be considered a malicious deserter. They would be subject to being shot on the spot, and their family members would be subject to arrest. It is very telling that even after two decades of propaganda, Stalin did not trust in the loyalty of his subjects.

Solzhenitsyn adds that "in the course of the big southern retreat [in the face of the German offensive of 1942] to the Caucasus and the Volga ... those who refused to stand to the death and who retreated without permission, the men whom, in the words of Stalin's immortal Order No. 227, the Motherland could not forgive for the shame they had caused her ... after accelerated processing by divisional tribunals, it was, to a man, herded into punishment battalions, and was soaked up in the red sand of advanced positions, leaving not a trace."

And it was not merely the paranoid Stalin, but the *Stavka* (Soviet high command) as well. Order No. 227 flowed from Stalin's insistence that retreat was tantamount to treason. "*Ni shagu nazad!*" ("Not a step back!") shouted the Man of Steel. With this ringing in their ears, the Stavka used Order No. 227 to instruct the army to create combat penal battalions and blocking detachments behind the front lines, but they had already been using blocking detachments since June 1941, only five days after the start of the war.

As Roger Reese reminds us, on June 27, 1941, "Marshal Timoshenko and General [later Marshal, Georgi] Zhukov signed Directive No. 35523, establishing conditions and procedures for their use. The first blocking detachments were implemented on 5 September 1941, when Stavka authorized their use at the request of the commander of the Briansk Front. One week later, Stavka ordered the forces of the Southwest Direction to create blocking detachments for every division under its authority. It spelled out their duties—namely, to detain and return to combat any soldiers who fled the field of battle in panic, as well as any soldier away from his unit without authorization."

Recalling how easily and arbitrarily her own father had been sucked under the metaphorical bus, a dread of being captured and repatriated would later become one of Lilya Litvyak's most consuming fears.

As has been recounted in numerous accounts of that winter, German officers were able to see the towers of the Kremlin through the Carl Zeiss lenses of their binoculars by the first of December. A sizable German force got within 20 miles of Moscow on two sides, but weather and determined Soviet counterattacks began pushing them away. No one realized at the time that the Germans would never again be that close.

From inside the city, Nina Kosterina wrote "There is endless firing. 'Tak-tak-tak' clatter the ack-ack guns. 'O-oh … o-oh …' the heavy artillery is booming. And now and then, infrequent but shattering, heavy explosions. Somewhere a house was blown up, people are dead. Moscow,

Moscow! How many years from Batyi's Golden Horde to Hitler? But never mind, Moscow is a phoenix."

Temperatures fell to around 30 degrees below zero and remained there. Without winter gear, the Germans were at a steep and miserable disadvantage. Having advanced more than a thousand miles since June, the Germans now were compelled to back away from Moscow to regroup.

The VVS, especially crews flying the new *Ilyushin Il-2 Sturmovik* (Stormbird) tactical bombers, played an important role in the counterattack. This aircraft, when used as "tank busters" against the German mechanized forces, would go on to earn a reputation as the most effective Soviet ground attack aircraft of the Great Patriotic War.

The VVS bomber pilots were aided by the weather insofar as the snow and ice that slowed the German armored vehicles also made them sitting ducks for air attack. And, of course, if the weather grew bad enough to ground the VVS, the Luftwaffe wasn't flying either.

Meanwhile, the VVS also had the advantage of operating close to its own infrastructure, and the Luftwaffe units were at the end of long, snow-covered supply lines. In the Battle of Moscow, the VVS was, for the first time, no longer completely overwhelmed by Luftwaffe superiority. Estimates vary, but both sides probably had between 500 and 600 aircraft operational at any given moment in time.

Moscow had survived Hitler's offensive—the phoenix described by a twenty-year-old budding poet—and the Soviet Union had inflicted a million casualties on his armies.

But the Wehrmacht still held half a million square miles of the Soviet Union, an area nearly three times the size of Germany, which was home to 75 million people, a population greater than that of Germany. The Soviet counteroffensive that had saved Moscow would soon run out of steam, and the German offensive in 1942 would carry the invaders ever deeper, especially in the south, where they pressed as far as the Volga River and the city named for Stalin himself: Stalingrad.

## Chapter 10

# WOMEN AT WAR

When the Soviet Union was invaded on June 22, 1941, there was an immense outpouring of eagerness by Soviet citizens, women as well as men, to take up arms against the Germans. "I am ready," Nina Kosterina, the young Komsomolka and geology student, wrote in her diary on that day. "I want action, I want to go to the front."

This was not mere empty hyperbole. Late in November, after returning to Moscow and an empty apartment, she volunteered to join a partisan militia group and defend her beloved Moscow from the Panzers of Army Group Center. In her last letter to her mother, dated December 8, she wrote "I have not written to you for a long time, but, really, it was impossible. I have just returned from a mission, and am resting now. Soon I shall go again ... Write me oftener, give my address to the family. Do not worry, mama darling, thus far everything is well."

In January 1942, her mother learned from the *Narodnyi Komissariat Oborony* (the People's Commissariat of Defense) that Nina had been killed by a German bullet.

Meanwhile, Yevgheniya Zhigulenko, a future combat pilot self-described as a "freedom-loving Cossack girl riding a horse along the Kuban steppes," also had an immediate urge to physically fight the Germans.

On June 22, Yevgheniya was in flight school at Tushino Airfield outside Moscow, while at the same time studying music at the Moscow Conservatory. As she later told Anne Noggle "I was returning to my college hostel room, full of joy and life, and I sensed something tense in the air. The war—the war has started, the girls told me. I had only a vague knowledge about war, from books, mass media, and propaganda. Now it was a reality to live with. I made up my mind to go to the front."

Natalia Nikitichna Peshkova, whose recollections are recorded on the Russian website *I Remember*, recalls the mood of the times among the generation of young women emerging from their school days, directly into wartime.

"When you are 17 you think more about romance than about politics," she remembers. "Sure, we were fooled by our propaganda. No, my generation didn't have any apprehension that the war would start soon. I left for war on July 6, 1941. I had just graduated from school [on June 21]. We had a traditional ceremony and walked on Red Square. The war began the next day. Well, I regarded myself as no less than Joan of Arc, so I immediately ran to a regional office of the Komsomol and they sent me to a group of medics."

Nadezhda Popova, who later as a combat pilot earned the Hero of the Soviet Union decoration, told Noggle that she had gone into shock in the early days of the war when her brother was killed. "We were close, and I cried for days and nights," she recalls. "When my mother heard that her son had perished—he was only twenty and had never even kissed a girl—she met me at our house and embraced me and sobbed, 'That damned Hitler!' I saw the German aircraft flying along our roads filled with people who were leaving their homes, firing at them with their machine guns. Seeing this gave me feelings inside that made me want to fight them."

She did.

For Lilya Litvyak, as for many who lost family members to the Great Purge, the determination to fight the Germans was almost cathartic. Lilya saw it as a means of vindicating her family's name, still obscured by the shadow of her father's arrest and execution.

In the coming months, she would meet many other young women who had endured the same thing and who also operated as though still beneath that dark and smothering cloud. It was something about which they rarely spoke, and when they did, only in whispers out of a mixture of guilt, embarrassment, and fear that a political officer might be listening.

Through the years since the war, there has been an ongoing debate among academics—comfortably removed, of course, from the horror of Gulag or battlefield—about the motivations of ordinary people for wanting to rise up to defend a regime as repressive as Stalin's had been since 1937.

Did the young men and women who had been born during the Revolution and Civil War rise up to volunteer out of a desire to defend the state—even though the state had recently killed or imprisoned so many fathers and brothers—or did they have deeper motives? Was their patriotism focused upon a defense of their "Father," Stalin, or their Mother Motherland?

The official view, as represented in Soviet media and in official propaganda during the war, insisted that the surge of patriotism "proved" that the people really did love Father Stalin and the Communist regime. Many postwar Soviet historians, and a few like-minded academics in the West, insisted that this perspective represented the vast majority of the people, including women, who fought to defend the Soviet Union from the Germans.

Others, meanwhile, have pointed out that patriotism for the Mother, the Rodina, ran far deeper than anyone's Party allegiance, and that the Soviet state was defended in spite of itself.

Arseni Rod'kin, a tank mechanic, summarizes the mood quite succinctly when he observed on the *I Remember* website that "the Kremlin bastards come and go, but Motherland stays forever ... I was defending my country, not the Soviets."

In his book *Why Stalin's Soldiers Fought*, Roger Reese writes that in basic terms "Most likely the fundamental reason that Soviet citizens fight was that their country had been invaded."

To the average person, it was just that simple.

Explaining how deeply the Rodina principle was ingrained in the thinking of average people, the famous Soviet war correspondent Ilya Ehrenburg wrote that Soviet patriotism was a natural extension of Russian patriotism, meaning the love of their Motherland. The Soviets succeeded when they were able to co-opt innate Rodina patriotism. Even in the songs sung by the Young Pioneers and Komsomolkas spoke of being "always ready" to defend the state by defending the Rodina. Indeed, the organizational structure of the Komsomol would play an important role in processing many of the younger, especially urban, volunteers.

In an oral history document in the Central Repository for Contemporary History in Russia's Kursk Oblast, accessed by Reese, a forty-seven-year-old Nikolai Kiriaev states that "Two times in my life I have fought for the motherland. The first time was in the imperialist war with Germany [World War I], the second in the Civil War. Now for a third time I will fight with all my strength. I have no military obligation and the state of my health is no secret, but when they talk about defending the rodina I am not able to sit with my arms folded. I know the business of war and will use it to crush the fascist vermin enemy."

Then too, the phrase "Great Patriotic War" used to describe the German-Soviet war was a constant reminder of the "Patriotic War," of which everyone who had grown up in Russia was aware—even though the Russia being defended against Napoleon in 1812 was ruled by a Tsar.

The people loved and defended their Mother in 1812 when Tsar Alexander was in the Kremlin, and they loved their Mother in 1941 when Josef Stalin was in the Kremlin.

Though Stalin's own paranoid insecurity would compel him to resort to the coercion of Order No. 270, he recognized the value of carrots as well as sticks, and he manipulated the prevailing mood of Rodina patriotism to his advantage.

After his moment of numbness immediately following the invasion, Stalin was able to regain his skills of manipulation and exploit the urge to defend the mother to his own ends. For him, as long as they fought, it really didn't matter whether it was for Motherland or Father. At least at the beginning of the war, he didn't really care why the masses rose up to defend him; it only mattered that they did.

As seen by these examples, the average persons included women as well as men. The example of Nina Kosterina illustrates that women were just as impassioned as men in their fiery urge to fight the fascists—even to fight to the death. Inspired by love of Rodina, these women considered themselves worthy warriors, certainly as worthy as their brothers, and they were prepared to fight.

Though there was no contingency plan to do so at the time of Operation Barbarossa, the Soviet Union would eventually utilize women in combat roles. While large numbers of women served in the armed forces of Germany, Britain, and the United States during World War II, it was only in the Soviet Union that women went on to serve in combat on a large and organized scale.

The Soviet Union eventually drafted women, but there was still a sizable proportion who, like Nina Kosterina, volunteered—even though they knew that they would being carrying weapons, dodging bullets, and killing people. In the book *The People's War: Responses to World War II in the Soviet Union*, edited by Robert Thurston and Bernd Bonwetsch, it is pointed out that 490,235 women were eventually drafted into the Red Army. This number is greater than the 310,000 who volunteered, but not by a lopsided proportion. Also of note is the fact that two thirds of the women who volunteered did so in the first month of the war.

The large number of male volunteers could have been anticipated under the circumstances of the massive invasion, and they were naturally welcomed. However, the huge number of women who volunteered caught the Stavka off guard.

Roger Reese writes that "Despite the precedents of women's volunteerism for war and the public acclaim of women as equals in the rural and urban workplace, the state and the armed forces were surprised by the number of women who wanted to serve and to fight. Unclear in the Western treatment of women's volunteerism for the Great Patriotic War, and opaque in the Soviet record, was what exactly these women volunteered to do. Of the 310,000 women who joined the military by volunteering or responding to the call of the Komsomol, an overwhelming number [like Nina Kosterina] ended up joining their local *opolchenie* [people's militia] divisions or *istrebitel'nyi*, or Komsomol battalions. Fewer attempted or were permitted to join the regular Red Army."

In July 1941, thousands of the women who volunteered were pressed into service as part of essentially civilian work brigades to help dig antitank ditches and build fortifications for the Mozhaisk Line, which was being constructed on the approaches to Moscow. One of them was Irina Lunyova-Favorskaya, who later served as an aircraft mechanic. She told Anne Noggle simply that "I wanted to join the army to help the country beat the fascist Germans, to liberate the motherland. My comrades in arms, I discovered, all joined for the same reason … I am a native Muscovite as were my parents and grandparents. All were born here, and it is the loveliest and dearest place in the world, and I didn't want it to be captured by the Germans—it was an emotion of my heart!"

By winter, young women such as Nina Kosterina would be carrying rifles, but during the summer, young women such as Irina Lunyova-Favorskaya were carrying shovels.

Trench-digging aside, the initial reaction of the state had been to discourage women from formally joining the Red Army and certainly from joining to carry rifles. Contrary to media reports and official propaganda releases from later in the war, entrenched stereotypes lived on. It was only after it became obvious that the Soviet Union was in for a war of long duration that the Red Army finally began integrating women into is ranks.

Because the Soviet armed forces had no formal doctrine to utilize women in combat roles when the war began, most of the early draftees and volunteers were channeled into jobs that were considered "traditionally" female, such as in the medical, clerical, and logistics fields. Men who knew, or at least could conceive of the horrors of war, did not wish to see women embroiled in combat.

As Klara Goncharova told Svetlana Aleksievich in the book *War's Unwomanly Face*, the volunteers were often faced with recruiting officers who had a hard time sending the unsuspecting young women into combat. "It was not easy for him to send naïve girls into the crucible of war," she recalls of a particular recruiter. "They did not know what awaited them. He, a regular officer, did. Feelings of guilt towards women because they, too, were involved in the fighting were shared by many men."

Some western observers during and since the war have attributed the large numbers of women volunteers to a sense of gender equality that came about as part of the change in society precipitated by the Revolution. Some point to the fact that gender equality was codified in Article 122 of the 1936 Soviet Constitution, and remind us of the integration of women into the industrial workforce during the Five Year Plans.

However, Roger Reese observes that "Many historians make the unfounded assumption that women joined men in the Stalinist socialist workplace as equals, which made their choice to join the army at the time of the German invasion all the more natural and easy. In fact, women had been part of the industrial workforce since the formative years of Russian industrialization in the late nineteenth century."

He goes on to say that "The regime did not induct women into the armed forces to make an ideologically based pro-feminist statement. It did so to get meaningful work out of them."

Though the women who volunteered during the summer of 1941 faced a brick wall when it came to their desire to join the regular Red Army, this was conveniently forgotten as the propaganda narrative was rewritten later in the war. By then, as women were fully integrated into the Red Army, the official position was that this had been arrived at as a seamless transition from the theoretical gender equality proclaimed in Article 122.

This perspective was eloquently described by Irina Aleksander in an article in the March 1944 issue of the pictorial monthly magazine *Soviet*

*Russia Today*, published in New York by the lobbying group Friends of the Soviet Union.

"In the quarter of a century before this war many feminine names have become famous in Soviet Russia," she writes. "They have been repeated all over the country with pride and admiration … These were the names of heroines of labor, science, art. They were great examples for the women of Soviet Russia to follow. And they followed these great examples, certain and proud of their new rights, conscious of their new duties … Since June 22, 1941, many thousands of new names have been inscribed on the glorious pages of Russia's recent history. Names of women as soldiers, nurses, war-plant workers, sailors, engineers, doctors and so on. For a quarter of a century they represented an important factor in the process of building a new land, a new state. For a quarter of a decade they represented an important factor in the bitter struggle for that land's and their own survival."

If the motivation of the state for incorporating women into the Red Army was to "get meaningful work out of them," the motivation of the women themselves was predominantly to fight back against an invasion they took personally. The German onslaught became personal when their Rodina was violated, and especially personal when someone they knew had been killed by the invaders.

Zheka Zhigulenko, a young woman from the Kuban region in southern Russia who later served as a combat pilot, was one of the thousands of women who helped to dig the Mozhaisk Line trenches. As she told Soviet journalist Vladimir Pozner in 1988, she had been studying at the Dirigible Manufacturing Institute when the Germans invaded, and she had found the notion of the Soviet Union being at war to be an abstraction until one day on the Mozhaisk Line.

"We were quite cheerful, playing all sorts of practical jokes," she recalls. "Sure, it was war, but we were just kids, only 17, 18 years old. Here we were digging, and suddenly someone yelled, 'Hit the dirt!' I and my friend Tanya fell to the bottom of the trench. In fact, everyone ran for shelter during the strafing. The planes flew by, and I raised myself and looked around. Tanya was still lying there, and she had blood oozing from her temple. Understand, we had just been conversing, laughing, discussing this, planning that, and suddenly—she is no more. Suddenly, this human being ceased to exist! At that moment, I understood finally what war was."

Once they were engaged in their "meaningful work," the women were determined to prove themselves, and it was as much to prove themselves equal to the task, as it was to prove themselves equal to the men doing the same tasks. Indeed, such was certainly present among most women, such as the American WACs and WAVEs, who volunteered to serve in uniform during the war.

"We wanted to be equal," Maria Kaliberda explained to Svetlana Aleksievich. "We didn't want the men saying 'Oh, those women!' about us. And we tried harder than the men. Apart from everything else we had to prove that we were as good as them. For a long time we had to put up with a very patronizing, superior attitude."

Irina Aleksander writes that Soviet women "were the spiritual resource of their country's strength." However, the women themselves were keen to prove themselves as a resource that was also of practical value.

Those women who had the practical skills that they perceived as important to the war effort naturally assumed that they had something unique to offer. This was certainly the case with all the young women who had been training as pilots in the Osoaviakhim flying clubs since their early teens—women such as Lilya Litvyak.

They perceived the need for qualified pilots and presented themselves as prepared to fly and fight. However, these women fliers were unprepared for the first major stumbling block that they encountered. As with most women who tried to volunteer for anything more than digging trenches in the summer of 1941, they were perfunctorily turned down by the VVS and the PVO.

This was despite the fact that women—albeit in small numbers—had been trained and commissioned as officers and pilots for many years. Someone in the Soviet bureaucracy had decided that, although there were not enough pilots to face the sudden challenge of a war on an 1,800-mile-wide front, there were enough women pilots.

In a 1990 interview with *Soviet Life* magazine, Zheka Zhigulenko explained that "in the first months of the war, women were not enlisted in aviation units. Women could only serve as nurses, communications operators, or antiaircraft gunners, even though many of [us] had been members of aviation clubs before the war … A friend and I wanted to be pilots. We camped out on many a doorstep, but we were always turned down."

She did eventually get her wish and went on to fly as a bomber pilot, later decorated as a Hero of the Soviet Union—although she almost spent the Great Patriotic War wrapping bandages.

As Militsa Kazarinova wrote in the postwar oral history anthology *In the Sky Above the Front*, which she edited and which was later translated by Dr. Kazimiera Jean Cottam, Militsa had already completed ten years of service with the VVS. She had "served as an attack pilot, trained in air tactics, took part in air shows over Moscow, graduated from the Air Force Academy, and finally enrolled in a postgraduate program." Nevertheless, even she was initially blocked from a combat assignment.

"After the war had broken out, many of us wrote letters to the Academy's commandant, asking to be sent to the front," she recalls. "Invariably, we were all told to await our orders. Meanwhile, the situation at the front continued to deteriorate."

It was in the darkest days of October 1941, when the Red Army seemed to be collapsing and it seemed that the VVS would be swept from Soviet skies, that the rules abruptly changed. Not only was the decision made to permit Soviet women to join the VVS as combat pilots, but the service announced that it would organize specifically all-women units.

The origins of this revolutionary idea, and of its official approval, are unclear. Though the paper trail is ambiguous at best, it is widely accepted that the idea originated with Major Marina Raskova, and that it was approved not by a bureaucrat somewhere in the VVS hierarchy, nor within the Commissariat of Defense, but by Stalin himself.

How all of this evolved has been an inexhaustible incubator of speculation. Decision making inside the Kremlin during Stalin's rule was done behind closed doors, from which much information never escaped to reside on any archive shelf.

Many sources, including historian Aleksandr Magid and General Aleksandr Belyakov, who flew with Valery Chkalov on the 1936 flight to America, have written that the idea for all-women VVS units did, in fact, originate with Marina Raskova. Indeed, this was the popularly held assumption by the women pilots themselves. In nearly every postwar account by women who served with the VVS during the Great Patriotic War, it is assumed out of hand that there were all-women units specifically because of Raskova's influence and initiative.

By the time that the Great Patriotic War began, Marina Raskova was the best-known and best-loved woman pilot in the Soviet Union. Of the troika of women who had taken part in the celebrated 1938 flight of the *Rodina*, Polina Osipenko had perished in 1939, and Valentina Grizodubova avoided the spotlight as much as Raskova embraced it. She is also recalled as lacking Raskova's extraordinary charisma and vision.

Marina Raskova was publicly outspoken in her opinion that women in general, and women pilots in particular, should volunteer and be allowed to serve.

A speech that she made to this effect in early September 1941, reportedly attended by Lilya Litvyak, was widely quoted in Soviet media. In the meantime, it had been to Marina Raskova that hundreds of young female Osoaviakhim pilots had addressed letters all summer long, asking to join the VVS. News of her speech elicited a further tide of requests to serve. A popular figure in the Soviet media in general, she had rock-star status among young, aviation-minded women.

The story that she made a personal appeal to Stalin has always been a part of the folklore, and it is probably true. Stalin's great attention to women aviators is certainly illustrated by his having served as a pallbearer for Polina Osipenko. He was particularly interested in Marina, and they kept in touch after having been seated next to one another at the 1938 Kremlin banquet celebrating the flight of the *Rodina*.

How well she knew Stalin, and how much influence she had on him, will never be known. Whether their relationship went beyond the professional has long been the subject of innuendo, but again, this is a case where the records, if they ever existed, have been erased.

An article in the April 1, 1940, issue of *Time* magazine suggestively insinuated that it was an open secret around the Soviet capital that Marina was intimate with the Man of Steel. In it, the magazine's correspondent writes that Spencer Williams, the long-time Secretary of the American-Russian Chamber of Commerce arrived in London "surprised because no Moscow correspondent has dared smuggle out the story of handle-bar-mustached Mr. Joseph Vissarionovich Djugashvili's latest heartthrob."

According to *Time*, "Mr. Williams reported that, in the early days of the Finnish War, plain, studious Soviet Aviatrix Marina Raskova began to be seen riding regularly in the Dictator's official car to the Kremlin and also to his country villa. Friends of neat Miss Raskova, who parts her shiny black hair in the middle and draws it back along her skull into a bun at the rear, confirmed to Secretary Williams before he left Moscow that she now seems to be accepted by everyone around the Dictator as his wife. That J. Stalin ever went through a marriage ceremony with even his acknowledged first or second wife is as doubtful as whether A. Hitler has been to the altar with Miss Evi [sic] Braun."

Though the question of whether she was Stalin's "heartthrob" will never be answered, the notion that she was his "wife" in a common law sense is clearly disproven by the fact that she continued to be thoroughly engrossed in her VVS career, and that this would keep her at some distance from the Kremlin apartment of the Man of Steel.

Had Marina actually traveled to Stalin's dacha? If someone had seen her in his car, she may have. However, there is no reason to believe that they were actually having an affair. Of course, one never really knows. If they were, Stalin certainly would have had the power to keep it out of the Soviet media and to erase all record of it.

To suggest that the only way a woman could influence a man is by having an affair with him, rather than through a logical discussion, is preposterous. Equally absurd is the notion that a woman of Marina Raskova's caliber would have done so in order to curry favor with Stalin.

Though *Time* did not give bylines to its correspondents in those years, it can be surmised that the unnamed correspondent was Richard E. Lauterbach, who served in this role in the Soviet Union for *Time* and *Life* magazines during the period of the Great Patriotic War, and who discussed the relationship between Stalin and Raskova in his 1944 book *These Are the Russians*.

In his book, Lauterbach backtracks to dismiss intimations of an affair between the two as "prewar gossip, mostly foreign," but the stories do confirm that Raskova probably had more access to Stalin than the average VVS junior officer, and that she was no stranger to the inner offices of the Kremlin in the early 1940s. It is also documented that Stalin took a personal interest in the all-women aviation units that were later formed and in the role Raskova played in the process.

Marina later told Zheka Zhigulenko that she did, in fact, have a spirited conversation with the Man of Steel on the subject of women flying in combat. Stalin had said, with empathy unheard-of from him, "You understand, future generations will not forgive us for sacrificing young girls."

"You know, they are running away to the front all the same," Marina reportedly told him. "They are taking things into their own hands, and it will be worse, you understand, if they steal airplanes to go."

In fact, as Stalin well knew, there had been an instance of young women stealing an airplane. As Zheka Zhigulenko recalls, "there were several girls who had asked to go to the front, and they were turned down. So they stole a fighter plane and flew off to fight. They just couldn't wait, because they knew there in occupied territory were mothers and children."

Also fresh in the minds of both Zheka and Marina, as well as Stalin, was the story of the young Ukrainian VVS pilot, Ekaterina Ivanova Zelenko, who had used her Su-2 to ram a Messerschmitt Bf 109 near Kharkov on September 12, 1941. Attacked by seven German fighters, she had run out of ammunition fighting them and rammed one of the Messerschmitts from above, ripping it in half.

Stalin's motivation may well have been just as simple as Roger Reese had suggested. He wanted to get "meaningful work" out of a cadre of trained pilots. Indeed, that was the motivation in the United States behind the creation of the Women Airforce Service Pilots.

When the decision was finally made in October 1941 that such regiments should exist, it was obvious to everyone in the Soviet hierarchy, especially Stalin, that the bright and personable Marina Raskova was not just the ideal candidate to head up the project of creating all-women VVS units, she was the only reasonable choice for the job.

Just as she had been responsible for charting the course of the flight of the *Rodina*, she would chart the course of an even more historic transformation in military policy.

*Chapter 11*

# MARINA'S FALCONS

O fficial orders were issued on October 8, 1941, by the *Narodnyi Komissariat Oborony* (the People's Commissariat of Defense). They called for the creation of the 122nd Aviation Group, commanded by Marina Raskova. It was formed as a precursor unit to train and process women into operational units. It was the first military aviation unit in history to be comprised entirely of women destined for combat.

Klavdiya Terekhova-Kasatkina, who was later the secretary of the Communist Party organization within one of the regiments, was working at the Central Body of the Komsomol in Moscow in October 1941, and was in the department that received letters from women pilots asking to be permitted to go to the front. She later told Anne Noggle that "there were so many letters that Marina Raskova … calculated that the number was equal to that required to form three regiments. This was the start of the female regiments. I too submitted an application asking to be admitted to such a regiment."

To be formed and designated later, when the 122nd Aviation Group was subdivided after training, there would, in fact, be three aviation regiments. Numbered consecutively, these would be the 586th Fighter Aviation Regiment (*Istrebitel'nyi Aviatsionnyi Polk*, IAP), the 587th Bomber Aviation Regiment (*Bombardirovochnyi Aviatsionnyi Polk*, BAP), and the 588th Night Bomber Aviation Regiment (*Nochnoi Bombardirovochnyi Aviatsionnyi Polk*, NBAP).

At that time, the aviation regiment (*aviatsionnyi polk*) was the basic building block of Soviet military aviation. It was the equivalent of a contemporary USAAF group or an RAF wing, and was comprised of *eskadrilya*, which were the equivalent of USAAF or RAF squadrons. In turn, the eskadrilya were comprised of *zveno* (flights). Though there were exceptions, three eskadrilya usually comprised a regiment, and there were three zveno in an eskadrilya. In turn, a zveno of fighter aircraft was composed of a troika of three aircraft, but this would be changed to four (two pairs) after the beginning of 1943. This arrangement, which was common to other major air forces and more effective in combat situations, allowed for each of two flight leaders to be paired with, and backed up by, a wingman.

Some of the women already serving in existing, mostly male, VVS regiments were transferred, or requested transfers to the 122nd, while others, who were well established or had been in the service for a number of years, chose to remain on their current VVS career tracks. Among the officers who did make the move to the 122nd were those who went on to serve as leaders of the new operational regiments. The women who were transferred included Major Tamara Kazarinova and her sister, Captain Militsa Kazarinova, who became Marina Raskova's chief of staff, as well as Major Yevdokiya Bershanskaya (also spelled Evdokiia Bershanskaia), who helped to oversee training.

Certainly most notable among the women aviators who remained in their previous VVS positions and did not join Marina Raskova's group was Valentina Grizodubova, the other surviving member of the crew on the 1938 flight of the *Rodina*. The VVS would later place her in command of the almost entirely male 101st *Aviatsiya Dalnego Deystviya Polk* (Long-Range Air Regiment). Nominally a bomber unit, the 101st ADD would achieve its most notable successes flying transport aircraft.

Once the orders were issued to form and staff the 122nd Aviation Group, things moved quickly. During the second week of October, hundreds of volunteers, as well as additional women recruited through the Osoaviakhim and the Komsomol, were assembled at the dark cream-colored building with peeling paint that housed the Zhukovsky Air Force Engineering Academy in Moscow, where Raskova had worked and trained in the 1930s.

Here, they were interviewed and vetted by Raskova and other VVS women officers, including Captain Vera Lomako, who had crewed with Raskova on the Sevastopol-to-Arkhangelsk record-setting flight in 1938. Hundreds of young women arrived here, excited at being in the proximity of Marina Raskova. They were awestruck to be personally interviewed by their popular role model.

Yevgeniya Zhigulenko, the "freedom-loving Cossack girl" who had made up her mind on the day the war began to go to the front but hadn't yet done so, pestered a VVS colonel with phone calls until he agreed to see them. When Yevgeniya and the other would-be warriors met face-to-face and explained what they wanted, he laughed and said "You girls should have told me about it at once! Marina Raskova is forming female flying regiments; she is to be here in a few minutes, and you may personally talk with her."

As Yevgeniya later told Anne Noggle, when Marina Raskova arrived, the young women "found her so alive and so miraculously beautiful—we were spellbound. We stood breathless, so great was our emotion. She smiled at us; she was well aware of her enigmatic beauty. We murmured affirmatively when she asked if we wanted to join the regiments. She gave us passes to the Zhukovsky Academy."

Larissa Rasanova, whom Bruce Myles identified as having been an instructor at the same flight school as Lilya Litvyak, applied to be considered for one of the regiments, and she received the coveted telegram ordering her to report to the Zhukovsky for an interview. It read tersely: "Bring suitable clothing. If selected for training, you will not be returning home."

When her mother saw that she had packed her entire closet and could not close her suitcase, she laughed at Larissa and pulled out most of the clothes. Myles wrote that Larissa later told him, "Mama saw that I'd tucked one of my favorite dolls from childhood into a corner of the case. She turned to me and said, 'Darling, you can't take that with you to the war— you're eighteen years old now.' Then the tears ran down her cheeks."

Like Vasilisa in the old folk tale, Larissa valued her doll, and perhaps imagined that she would prove to be as useful as a companion as Vasilisa's doll had been. For every woman like Larissa, whose perspective was one of nostalgia for cozy childhood, there were many others who were ready and more than willing to put the past in its place and look outward toward the emotionally charged urge to face down the real, not allegorical, enemies at the gates.

"When we heard it was Raskova that was forming regiments, and she was so attractive, so intelligent, we all wanted to serve under her very much," Irina Lunyova-Favorskaya told Anne Noggle. "It happened that on October 10 all of us had submitted our papers to the Central Committee asking to be allowed to go to the front. On the sixteenth the Hitlerite fascists were located only 24 kilometers from Moscow."

The VVS officers had their pick of scores of skilled women pilots, each of whom had accumulated more than a hundred hours in the cockpit. Not all would be chosen to move on to join one of the new regiments, so it was a proud moment to receive a thumbs-up from Raskova.

Lilya Litvyak, whose skills as a pilot and flight instructor were attested to in letters of recommendation from her Osoaviakhim instructors, made the cut. So, too, did another young woman who would become her close friend, and with whom she would fly for the rest of her career.

Ekaterina Vasylievna Budanova, known as Katya, was nearly five years older than Lilya, having been born before the Revolution, on December 6, 1916, in the small village of Konoplyanka, near Smolensk, about 200 miles southeast of Moscow. As recalled by Inna Pasportnikova in the oral history anthology *In the Sky Above the Front*, Katya Budanova exuded "cheerfulness, decisiveness, and determination."

She had a good singing voice and was an exceptional student, but she had to drop out of school because of the death of her father. According to Inna Pasportnikova, the defining moment in Katya's life came when she was a young girl and an airplane landed near Konoplyanka.

"Finally, she was given the opportunity to see a real aircraft and a real live pilot, whom one could even touch; all one had to do was to extend one's arm," Pasportnikova writes. "The pilot turned out to be not as stern as she imagined he would be; he was merry and friendly. The emboldened girl climbed onto the wing of his machine and with her eyes soaked in the instrument panel."

It was at that moment that Katya Budanova decided to become a pilot.

In 1930, shortly after the death of her father, Katya had gone to Moscow to live with her sister Olya, who got Katya a job as a carpenter in the airplane factory where she worked. She immediately joined an Osoaviakhim club, learned sky diving, then took flying lessons and soloed when she was seventeen years old. She joined Moscow's Kiev District Flying Club, and became an instructor in 1937. She later became an air show performer, flying a Yakovlev UT-1 trainer.

Another woman who was accepted into the 122nd was Nina Raspopova, the young woman who had told Anne Noggle that she "sang, cried, and sobbed with happiness" on her first solo flight. Though she had only been in her early twenties, she had already suffered the experience of losing many comrades to adversity. During the Great Purge, sixteen Komsomol members at her glider school were denounced as enemies of the people, and one was executed. She, too, expected the worst, but suddenly and unexpectedly, her Komsomol membership card was returned and she was reinstated at glider school. By 1941, she was an instructor at the Central Air Club in Moscow.

It is important to underscore the facts that the recruits chosen by Marina Raskova were all above-average individuals and that they were all volunteers. Zheka Zhigulenko reminded Vladimir Pozner in 1988 that "we had absolutely extraordinary people. All of our girls generally had come from universities. You understand, they called up the boys for service, but we volunteered. We knew with our hearts that we were ready to give up our lives for victory."

For Lilya, Irina, Katya, Nina, Yevgeniya, Zheka, and hundreds of others, the initial excitement of being chosen by Marina Raskova for the historic regiments was quickly superseded by practical issues—especially when it came time to pass out the uniforms and flight gear. Because the VVS, like the Red Army, had no preexisting plan to incorporate women into their ranks, their quartermasters stocked no uniforms cut for women, nor even sized for women. In some cases, the men's uniforms that the VVS had in stock in October 1941 were a half-dozen sizes too large.

Alexandra Makunina told Anne Noggle that she recalled the uniforms, including jackets, overalls, and pants, all being men's clothing, and all being much too large. The women, many of whom reported to Zhukovsky in fashionable dresses, now found themselves in uncomfortable and clumsy uniforms.

"Like all young girls we were pretty fashion conscious, even though there was a war on," Bruce Myles writes, attributing the quote to Larissa Rasanova. "Most of us had slim waists and, though we didn't expect uniforms tailored for us by a Paris couturier, we hoped that they had made some little concessions to the fact that we were a different shape from most soldiers … We didn't know whether to laugh or cry."

The women felt ridiculous in the oversized garments, especially the huge boots, which, over the coming winter, evolved into an oft-cited symbol of the failure of the Soviet armed forces to anticipate having women in their ranks. Of course, in light of the debacle of the summer, this oversight was very low on the list of things the Soviet armed forces could be criticized for failing to anticipate.

"Some of the girls were very good with scissors, needle, and thread, and we managed to get some semblance of fit out of the uniforms over the next few days," Larissa Rasanova continued. "But we must have looked like nothing on earth … We could hardly walk with these boots—we hobbled.

Lidiya Vladimirovna Litvyak, known universally as "Lilya," was the highest scoring woman air ace in history. They called her the "White Rose of Stalingrad," though it was actually a white lily that she painted on the side of her aircraft. (Anne Noggle Collection, Harry Ransom Center, University of Texas)

Marina Mikhailovna Malinina Raskova as a young air force officer and aviator in 1938. In September of that year, she participated in a record-setting long-distance flight that earned her one of the first Hero of the Soviet Union medals awarded to a woman. (Anne Noggle Collection, Harry Ransom Center, University of Texas)

The smiling crew of the *Rodina* pose with their ANT-37 aircraft ahead of their record-setting flight in September 1938. From left to right, they are Polina Osipenko, Valentina Grizodubova, and Marina Raskova. (Photo courtesy of RIA Novosti)

Josef Stalin, born Iosif Vissarionovich Dzhugashvili, became the leader of the Soviet Union in the 1920s. Stalin would be a dominant, and dominating, presence throughout Lilya's entire life. He was regarded by the masses and the state-controlled media as a father figure, but when his dark side was turned, his enemies were exiled or executed by the tens of thousands. (Library of Congress)

A poster admonishing the viewer to join the Osoaviakhim (The Society for Assistance to the Aviation and Chemical Industry). At the flying clubs it sponsored, this organization turned a million Soviet young people into Soviet pilots. One of them was Lilya Litvyak. (Author's collection)

The Yakovlev Yak-1, which made its debut shortly before the Great Patriotic War, was the best Soviet fighter plane in service in the early years of the war. Lilya Litvyak spent her early career as a combat pilot flying the basic Yak-1, and later she flew advanced Yak-1 variants. (Author's collection)

Major Marina Raskova, seen here wearing her Hero of the Soviet Union decoration as well as two Order of Lenin medals, conceived of the idea of forming all-women air combat regiments during the Great Patriotic War. (Author's collection)

A smiling Marina Raskova enjoys a lighter moment, probably at Engels in 1942. Note that she is wearing her Hero of the Soviet Union decoration, indicating that this was probably an official photo opportunity. (Photo courtesy of RIA Novosti)

A group of female pilots assigned to the 586th Istrebitel'nyi Aviatsionnyi Polk (Fighter Aviation Regiment) make their way from their briefing room to the flight line. A Yak-1 can be seen parked at the edge of the field in the background. (Anne Noggle Collection, Harry Ransom Center, University of Texas)

Lieutenant Valeria Ivanovna Khomiakova (third from left) is the center of attention in this photograph of 586th IAP pilots. In September 1942, she was celebrated as the first woman fighter pilot to shoot down a Luftwaffe aircraft. This distinction actually belongs to Lilya Litvyak, although Khomiakova was the first to shoot down an enemy plane at night. The women on the left are Galina Burdina and Tamara Pamyatnykh. On the right is Valentina Lisitsyna. (Photo courtesy of RIA Novosti)

Soviet women pilots of the 586th IAP share a lighter moment on the flight line in 1942, probably at Engels, posing with one of their Yak-1 fighters. The officers with the large shoulderboards have been identified as Major Tamara Kazarinova, the regiment's commander, and political officer Olga Kulikova. (Photo courtesy of RIA Novosti)

Several dozen Yakovlev Yak-1 fighter planes take shape on the assembly line, circa mid-1942. There was an assembly line such as this located at Saratov, just across the Volga River from Engels, where the all-women aviation regiments trained. (Library of Congress)

A pilot enters the cockpit of his Messerschmitt Bf 109G-6 fighter. The Bf 109 series aircraft were the most widely used fighter planes of the German Luftwaffe during World War II. These aircraft were the German planes most often encountered by Lilya Litvyak. Though it was superior in many respects to her Yakovlev fighter, Lilya scored at least half a dozen solo victories against the great Messerschmitts. (Author's collection)

A German Junkers Ju 88A bomber in flight. The type was widely used by the Luftwaffe against Soviet targets during the war. Lilya Litvyak scored her first aerial victory against such an aircraft and went on to shoot down three more during her career. (Author's collection)

Though he panicked when the German armies first invaded the Soviet Union, Josef Stalin regained his composure, had himself declared a Marshal of the Soviet Union, and led millions of men and half a million women to victory in the Great Patriotic War. (National Archives)

Ekaterina Vasylievna Budanova, known as Katya, was the second highest scoring woman ace in history. Like Lilya Litvyak, she scored her first victory with the 437th Fighter Aviation Regiment and eventually flew with the elite 73rd Guards Fighter Aviation Regiment. (Author's collection)

Standing before a Yak-1, Mariya Batrakova and Valentina Petrochenkova, fighter pilots with the 586th IAP, prepare for a mission, circa 1943. (Photo courtesy of RIA Novosti)

Valentina Guozdikova, Klavdiya Pankratova, and Lilya Litvyak in a 1942 photograph taken when the three women were flying with the 586th Fighter Aviation Regiment. (Anne Noggle Collection, Harry Ransom Center, University of Texas)

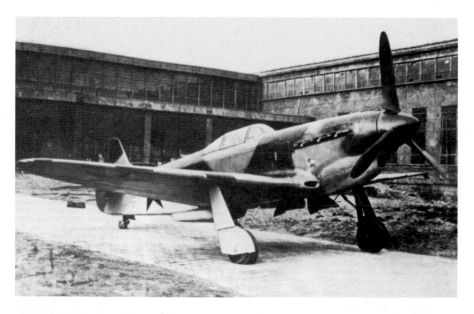

The Yak-1M, in which the "M" stands for *Moskit*, or "Mosquito," was the most advanced of the early generation of Yakovlev fighters. It was designed as a stepping stone to the Yak-3, the "ultimate" development of the Yak family. The last fighter flown by Lilya Litvyak, it had increased maneuverability and performance as well as a bubble canopy that afforded her excellent 360-degree visibility. (Author's collection)

Lieutenant Lilya Litvyak, in full uniform, poses with her aircraft for a publicity photograph in 1943. (Photo courtesy of RIA Novosti)

Lilya Litvyak, Katya Budanova, and Mariya Kuznetsova are seen here studying paperwork on the tail of a Yak-1. They all started out with the 586th Fighter Aviation Regiment but transferred to the 437th Fighter Aviation Regiment in September 1942. It was with the latter regiment that Lilya and Katya began scoring their early aerial victories. (Anne Noggle Collection, Harry Ransom Center, University of Texas)

Lilya Litvyak, a veteran fighter pilot by the summer of 1943, sits down to rest after a difficult mission. The age in her eyes tells of a woman old beyond her years, despite her being several weeks short of her twenty-second birthday. (Photo courtesy of RIA Novosti)

The monument to Lilya Litvyak in Krasny Luch in Ukraine is seen here surrounded by a group of Young Pioneers, possibly at its dedication. Her last duty station, during the summer of 1943, was at the airfield near Krasny Luch. The monument currently bears fifteen stars. (Photo courtesy of RIA Novosti)

The Order of the Red Banner was awarded in recognition of extraordinary heroism, dedication, and courage on the battlefield. Lilya Litvyak received hers after demonstrating her heroism in the skies over the Stalingrad battles.

The Order of the Red Star medal was awarded for personal courage and bravery in battle, as well as outstanding service in nonmilitary affairs involving public safety. Lilya Litvyak received her medal in February 1943 for "exceptional service in the cause of the defense of the Soviet Union in both war and peace."

The Order of the Patriotic War was established in 1942 and awarded for specific acts of heroism. Fighter pilots received the medal for shooting down three enemy aircraft, and a second medal for a second three victories, or ace status plus one. Lilya Litvyak earned her first Order of the Patriotic War in September 1942 and her second in February 1943. A third Order of the Patriotic War was not issued for nine victories, but ten typically brought a recommendation for the ultimate decoration, the red star of the Hero of the Soviet Union.

The Hero of the Soviet Union was the highest decoration for military valor issued by the Soviet Union. The medals were usually awarded to fighter pilots after ten aerial victories. Lilya Litvyak had earned hers by May 1943, but did not receive it before she was declared as missing in action in August. Because Stalin's paranoia did not allow the decoration to be awarded posthumously without confirmation of a person having been killed, Lilya's medal was delayed for half a century. Mikhail Gorbachev finally awarded Lilya's posthumous HSU on May 5, 1990, as part of commemorations of the forty-fifth anniversary of the end of the war. Hers was among the last ever issued.

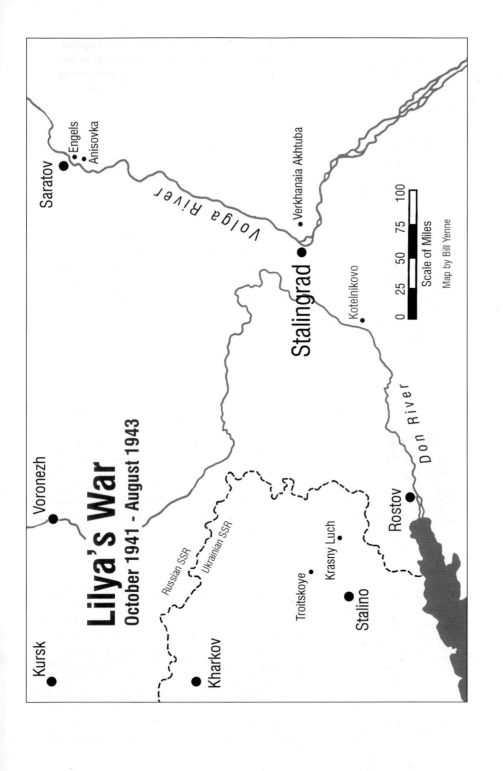

**Lilya's War**
October 1941 - August 1943

Kursk

Voronezh

Kharkov

Russian SSR

Ukrainian SSR

Troitskoye

Krasny Luch

Stalino

Rostov

Don River

Kotelnikovo

Stalingrad

Verkhanaia Akhtuba

Volga River

Saratov

Engels
Anisovka

Scale of Miles

0   25   50   75   100

Map by Bill Yenne

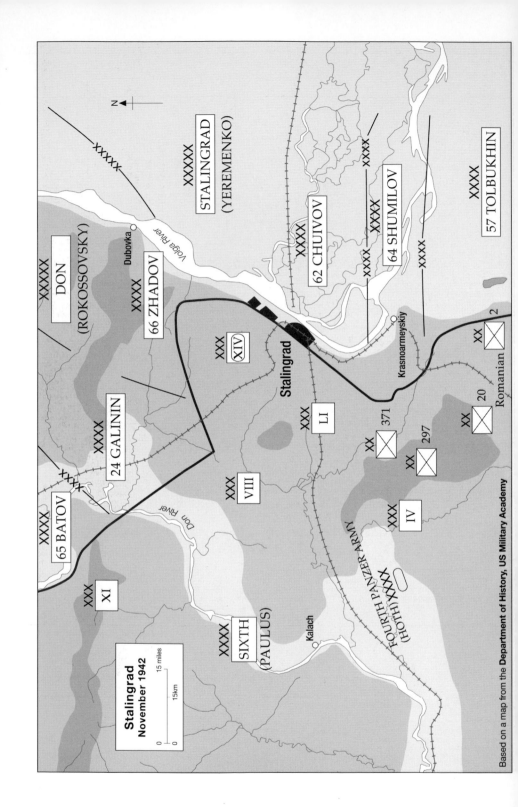

Based on a map from the **Department of History, US Military Academy**

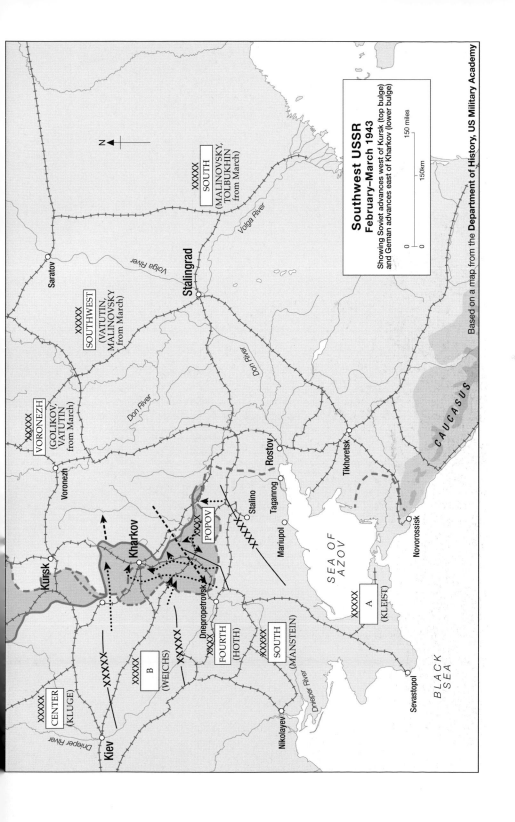

**Southwest USSR**
**February–March 1943**

Showing Soviet advances west of Kursk (top bulge)
and German advances east of Kharkov (lower bulge)

0      150 miles

0      150km

Based on a map from the **Department of History, US Military Academy**

N

CENTER
(KLUGE)
XXXXX

B
(WEICHS)
XXXXX

FOURTH
(HOTH)
XXXX

SOUTH
(MANSTEIN)
XXXX

A
(KLEIST)
XXXXX

POPOV
XXXX

SOUTH
(MALINOVSKY,
TOLBUKHIN
from March)
XXXXX

SOUTHWEST
(VATUTIN,
MALINOVSKY
from March)
XXXXX

VORONEZH
(GOLIKOV,
VATUTIN
from March)
XXXXX

Kiev
Kursk
Voronezh
Kharkov
Saratov
Stalingrad
Dnepropetrovsk
Stalino
Taganrog
Rostov
Mariupol
Tikhoretsk
Novorossisk
Sevastopol
Nikolayev

*Dnieper River*
*Don River*
*Don River*
*Volga River*
*Volga River*
*Dnieper River*

*SEA OF
AZOV*

*BLACK
SEA*

*CAUCASUS*

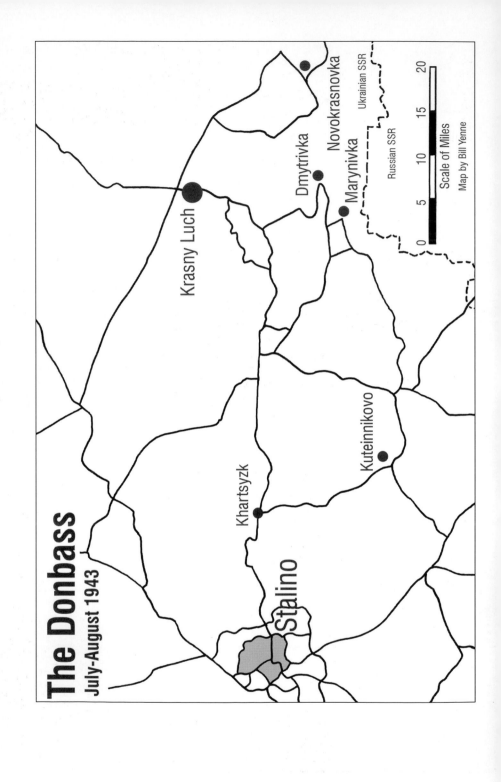

# The Donbass
## July-August 1943

Krasny Luch

Dmytrivka

Novokrasnovka

Marynivka

Ukrainian SSR

Russian SSR

Khartsyzk

Kuteinnikovo

Stalino

Scale of Miles

0　5　10　15　20

Map by Bill Yenne

Some of the trousers had been shortened simply by cutting some length off the leg, so that they divided just above the knee, and most of the coats were still trailing on the ground at that time. God knows what the Germans would have thought."

The events surrounding Marina Raskova and her young acolytes during their first week, as they oriented themselves to the reality of military life, were not happening in a vacuum. These were supercharged times, electrified not only by excitement among the young women milling about in the halls of the Zhukovsky Academy. Everyone present was aware that less than a hundred miles away, the Germans had reached the Mozhaisk Line on October 13, the day after the uniforms were handed out, and were threatening Moscow from both the West and the North.

Even as the last of the pilot interviews were still ongoing, the halls were buzzing with the information about Stalin's sudden decision to order the evacuation of government and Party officials from Moscow. This precipitated an impulsive flight of civilians from the city, which nearly turned into pandemonium until Stalin announced that he would remain.

According to Gregory Malloy Smith in his 1989 Ph.D. dissertation *The Impact of World War II on Women, Family Life, and Mores in Moscow*, 150,000 civilians left Moscow on crowded evacuation trains on the night of October 16 alone.

Lieutenant Galina Chapligina-Nikitina, an experienced VVS pilot who had been assigned as Marina Raskova's adjutant, was asked to take on the task of evacuating Marina's little daughter Tanyusha, who was studying at the ballet school in the Bolshoi Theater.

"Raskova sent a letter along with me asking her daughter to please give Galina some milk," Galina told Anne Noggle many years later. "She knew that I had in the past flown a number of high ranking officers, and they had eaten in the plane and offered me nothing. She trusted me and my flying to put her daughter in my hands."

Against this backdrop of fear and confusion, the several hundred young women newly selected for the 122nd Aviation Group joined the exodus from the Soviet capital. On October 15, Marina Raskova had received orders from VVS headquarters to move her base of operations and her recruits out of Moscow.

Though most of the women were not briefed on their destination until they were underway, the 122nd was being relocated to the city of Engels, a river port city on the east bank of the Volga River, about 425 miles south by southeast from Moscow, and 200 miles north of Stalingrad. Engels was, and continues to be, home to a major military aviation complex.

The chaotic moment of their departure, simultaneous with the government evacuation and civilian exodus, put Marina Raskova's troops in a position of jockeying for space aboard the trains gridlocked in Moscow's rail yards. Like many who were leaving Moscow, the would-be falcons wound up being crowded into freight cars. On October 25, after a cold and miserable eight-day journey, the women arrived at the rail station at Engels, on the bleak and windswept steppes, with only a vague idea of where their airfield might be.

Marina Raskova's chief of staff, Militsa Kazarinova, wrote in *In the Sky Above the Front*, the postwar oral history anthology she edited, that the women arrived in Engels in the dark. To make matters worse, it was raining and the town was blanketed by fog. Marina wondered out loud whether this was even the right town.

"Not a soul came to meet us at the platform," Kazarinova recalled. "Not a single light burned anywhere."

She assured her commander that this was the right place. She had earlier attended flight training here, and she knew the way to the airfield where she had first soloed seven years earlier.

When they finally found them, their quarters at the VVS base were a dormitory set up in the gymnasium that were hardly more hospitable than the freight cars, and winter was coming on. It was a very inauspicious beginning.

The exception was the private room that had been set aside for Marina Raskova. It had a carpet on the floor, a wide double bed, and a vase of fresh flowers.

"Is this some kind of a boudoir?" Marina responded angrily, according to her chief of staff's recollection. "Take the bed away. Exchange it for two ordinary cots. My chief of staff and I will share this room. Take the carpet and the flowers away, too. After all, the girls don't have them either!"

At first, the men of the all-male VVS units at Engels greeted the women with a mixture of curiosity and—among those for whom entrenched stereotypes persisted—disgruntlement. The women reacted with a resolve to prove themselves by their skill and determination, and, gradually, they succeeded.

Despite the confusion and their clumsy appearance, the women aviation recruits were volunteers, and therefore more highly motivated than the average conscript. They were definitely above average in their educational background and general literacy. Indeed, most were from urban backgrounds, and were not peasants, as was the case with many conscripts, both male and female. As Nina Shebalina, later an aircraft mechanic, told Anne Noggle, "the regiment consisted of very intelligent girls, graduates of universities and institutes. We even had a poet. She studied at Moscow University in the philology department, and she composed verses and we recited them; moreover, we sang those verses using the melodies of well-known songs … All of us at the front were obsessed by the idea that our land must be liberated."

In the words of the "March of the Happy-Go-Lucky Guys," which all the young women remembered from their teenage years, "When our country commands that we be heroes, then anyone can become a hero … A song helps us building and living, Like a friend, it calls and leads us forth."

Shortly after arriving at their duty station, the young women learned that they were to be led forth for haircuts. After the indignity of being issued men's uniforms, they now endured the further embarrassment of losing their long braids to regulation male haircuts.

Klavdiya Terekhova-Kasatkina told Anne Noggle that "when the girls came to join the army they all looked like girls, with long, curly hair and high heels. The first thing to do was make them look all alike, like soldiers, with hair cut short … It was really very difficult to make the girls part with their hair and feminine things and put them into men's military clothing."

She also pointed out that it was on the day of the haircuts that everyone first began to notice Lilya Litvyak's stubbornly independent streak. "When the girls were ordered to cut their hair very short, only one girl, Lilya Litvyak, refused to do it," Klavdiya recalled.

Having been charged with making sure that all the women turned up at the barber for their shearing, she reported the lone refusal to Marina Raskova.

"Comrade Major, your order has been carried out; everyone has had their hair cut but Lilya."

Ordered to get the job done, Klavdiya went back to Lilya "with tears in my eyes and asked her to please to do it, and at last she agreed."

An attractive young woman whom her comrades described as looking like the famous Ukrainian film star Valentina Polovikova Serova, Lilya Litvyak sadly allowed herself to be shorn.

It would hardly be an exaggeration to say that no one was happy with the haircuts. Indeed, they probably admired Lilya for her attempt to stand up to the humiliation of the boot camp hairstyle. Once they were deployed to operational regiments in 1942, however, the rules were relaxed and most of the women began allowing their hair to grow out once more.

Though the postwar oral history accounts frequently mention the recruits having their hair shorn, Marina Raskova is always recalled as having retained her long, dark hair. Echoing Richard Lauterbach in his *Time* magazine description, Militsa Kazarinova writes that her hair was "parted down in the middle; under the beret her braids were piled up tightly at the back of her head."

While their boxcar journey from Moscow and the onset of winter had convinced the women of the practicality of their new padded uniforms, the oversize boots were anything but practical and continued to be objects of scorn. In one of her letters to her mother, Lilya wrote that her boots were not only too big, but one was shorter than the other.

Her comments were not unique. There were numerous similar situations, many of them almost comical in retrospect. Alexandra Makunina, later the chief of staff for the 586th IAP, told Anne Noggle about a flightline mechanic who "received very, very large boots. While she was checking the aircraft and getting it ready for a mission, she took off her boots and performed her job bare-legged. At this moment the staff of the regiment was approaching. She realized that it was going to be a uniform violation and she would be punished, so she had to leave her job, jump into the boots, and stand straight in order to report to the staff."

Another incident cited by Klavdiya Terekhova-Kasatkina also occurred that winter. "Once in the morning, when we were in training, we all lined up, and Raskova faced us and gave the command: 'To the right.' One of the girls turned to the right, but her boots remained in the same place ... she swerved and the boots didn't move. Raskova was a very strict woman, and she was young, just 27; she could have reprimanded her, but she didn't—she burst out laughing. Soon after that, one girl was to show that she could pack her parachute rapidly and then jump. When she was jumping one boot fell off, then the other, then the leg wrappings that replaced socks, and only then did she come to the ground—barefoot! Then we were allowed to resew the boots."

As perceived by the officers with military experience, the young women hardly seemed like soldier material. As training officer Major Yevdokiya Bershanskaya later told Bruce Myles, "the girls seemed little more than children in many ways. Training was a very difficult time for all of us. Although most of them were good basic raw material, with a certain standard in their various skills, they had an awful lot to learn. And don't forget many of them had never been away from home in their lives before. Marina and I both realized that they needed a certain motherly kindness just as much as they needed to be pushed along with their training. I didn't think of myself as a mother figure at first—I still thought I was a girl myself [Bershanskaya was thirty-two]—but these teenagers didn't give me much choice."

Everyone's biggest complaint, though, was about the weather. As Irina Lunyova-Favorskaya told Anne Noggle, "in the winter of 1941, the cold was the most severe of the whole war. The temperature dropped to 35 degrees below zero centigrade; it was unbearable. We had to fix instruments on the aircraft with our bare hands, our skin stuck to the metal, and our hands bled. I wrote to my mother saying that it was unbearable to work with bare hands, and she sent a parcel to the front with a pair of pink silk ladies' gloves! I wore them, and all the girls laughed and made fun of me."

As their hair began to grow, the women began to slowly reassert their femininity. Occasionally, Marina's falcons have been compared to that other well-known heroine from Russian military history, Nadezhda Durova, the "cavalry maiden" of the Napoleonic wars. However, while she was both resolute and successful in suppressing and concealing her feminine identity, the women at Engels were just the opposite. Indeed, they frequently bent the rules as far as possible. Valentina Kovalyova-Sergeicheva told Anne Noggle that "One of our pilots kept a little bit of perfume in the cockpit, and she was punished for that. It was a violation of rules; not even a lipstick in the cockpit."

Again, as with the haircuts, it was the spunky Lilya Litvyak who asserted her independence and individuality when she cut the fur tops off her winter uniform boots to make a fur collar for her winter flying suit. As Inna Pasportnikova told Anne Noggle, "Lilya wanted to have this fashion."

When Marina Raskova asked when she had done it, Lilya replied, "During the night."

Marina then demanded that she should not sleep again the next night until she removed the fur collar off and sewed it back on the boots. As Inna explained, Lilya "was arrested and put in an isolation room, and all night she was changing it back … It was strange: the war was going on, and this blonde, this girl, was thinking about her collar. I wondered, what kind of a pilot will she make when she doesn't think of more important things than the collar and how she looks!"

The training schedule at Engels was rigorous, with up to fourteen hours a day of classroom work and flying time, most of the latter conducted in the same type of Polikarpov U-2 biplanes in which the women had first learned to fly before the war. As with all their recruits—male and female— across the Soviet Union, the VVS was anxious to squeeze two years of combat pilot training into six months.

Meanwhile, however, the young pilots were eating well, and the presence of men at the base gave the women an appealing diversion. The same men who had scorned them in October had long since come to accept—albeit grudgingly in some cases—and take an interest in the women in their midst.

As Lilya Litvyak put it in a letter home, "We eat normal meals three times a day in the mess, where we meet male pilots we know and, frankly, the girls powder their noses for half an hour before each meal. I must admit I don't yet wear make-up. I am very sorry I didn't take the blue high-collared shirt."

No lipstick in the cockpit, though, did not mean no lipstick in the mess hall.

"In our regiment the girls were attractive," Alexandra Makunina recalls. "They were very young and fresh, and nearby was a male regiment. Well, they got acquainted and they loved each other … It is a fact that girls were arrested for some violations. Sonya Tishurova was keen on dancing, and she even formed a special group of girls who performed national dances in the regiment. She tried to teach the Byelorussian national dance to everybody. Once she was arrested for three days for absence without leave … She was put in a guardhouse, a room where she could do nothing … and a brass band arrived at the regiment. It grieved her not to attend, because bands almost never came to the front. Besides, there were a lot of male regiments, and she was so popular among all the dancing fans who knew Tishurova was the best at performing the dances. So they came to her rescue … She escaped from that room and came to the dance and then returned to the guardhouse!"

Although she was strict, the women under Marina Raskova's command continued to idolize her. In her oral history anthology, Militsa Kazarinova wrote that "the girls liked Raskova, trusted her, and unswervingly followed her lead."

Despite later speculation that it might not have been Marina's first choice to have the Kazarinova sisters in her unit, Militsa spoke almost reverently of her commander.

"Her inner strength manifested itself in her movements, in the firm lines of her mouth, and in her penetrating eyes," writes Militsa, echoing the impression that she seems to have made on everyone who knew her. "She was so valiant and at the same time looked so very feminine! We listened to Raskova, trying not to miss a single word. Her simple and clear speech went straight to the heart of each of us. She spoke in a somewhat toneless voice, unhurriedly yet passionately; and her words took on a special meaning and significance as she uttered them."

Militsa adds that Raskova's popularity was "enhanced by her cheerful disposition. She was merry and loved to sing." Though classically trained, she was fond of popular songs. One of her favorites was "O Dnipro, Dnipro," and she enjoyed leading the women around her in singing its lines about cranes soaring heavenward above the wide and powerful Dnieper River.

Penned by the popular poet and songwriter Yevgeniy Dolmatovsky, it was one of those touching yet patriotic songs of the type that was extremely popular on every side during World War II. The British and Americans had songs such as "The White Cliffs of Dover" and "When the Lights Go on Again (All Over the World)," which spoke poignantly of the hopes and dreams of a peaceful world after victory was won.

The Soviets, especially the Ukrainians, had "O Dnipro, Dnipro." As Sergei Khrushchev wrote in his biography of his father, Nikita Khrushchev, "During the most difficult times of our retreats and defeats and our retreats and our abandonment of Ukraine, many Ukrainians drew from this song, the hope that we would some day return to the Dnieper."

It would be a long, arduous march back to the Dnieper, and Marina's young falcons would be part of it.

## Chapter 12

# OPERATIONAL ASSIGNMENTS

Before the women of the 122nd could be formed into their three operational regiments, Raskova and her staff officers had to train them and organize them by their skills and abilities. Those with flying experience or perceived aptitude for flying would become pilots; others with the necessary propensity would be trained as navigators for the bomber regiments.

While they all had some flight training, relatively few had skills as navigators, so they were in high demand. Although a handful of select VVS women had been making record long-distance flights in the 1930s, most of those who had trained at Osoaviakhim flying schools were used to relatively short flights in their Polikarpov U-2s, in which navigational requirements were fairly simple. Recognizing the need for navigators, Raskova disappointed many a pilot by diverting her to navigation training, while others, who had limited experience as pilots but who showed promising technical skills were delighted with being picked as potential navigators.

Still others faced the frustration of being assigned as ground crew. Among these women was Inna Pasportnikova, whom Marina Raskova recognized as having been trained as an engineer at the Zhukovsky Academy in Moscow where Marina had once been on the faculty. She told Inna that it was easier to turn a pilot into an engineer than to turn an engineer into a pilot.

Though disappointed, she had no choice, and she accepted her life on the ground. As she later explained to Bruce Myles, "When you can fly an aircraft as well as any other girl and you're told that you'll spend your war on the ground watching others do the fighting, it's hard to bear. But because I was a flier, too, Lilya and Katya were able to discuss their problems with me and I know I was a help to them when the going was tough."

The pilots among the women of the 122nd had learned to fly, but they had yet to learn to fly in formation, or to fly in combat. Their initial training at Engels would be in the familiar U-2 trainer. It was one aircraft that, even after the disastrous summer, the VVS still had in abundance. It was an open-cockpit aircraft, though, so the flights amid the blowing snow of the harsh winter were far more difficult than in the sunny summer skies over Moscow.

The routine was what one would expect of a boot camp during wartime. Reveille was at 0600 hours, whereupon the women marched though the snow to breakfast, singing in cadence: "Where infantry can't get through/An armored train can't rush past, too/A sullen tank can't crawl by/A bird of steel will overfly!"

As Inna Pasportnikova recalled, Katya Budanova would often lead the singing, noting that her strong voice woke up her half-asleep comrades as they marched.

For the women destined for the *nochnoi bombardirovochnyi*, the night bomber regiment, the learning curve would be the quickest, because they would be flying variants of the same aircraft on which they had trained. Originally called U-2, and later redesignated as Po-2 in honor of its designer Polikarpov, the 1920s-vintage biplane proved more reliable than many of the aircraft that had debuted in the 1930s, such as the bomber assigned to the day bomber pilots.

These women would ultimately fly the new, twin-engine Petlyakov Pe-2 dive bomber, but these were not authorized for them until June 1942, so the women at Engels were obliged to train with the obsoleste, unreliable, single-engine Su-2. This low-wing monoplane bomber had evolved from the Tupolev ANT-51, but received the Su-2 designation when Pavel Sukhoi, its designer, left Tupolev to head up a new design bureau. While the Pe-2 was a rising star within the VVS stable as 1941 gave way to 1942, the Su-2 was considered obsolete for anything but training. At least it had an enclosed cockpit, unlike the U-2/Po-2, and for those being trained, this offered some protection from the bitter cold of the winter.

On December 9, the fighter regiment, the 586th IAP, became the first of the three operational regiments to be officially activated. Both Lilya Litvyak and Katya Budanova had earned coveted slots in this regiment, as did Inna Pasportnikova, as a mechanic. As she told Anne Noggle, Lilya "was one of the best pilots; she flew her program perfectly."

Larissa Rasanova, the woman who, according to Bruce Myles, had trained and flown with Lilya before the war, told him that "at our old flying club, Lilya was always getting into trouble with the chief instructor for doing aerobatics too near the ground. It wasn't so much showing off as a total exuberance for throwing the aircraft around the sky. I think she was determined to show the instructors at Engels, from the very start, that she was the stuff fighter pilots are made of."

She was, and she had proven it to the instructors—and to Marina Raskova.

To command this unit, Marina Raskova picked Tamara Kazarinova, the sister of her chief of staff, Militsa Kazarinova. Although Tamara had been awarded the Order of Lenin in 1937 and had a good record with the VVS, Reina Pennington cites frequent conflicts between Raskova and the two sisters to suggest that Tamara Kazarinova was not her first choice to command the 586th IAP, and that the decision may have been influenced by higher authorities within the VVS with which the sisters had some measure of influence.

Alexandra Makunina, the chief of staff of the 586th IAP, wrote in that anthology that Tamara Kazarinova had not accompanied the women to Engels in October. Rather, she had gone to a flight school in the Chechen-Ingush city of Grozny (today the capital of autonomous Chechnia) to learn to fly advanced fighter aircraft and did not arrive in Engels until February 1942. Makunina described the new regimental commander as having "a slight limp in her left leg … black, piercing eyes and the little furrow-like wrinkle across the bridge of her nose underlined her strong-willed character." Her limp was attributed to her having been injured in an air raid while she was in Grozny.

In the anthology *In the Sky Above the Front*, Makunina recalled Tamara Kazarinova as a stern but effective taskmaster who worked long hours and kept to herself. Two decades later, in 1993, she revealed to Reina Pennington that Kazarinova was unable to pilot an airplane because of her injury and that she never flew one of the regiment's fighters. To have a regimental commander who was not on flight status was an extremely unusual, not to mention awkward, circumstance.

The 586th IAP was a relatively small organization, consisting of only two eskadrilya, each comprised of three zveno of three aircraft each, giving the regiment a minimum strength of eighteen aircraft, plus spares. Including pilots, staff officers, and support personnel, the regiment had a personnel strength that fluctuated around 250.

While the regiments were usually commanded by majors, many of the pilots were noncommissioned officers. Indeed, women such as Lilya Litvyak and Katya Budanova held the rank of *serzhant* (sergeant) during the early months of their combat flying careers. In the USAAF and the RAF, most pilots were commissioned officers, but in the Soviet Union, as well as in Germany and Japan, it was not uncommon for fighter pilots to be noncommissioned. The ranks in the 586th IAP held by the women, it should be added, were the equivalent of those held by Soviet male pilots starting out in other regiments.

Sergeant Litvyak and the other women destined to fly fighters with the 586th IAP were assigned the Yakovlev Yak-1, which had emerged as perhaps the best fighter in the VVS at the time. It was the first fighter aircraft from the design bureau headed by Aleksandr Yakovlev, who also had been serving as a deputy commissar for aviation production and who had been involved in the emergency relocation of Soviet aircraft factories beyond the Urals earlier in 1941.

How Marina Raskova managed to get Yak-1s for her fighter pilots is a story of the active networking that she had done since she became a prominent figure in Soviet aviation circles after the flight of the *Rodina*. Back in 1938, she had gotten to know I. S. Levin, who was an associate of Yakovlev himself and who knew Stalin. As it turned out, in 1940, Levin had been transferred from his post at the aircraft factory in distant Irkutsk, to manage the factory at Saratov. Coincidentally, this was just across the Volga from Engels. Furthermore, this factory was one of those now manufacturing the Yak-1.

In her book, Reina Pennington points out that there was opposition within the VVS ranks to the women receiving the Yak-1s at a time when they were "needed" by male pilots, but that Raskova's having the official sanction of VVS headquarters paid off.

In his own memoirs, quoted by Pennington, Levin notes that the delivery of two dozen factory-fresh Yak-1s to the women at Engels was signed off by General A. V. Nikitin, who was chief of the VVS Organization and Staffing Directorate. Von Hardesty, in his history of the VVS during the Great Patriotic War, credits Nikitin with being responsible for doing much to streamline VVS training "to achieve combat effectiveness." Stalin had taken a personal interest in Raskova's regiments, and Nikitin was keen to see that they received the equipment necessary to succeed.

The original prototype of the Yak-1, designated as I-26, had first flown in January 1940 as one of three prototypes then being considered by the VVS as potential frontline fighters. The others were the Lavochkin-Gorbunov-Gudkov LaGG-3 and the Mikoyan-Gurevich MiG-3, the piston-engined forerunner to the well-known series of MiG jet fighters that would be ubiquitous in the Soviet air force after World War II.

The experience of the VVS in fighting German Messerschmitt Bf 109s with underperforming Polikarpov I-15 and I-16 fighters during the Spanish Civil War manifested the need for a significantly better aircraft. When the Great Patriotic War began in June 1941, the Yak-1, LaGG-3, and MiG-3 were all finally in production, though only a handful had reached frontline units by that time. The bad news was that the VVS did not have sufficient quantities of these aircraft with which to face the Germans. The good news was that the VVS did not have too many on hand to lose when the Luftwaffe destroyed most of the VVS fleet on the ground in June and July.

As the VVS rebounded from its initial disaster, experience soon ascertained that the Yak-1 was the best of the three and the LaGG-3 was the worst. The MiG-3 was deemed to be the best at high altitude, but most combat actions were taking place at the lower altitudes where the Yak-1 proved ideal. Thanks to Aleksandr Yakovlev's prewar experience designing light sporting and aerobatic aircraft, the Yak-1 was nimble and highly maneuverable, important attributes for air-to-air combat.

It was also well armed, carrying the 20-mm ShVAK (*Shpitalnyi-Vladimirov Aviatsionnyi Krupnokalibernyi*, or Shpitalny-Vladimirov large-caliber aircraft cannon), with a rate of fire in the range of 700 to 800 rounds per minute.

Powered by variants of the Klimov M-105 V-12 liquid-cooled engine, delivering more than 1,000 horsepower, the Yak-1 had a top speed of nearly 400 mph and a service ceiling of around 35,000 feet depending on variant. The Yak-1 was the first Soviet-developed fighter that was capable of holding its own against the Luftwaffe's outstanding Bf 109. It was also a precursor to the improved Yak-3, Yak-7, and Yak-9 fighters which appeared later in the war. Von Hardesty and Bill Gunston both reported that a total of 8,721 Yak-1s were produced.

Those Yak-1s that reached the 586th IAP were all equipped with radio receivers, but there were only enough aircraft with radio transmitters for the eskadrilya commanders. This was, in fact, typical for aircraft delivered to VVS units at the time and not specifically a practical joke being played on the women. VVS doctrine had been, and continued to be, for operational units to be under more strict centralized control than they were those in non-Soviet air forces.

Nevertheless, Marina Raskova and her crews took exception to the usual way of doing things. As Irina Ivanovna Danilova-Emel'ianova, an engineering officer with the 586th told Reina Pennington in a 1993 interview, "our girls refused to fly without transmitters, and they won." The transmitters were installed.

Pennington adds that the Po-2 biplanes flown by the women of the 588th NBAP never had radios, and the Pe-2s of the 587th BAP did not receive radios until much later in the war.

For new pilots making the transition to the Yak-1, their first flight was also their first solo flight. Because it was a single-seater, there was no way that an instructor could take a student pilot up to demonstrate the flight characteristics before handing off the controls.

For pilots like the women assigned to the 586th IAP, this was particularly challenging because they had learned to fly in the slow and stable U-2/Po-2 biplanes, and now they were stepping into a high-performance fighter. Because it was designed for speed and maneuverability, it was inherently unstable, and therefore it presented a steep learning curve. Even for a daredevil pilot with a proclivity for aerobatics like Lilya Litvyak, the Yak-1 was challenging.

On their first day with the new aircraft, they took it easy. Bruce Myles writes that a fighter pilot named Galia Boordina told him "We only did a series of circuits and bumps, flying round the airfield boundary, landing and then immediately taking off again. But we were all trembling with excitement. Imagine it—there we were, young girls, up there throwing these fighters around. The power of the Yak was incredible, compared to what we'd been flying before. Everything seemed to happen so much more quickly. None of us—not even Lilya—tried anything too adventurous that day."

Some sources note that the young women who would be fighter pilots began to train with their Yak-1s in February 1942, although Lilya Litvyak wrote to her mother and younger brother that she had first flown the aircraft on January 29.

"You may congratulate me," she wrote proudly. "Finally, my long-standing dream has come true. You may consider me a 'natural' fighter pilot."

In letters Anna Vasil'yevna saved and shared with the journalist Gribanov two decades later, Lilya extolled the virtues of her Yak-1, writing in February that she had practiced flying without oxygen at an altitude of 5,000 meters, and that "the machine is splendid! What a speed! A few times I fell into a spin, but in the end I learned how to turn."

When her bother Yuriy wrote back with pride, she cautioned him, writing that "I value your affection, but it is too early for you to be so proud of me. I've not yet finished the prescribed training. Wait until we actually score victories over the enemy."

There was still a lot of work to do, the worst winter in memory still raged, and living conditions for the 586th IAP were still deplorable.

"Our airfield was located on the left bank of the Volga," as Nina Siovokhotova later described their setup. "[There were] two wooden cottages, several dugouts constructed by the girls themselves, and farther away, aircraft hardstands and the runway."

"Each [ground] crew lived together in one dugout," Valentina Kovalyova-Sergeicheva told Anne Noggle. The pilots lived in the buildings. "In our dugout we had a *pichka*, a Russian fireplace, a stove. When it rained we always knew it because the water came in. We would ask the girl next to the entrance how much water had flowed into the dugout, and she would put her hand into the water and say, 'No, no, not much yet, sleep! Quietly, not much yet!' And then when we came to realize that there was so much water in the trench that everything was floating, we would jump up and go out in our underwear to ask the men on the truck with a pumping machine to come and pump out the water so we could go back to sleep."

The women later moved into wood frame buildings, but the conditions were hardly an improvement. Valentina explained that it was a "house of wood with very thin boards, and the temperature was as low as forty degrees below zero centigrade, and it was dangerous to live in under those cold conditions. We had lower and upper bunks, and on entering the house you could see two containers of water brought into our quarters by the logistics battalion to use for washing ourselves. We washed immediately and very quickly, because the water might freeze before we finished. … When we washed the floor, it was so unbearably cold outside that the floor dried only by the fireplace, and the rest of the room was slippery-covered with ice."

By March, the icy cold and blowing snow had abated. As Lilya wrote in a letter to her mother on March 20, "the weather is ideal; not a single non-operational day." She happily wrote that "it is very warm aboard fighters not like in the U-2. The cockpit is heated; sometimes, it is even too warm in it."

In a letter written on March 29, Lilya mentioned that some of the girls were making occasional furlough visits to Moscow, bringing simple personal items back with them on the train. Like any young person away from home, such as off to college for the first time, she requested that her mother put together a package for her.

"I look forward so to getting nice things from home," Lilya wrote. She asked for toothpaste and notebooks, as well as for gloves and socks. She also asked for a cloth flying helmet, such as aviators wore, and, recalling that there had been spare pieces of material around their home, she asked her mother make her some handkerchiefs.

In the meantime, Lilya had also written to her mother asking for a picture of roses. As Inna Pasportnikova recalled, "her mother couldn't find a picture, so she asked me to write to my mother, who sent a postcard with roses, but the roses were yellow and Lilya liked red. She put the picture of roses on the left side of the instrument panel and flew with it."

The 586th IAP was officially declared to be operational on April 16. As Lilya had written, "I daresay I finally got the complete feel of my machine."

Having digested the excitement of becoming the first operational all-women combat aviation regiment in history, the crews absorbed the anticlimax of being assigned to the PVO to fly air defense for the industrial complex at Saratov. Instead of going west toward the front lines to fight the Germans, they remained on the east bank of the Volga, assigned to an air base at Anisovka, a few miles south of Engels. Though the three cities would remain far from the front of the land war as the Wehrmacht began its summer of 1942 offensive, the Luftwaffe would occasionally fill the skies overhead with bombers—and therefore with potential targets for the women of the 586th.

Nevertheless, German bombers rarely flew as far east as Saratov during the spring of 1942. The women spent much of their time waiting—and daydreaming. As Lilya wrote to her mother on May 8, "Today we are sitting in our aircraft on a scramble alert. Saratov sleeps peacefully. Seeing the new day in at my post, I am with you mentally; in my mind's eye I see myself sitting behind a table at home, and I imagine that I am eating pancakes, my favorite dish. It is very pleasant to daydream sometimes."

Two weeks later, Lilya observed the facts that May had almost ended and that life in a PVO air defense unit was "quite monotonous." She went on to say that "We are training a great deal now and this fills us with enthusiasm, since it brings us nearer to the attainment of our common goal—to fight at the front. Virtually no one among us wants to live in wartime as peacefully as we do now. We are all so confident, and feel so strong and energetic that we consider our presence at the front indispensable. All of us are thirsting for battle, especially me. I am not going to be indebted to anyone; if the need arises, I'll do my utmost for the common good."

In the meantime, the monotony was punctuated by the occasional get-together with their fellow aviators from the male regiments. The women, who had been forbidden to carry perfume and lipstick in their cockpits, made up for it on the ground. Bruce Myles writes at length of a dance in May 1942 that was described to him by Nadia (perhaps he meant Nadezhda) Popova. He describes an "impromptu band [that] certainly would not have passed an audition for Radio Moscow, but as the evening progressed and the vodka flowed, the combination of accordions, banjos, piano, and drums sounded better and better."

According to his account, Popova mentions one young man, an instructor in the Yak-1 conversion squadron, who had taken a particularly keen interest in Lilya.

"I could not help overhearing what they were saying," she recalls. "He had obviously fallen very heavily for Lilya. He was pleading with her not to see any other man, not to write to anyone but him when she left Engels. And she had only just met him, remember. She did look dazzling that night with her big gray eyes and blonde hair, and I could see that she was enjoying the adulation of this attractive boy, but she didn't want to hurt him. She said to him, 'Let's get the fighting over first, darling—then maybe we can talk about love, eh?' Then she got up and danced with someone else. But as soon as she'd finished the dance, he dragged her down to the bench beside him again. She had this extraordinary effect on men."

As June came, the boredom faded into wistfulness. On June 16, Lilya wrote of having spent an entire day, since 0200 hours, waiting in her cockpit on scramble alert. "A steppe and the airfield are stretching before me," she wrote pensively. "Here, on my right I see a train travelling to Moscow. And I feel so sad, so alone Yura! If you can, send me a photograph of our father."

One assumes that she meant the late, discredited Vladimir Litvyak, and not the Man of Steel, whose photographs were everywhere.

For Lilya's comrade Katya Budanova, the sadness of homesickness took on a much more tragic dimension when she received notice that her mother and sister had been killed in the fighting west of Moscow.

During the late spring of 1942, though, both sides were still amid the relative calm before the storm. In contrast to the vast sweeping actions throughout 1941, the spring of 1942 was marked by a period of comparatively little movement on the ground. Soviet forces had gained ground north and south of Moscow, but the Germans gained ground in the south, and in their campaign against Leningrad. After a round of Soviet counterattacks in January had succeeded in pushing the Germans back from the gates of Moscow, both sides had slowed to regroup.

The climactic actions at Moscow in December had marked the end of the beginning for Hitler's legions, which had failed to achieve the quick victory for which they had planned, but to paraphrase Winston Churchill, the beginning of the end still seemed a long way off.

On the ground, the Germans still occupied an area of the Soviet Union much larger than Germany. In the air, the Luftwaffe maintained its superiority wherever it chose to operate. For the VVS, it was a period of frantic rebuilding. As Von Hardesty points out, however, the Soviets may have lost a staggering number of aircraft during Barbarossa, but the fact that so many were destroyed on the ground meant that a large proportion of experienced pilots had not been lost.

The VVS had also reorganized its command staff, with Marshal Aleksandr Alexandrovich Novikov replacing Pavel Fyodorovich Zhigarev as VVS commander in April 1942. Impressed by the effectiveness of air-ground operations under the German blitzkrieg doctrine, Novikov worked to improve the coordination between Soviet air and ground units. Throughout the spring and summer of 1942, the emphasis was placed on rebuilding the VVS, as well as the factories that could deliver the waves of new and improved aircraft that would make it an even match for the Luftwaffe. He also accelerated the formation of new VVS units, among which were the three new all-women regiments.

The 588th Night Bomber Regiment (NBAP) became operational on May 23 with Major Yevdokiya Bershanskaya, formerly in charge of training for the 122nd, as its commander. A graduate of the Bataysk Flying School, she had worked for ten years as an airline pilot before joining Marina Raskova's staff.

"Appearing severe, and with a sharp look in her greenish eyes, she was not yet close to, or understood by us," wrote Natal'ya Meklin, one of the pilots in the 588th NBAP, in *In the Sky Above the Front*. "We all tried to pretend that she reminded us of Raskova, but they did not resemble each other externally. However, they were similar in terms of their strong character and will, energy, and a manner of smiling. Bershanskaya had the habit of frowning and screwing up her eyes into narrow slits. At such times, she seemed to us strange and remote. Therefore, when we saw her smile for the first time, were all unexpectedly struck by the amazingly gentle, embarrassed, and shy quality of her smile, characteristic of very kind people."

In turn, the 588th NBAP was assigned as a component of the 4th Air Army (*4 Vozdushnaya Armiya*), which had been formed one day earlier as an umbrella organization for VVS assets operating on the Soviet Southern Front in the campaigns across southern Russia and the Caucasus.

As Zheka Zhigulenko, now assigned as a pilot with the 588th NBAP, recalled, General Konstantin Andreyevich Vershinin, the commander of the 4th Air Army learned about the assignment of the women's regiment in a phone call from Novikov himself.

"Konstantin Andreyevich, how are things with you there?" Novikov asked. This being a dark moment in the Great Patriotic War, the question was full of irony. "Why haven't you asked me for help?"

"What help," thought Vershinin, according to Zhigulenko. "We have no planes; our pilots are all lying about in hospitals."

"Well, since you have been most disciplined and haven't asked for anything, we've decided to send you some reserves," Novikov continued. "It's a woman's aviation regiment."

"Oh God, what are you punishing me for? This is all I need!" Vershinin groaned after he had hung up the phone.

According to Zheka Zhigulenko, when the 588th NBAP flew to the front and settled in, "nobody came; nobody received us. Vershinin came only after a week. Well, we all lined up at attention on the airfield. We had our hair cut like boys. Imagine, these were girls of 17, 18, 19 years of age. They had boy's haircuts, but not like today; our forelocks were two fingers long, and the rest was shorn off … Everyone stretched, stood on tip-toe, puffed out their chests. We were a funny sight. Well, what can I say—we were kids … Vershinin walked along the formations, looked us over, and then, without even saying hello, turned on his heel and left."

"No one made any allowances for us," recalled Natal'ya Meklin, who later was awarded the Hero of the Soviet Union while serving with the

588th NBAP. "We were not considered the 'weaker sex' and never lagged behind male regiments."

The 587th BAP, meanwhile, did not receive its first twenty Pe-2 dive-bombers until July, but it was worth the wait. In her memoirs, as quoted by Reina Pennington, one of the pilots recalled the women's sense of accomplishment in getting their hands on such an advanced aircraft.

"The news that the women's regiment was transitioning to the Pe-2 created a real sensation in our garrison," Ekaterina Migunova said with great satisfaction in a postwar journal article. "Male pilots took it as a great insult."

The Pe-2, which had begun to prove itself as an extraordinary attack aircraft during the defensive campaign in late 1941, was now highly prized by the units to which it was assigned. A fairly large aircraft with a wingspan of more than 56 feet, it was powered by a pair of Klimov M-105 engines and carried a crew of three. In addition to the pilot, there was a navigator-bombardier and a radio operator who doubled as a defensive gunner, operating a pair of rearward firing 7.62-mm machine guns.

Compared to the U-2/Po-2 night bomber of the 588th NBAP, the performance of the Pe-2 seemed as different as the environments of night and day in which the respective aircraft operated. While the older biplane had a top speed of barely 100 mph and a range of 400 miles, the Pe-2 could reach speeds in excess of 350 mph and had a range of more than 700 miles. The 3,520-pound bomb load of the Pe-2 was five times that of the night bomber. An advantage of the U-2/Po-2, however, was that it was so slow that German fighters often stalled out trying to chase it. Another advantage was that it could fly very low and very quietly, both ideal characteristics for night attack missions.

In an ironic circumstance peculiar to Stalin's rule, the Pe-2 had been designed by Vladimir Petlyakov while he was imprisoned. A prewar member of Andrei Tupolev's team, he had been arrested in 1937 on charges of delaying work on the Tupolev ANT-42 bomber. Though he had to watch the first flight of the Pe-2 from behind bars, Petlyakov was released from captivity later in 1940 and politically "rehabilitated."

Meanwhile, on June 28, as the 587th BAP was waiting for its Pe-2s, the Germans launched their much anticipated, and much feared, major summer offensive, and the war entered a new and dangerous phase. Though the Germans had insisted that they intended to finish what they started and capture Moscow in 1942, their offensive was primarily in the south. Operation Braunschweig (initially code-named Case Blue) was aimed at driving eastward from German-held Ukraine to capture the oil fields of the Caucasus, from which the Soviet Union derived 80 percent of its oil.

Beginning one year and six days after Barbarossa, the 1942 summer offensive was nearly as effective in achieving its more limited objectives as Barbarossa had been in 1941. Within a month, the Wehrmacht's Army Group South had pushed 250 miles into Soviet territory. They had captured Rostov, the port city where the Don River flows into the Sea of Azov.

The Germans also captured Voronezh, 300 miles upriver on the Don, the city where the Five Year Plans had so recently constructed apartment blocks with neither running water nor sewer connections. The people who lived in these dreadful places were now either forced to live there under the Hitlerite fascists or become homeless refugees drifting, cold and hungry, across the steppes. As bad as life in the Soviet Union had been in the 1930s, it was even worse under the German jackboot.

From the Don, the German armies pressed south into the oil-rich Caucasus and eastward toward the Volga, reaching the outskirts of Stalingrad in early September.

The battle lines were drawn at the threshold of the city named for Stalin—the threshold of the war's most terrible battle. The women of the three regiments had their work cut out for them.

## Chapter 13

# LILYA AT WAR

On September 24, 1942, Lieutenant Valeria Ivanovna Khomiakova of the 586th IAP, flying her Yak-1 on a night patrol over Saratov, shot down a Luftwaffe Ju 88 bomber flown by Oberstleutnant Gerhard Maak of *Kampfgeschwader 76* (Bomber Group 76), a veteran unit that had taken part in Operation Barbarossa and the Battle of Moscow the year before.

*Ogonek*, a Moscow-based illustrated magazine aimed at young adults, reported that this was the first time in history that a woman fighter pilot had shot down an enemy aircraft. Because Khomiakova (alternatively spelled Khomyakova) had been a popular member of a Moscow-based women's aerobatic team before the war, this made good copy. Indeed, it was such good copy that the story was repeated in the Soviet media and quoted in the Western aviation media for decades.

"Your very first kill—that's good," Tamara Kazarinova, the regimental commander, said to her young pilot. "But it wouldn't be easy to keep up the good work. From now on, you should demand even more than before from yourself and your subordinates. You'll be expected to perform even better, as befits a true combat pilot … Because we are women, we must never allow ourselves [to] become negligent."

*Ogonek* had left out one important detail in its reporting. In fact, Valeria Khomiakova was not the first woman fighter pilot to shoot down an enemy aircraft. She was merely the first woman pilot with the 586th IAP to shoot down an enemy aircraft.

As more detailed information has come to light since the fall of the Soviet Union, the history books have been rewritten. Since the 1990s, books written by Tomas Polak and Christopher Shores, as well as by Hugh Morgan, Henry Sakaida, Hans Seidl, and Reina Pennington, have clarified that the first woman to down an enemy plane in combat was not Valeria Khomiakova. Except for Ekaterina Zelenko, who had rammed a Messerschmitt Bf 109 near Kharkov one year earlier, the first woman to shoot down a German aircraft in air-to-air combat was someone who had been transferred out of the 586th IAP and was now flying with the 437th IAP, a mostly male regiment.

That woman was Lilya Vladimirovna Litvyak.

Lilya Litvyak had scored her first aerial victory on September 13 over Stalingrad, eleven days before Khomiakova. In fact, Lilya had probably scored two victories on that date, and a third on September 14.

Lilya's move from Saratov to Stalingrad in September 1942 was her first step along the road that would take her to the unique prominence she would achieve among all the women who fought for the Rodina during the Great Patriotic War.

Throughout the summer of 1942, Lilya and her fellow 586th IAP pilots had been flying their patrols over Saratov, painfully aware that they were stuck on the sidelines of the Great Patriotic War. Great events in the march of history were passing them by.

In June, on the anniversary of Barbarossa, Lilya had written that the 586th pilots, flying their routine sorties over Saratov, were "leading a life of leisure [while] our already tired out male regiments could well use such a 'rest' here."

As Lilya well knew, the main action of the Great Patriotic War was more than 250 miles southwest of Saratov, where the German offensive was pushing eastward toward the Volga and south into the Caucasus. When it became clear that the Wehrmacht was bent on capturing Stalingrad, both a strategically important city and a city named for Stalin himself, the Soviets began concentrating both air and ground assets to prevent this.

The city itself was, like Saratov, a Volga River port, but one that had grown into an important railroad hub and industrial center under the rule of its namesake. Stalingrad was home to the Barrikady ordnance factory, the *Krasny Oktyabr* (Red October) steel mill, and the sprawling Dzerzhinsky tractor factory, which had been retooled as a tank factory.

As the city of Tsaritsyn, Stalingrad had greeted the twentieth century with a population of around 84,000. By 1940, it was home to 450,000, making it twice the size of Saratov. In the wake of the German invasion a year later, Stalingrad's population had nearly doubled with the influx of refugees from regions to the west that had been occupied by the Germans during Barbarossa.

By the summer of 1942, Stalingrad was a city bursting at the seams as well as a city of great strategic and symbolic importance. It was a city which Adolf Hitler had ordered his legions to capture at all costs, and a city which the Man of Steel had decreed must be defended at all costs. It had been the threat to Stalingrad that was the catalyst for Josef Stalin's infamous Order No. 227 of July 28. It contained the famous admonition, memorialized in posters and even on a postage stamp, which read, "*Ni shagu nazad!*" ("Not a step back!").

There was a firmness in Stalin's order, which reverberated through the Soviet state government and startled even the most jaded of Western observers in Moscow. Alexander Werth, who was the *London Sunday Times* correspondent in Moscow at the time, writes that "something must have happened ... in high Government, Military and Party quarters, for on the 30th [of July] the whole tone of the Press radically changed. No more lamentations and imprecations ... but orders, harsh, strict, ruthless orders. Clearly what was aimed at above all was precise military results."

Stalingrad would be the end of the line for Soviet forces giving ground to the invader. It would be the high tide of Hitler's gluttony for Lebensraum in the East. The Man of Steel had so decreed.

The message was telegraphed from the *Stavka* (the Soviet high command) to the senior commanders, from them to the junior officers, and from them to the men and women in the field. "*Ni shagu nazad!*"

At the end of August, Stalingrad was in the same predicament as Moscow had been at the end of the previous November. A pincer was closing around it. German units were less than two dozen miles from its gates at several points on the compass. A major difference was that the snow and cold that had helped save Moscow was entirely absent.

Geographically, the long, narrow urban area was approximately 5 miles wide and extended southwest to northeast for about 25 miles along the west shore of the Volga River. The main part of the city was more compact, being a narrow strip, just 2 miles wide, along the river bank. Because the river was opposite the city from the German advance, it could not be used as a defensive feature. Meanwhile, the terrain on the western approaches was relatively flat, easily favoring the mechanized German forces and their tactics. Close to the city, a deep gorge and some low hills afforded some defense, but only at the virtual city limits.

It was obvious to all concerned that the battle that was forming would be a major one. The German 6th Army, commanded by General Friedrich Paulus and supported on the right flank by General Hermann Hoth's 4th Panzer Army, formed the centerpiece of a quarter-million-man force bearing down on the city, where Soviet defenders were initially outnumbered by a large margin.

Though both sides realized that Stalingrad would be a strategically significant contest, few realized what we know in retrospect: It would be the turning point of the Great Patriotic War.

In the air, the Luftwaffe still reigned supreme, able to maintain air superiority over any portion of the battlefield it chose. Mounting a credible challenge to the Germans in the skies over a major battlefield had heretofore eluded their grasp, and Soviet air commanders knew that there would be no saving Stalingrad without a reversal of the Luftwaffe's fortunes. The months of rebuilding Soviet air power were about to be put to the test as the best pilots and the best warplanes that could be mustered were being brought together at Stalingrad.

Von Hardesty writes that on the eve of the battle, the Luftwaffe had 1,200 combat aircraft, outnumbering the VVS on the Stalingrad area by a factor of four to one. He goes on to say that Soviet air defenses were in even worse shape. The PVO's 102nd *Istrebitel'naia Aviatsionnaia Diviziia* (Fighter Aviation Division, IAD), had only eighty fighters, mainly aging I-15s and I-16s, and they had reached out to the VVS and other PVO divisions for backup. The VVS responded with several regiments, and from the Saratov defenses, the PVO reassigned an eskadrilya of women warriors from the 586th IAP.

Just as women who were serving with mostly male units had been transferred to the all-women regiments a year earlier, the PVO now transferred women to previously all-male regiments. It is a testament to the work that Marina Raskova had done, and to the skills of the women pilots themselves, that they were chosen to ride into the simmering cauldron of Stalingrad as reinforcements for men.

The eight women transferred from the 586th IAP were split between two regiments, the 434th IAP and the 437th IAP. Klavdya Blinova, Antonina (Tanya) Lebedeva, Klavdya Nechayeva, and Olga Shakhova were assigned to the 434th IAP.

Commanded by Lieutenant Raisa Beliaeva (also written as Raya Belyayeva), who had flown in the same prewar aerobatic group as Valeria Khomiakova, the contingent assigned to the 437th IAP included Mariya Kuznetsova and Katya Budanova, as well as Lilya Litvyak. As with Lilya's father, Mariya's had been arrested during the Great Purge. He had survived the executioner's axe that took Vladimir Litvyak, only to die fighting the Germans.

The young women destined for the 437th IAP arrived on September 10, flying in with their Yak-1s as Stalingrad was under siege and the Germans were preparing for their climactic assault. It was immediately obvious that they were in a war zone, not simply in a position of defending against occasional air attacks, as had been the case for months over Saratov. Columns of smoke could be seen rising into the sky just a few miles away. When they landed on September 10, the women discovered that the airfield to which they had been assigned was nearly abandoned—and had been taking German artillery fire just a short time before their wheels had touched the tarmac.

A mechanic who met them explained that everyone else had evacuated this field. He told them that if they knew what was good for them, they would take off immediately. They did.

They flew on to another field at Verkhnaia Akhtuba, about 25 miles due east from the Volga and the southern end of Stalingrad. This would be their home or the coming weeks as they experienced their baptism of fire.

The women mechanics who were transferring from the 586th IAP came in as passengers crammed into Il-2 Sturmoviks and arrived at Verkhnaia Akhtuba the following day. As she recalled in *In the Sky Above the Front*, Inna Pasportnikova found that arriving in Stalingrad was like arriving in a surreal vision of hell. "Endless waves of enemy aircraft bombed the city and the bridge across the Volga," she writes. "Buildings, vessels, and the oil spilled on the Volga were all blazing up. The thick smoke covered the sun for many a kilometer, and turned a bright day into a night. The maimed and tormented city was pouring out its life-blood but refused to surrender."

"The first shock of being at the front came at Stalingrad," Sergeant Nina Shebalina, another mechanic, told Anne Noggle. "We arrived by fighter-bomber, and when our aircraft landed and we emerged from the plane, the artillery shelling began; we were caught in the shelling. I was a young girl and I was frightened. The [437th] regiment had not been informed of our arrival, and they didn't come to meet us. When the girls began jumping from the fighter-bomber and the men in the regiment saw us being shelled, they ran to us and pushed us into their trenches, covering us with their bodies. Thus we lay still all together until the shelling ceased. None of our flying personnel perished in the bombings and strafing during this period, but I did see one girl from the logistics battalion, who had served us our dinner, killed carrying a tray with dishes."

The 437th IAP was still flying the obsolescent LaGG-3 at the time the women arrived in their Yak-1s, so there was probably a bit of jealousy and "Yak-envy" at Verkhnaia Akhtuba on the night of September 10.

According to a postwar account by L. P. Ovchinnikovna quoted by Reina Pennington, the commander of the regiment, Major M. S. Khostnikov, derided the women, exclaiming that "We're waiting for real pilots, and they sent us a bunch of girls."

To say that the men looked down with disdain upon this "bunch of girls," would be an understatement. Even the mechanics were scorched by the angry disgruntlement. Soon after arriving, Inna Pasportnikova was working on one of the Yak-1s, adjusting a fuel line, when a male pilot walked by and stared at her.

"I asked him if he was to be flying that aircraft, but he didn't answer me," she told Bruce Myles. "He just gave me a look that was angry and contemptuous at the same time, and strode off toward the command bunker."

When he returned five minutes later with the chief regimental mechanic, she explained that the aircraft was ready to fly. "The chief mechanic went red in the face," she recalled. "He was clearly embarrassed. I asked him very respectfully if there was something wrong with my work. He said there was nothing wrong with my work as far as he could see. He had been watching me yesterday, he said. However, this pilot did not want to fly this aircraft because it had been prepared by a woman … I was so angry. I really understood what Lilya and Katya were feeling now. I forgot all the discipline I'd been taught and I spat on the ground in the direction of the pilot's back. I told the chief mechanic that the pilot was more of a woman than I. He was a decent sort. He pretended he hadn't seen what I'd done and said. I could see that he sympathized more with me than with the pilot. But now we were all intrigued to see what the commander would do about the pilot's refusal."

The pilot used a different aircraft later that same day and was shot down.

The Luftwaffe attacked the Stalingrad defenders with its Junkers Ju 87 "Stuka" dive-bombers and twin-engine Junkers Ju 88 bombers, while the VVS attacked the advancing Germans using their own single-engine Ilyushin Il-2 Sturmovik and twin-engine Petlyakov Pe-2 attack bombers.

To illustrate the vertical battlefield into which the women would soon be flying and fighting—perhaps with a bit of oversimplification—one might say that it consisted essentially of three layers of warring aircraft. At the lowest level were the ground attack bombers of the respective sides. Above them were the fighters of the opposing side, whose mission it was to destroy the bombers. On the next level were fighters tasked with protecting the bombers. In turn, the Soviet fighter pilots often added layers to their layers, creating an *etazherka*, or stack of fighters, spaced at varying altitudes.

Above their bombers, the Luftwaffe fighter pilots were armed with Messerschmitt Bf 109F and newer Bf 109G fighters. Meanwhile, Soviet pilots flew whatever they had available—ideally various model Yakovlev designs, such as the Yak-1, as well as later model Lavochkin fighters, such as the La-5, which was a refinement of the disappointing LaGG-3.

It is axiomatic that outnumbered fighter pilots like to ironically describe the skies in which they are operating as a "target-rich environment," and such was the case over Stalingrad in September 1942. There was plenty of Luftwaffe aircraft at which to shoot—and from which to dodge bullets.

On September 13, the "bunch of girls" of the 437th IAP would be dodging the bullets of the Luftwaffe's vaunted Jagdgeschwader 53, veterans of campaigns from the Battle of Britain to Operation Barbarossa. Known as the *Pik As Geschwader* (Ace of Spades Fighter Wing), it had once claimed forty-three victories in a single day during the Battle of France in 1940. The "Pik As" had been the top-scoring Luftwaffe fighter wing in the Battle of Britain with 258 kills, and they added 762 Soviet aircraft to their unit tally during Barbarossa. After several months in the Mediterranean Theater, JG 53 was assigned to Luftflotte 4 (Air Fleet 4), commanded by General Wolfram Freiherr von Richthofen (a cousin of World War I's Red Baron) for the summer 1942 offensive.

Now, Luftflotte 4 and its mass of warplanes were on the doorstep of Stalingrad.

Unteroffizier Erwin Meier was an aggressive young pilot, perhaps typical of the fresh, young Luftwaffe pilots who had joined JG 53 ahead of Operation Blau/Braunschweig. He had scored his first aerial victory on July 26, shooting down a LaGG-3, and his second, against a Sturmovik, on August 2. He became the Luftwaffe's newest ace on August 12 and scored his eighth kill, another Sturmovik, on September 8. It has been reported that he had already been awarded the Iron Cross, both first and second class, and possibly the Knight's Cross of the Iron Cross. The following day would be the best of his career.

On September 9, Erwin Meier was on fire. He bagged a VVS Sturmovik flying a low-level strike against German forces, and then tangled successfully with a Yak-1 at 3,900 feet. Before he touched the earth again in his Bf 109G, Meier had scored against yet another luckless Soviet pilot in one of the new Lavochkin La-5s.

Three in one day, especially for a man who had been in action for only two months, was remarkable. That night, the eleven-victory ace celebrated. Frothy mugs of beer clicked sharply against one another.

Four days later, on September 13, young Erwin Meier took off to add a twelfth kill to his tally.

His flight was in the middle layer, escorting a group of attacking Ju 88s, when the bombers were jumped from above by several Soviet fighters. A Ju 88s went down in flames, and one of the Yak-1s turned on Meier. He had no way of knowing that it was being piloted by a woman.

When she deftly maneuvered out of the sights of his two MG 131 13-mm machine guns, he might have been willing to believe that this pilot had once flown with an accomplished aerobatic team, but he would never have guessed that this pilot, young Raisa Beliaeva, was a woman.

When he finally lined his Messerschmitt up behind the tail of the Yak-1 and began chewing its tail apart with his punishing MG 151 20-mm cannon, Meier had no idea that he was seconds away from killing a woman.

When he felt 20-mm cannon rounds starting to hit his Messerschmitt, Meier pulled his stick to the side and broke off from his almost certain twelfth victory. He believed that a little evasive action would get him out from the sights of the second Yak-1.

He had barely gotten out of the Yak-1's sights when it was back on him. The pilot was using the Soviet fighter's maneuvering capability to maximum advantage. Meier could not break free of his pursuer.

If Meier had been hoping to get back to the first Yak-1 and add the second Yak-1 as his "lucky thirteenth" victory, this thought vanished into the ether as clouds of smoke began boiling from his mortally damaged Daimler-Benz DB 605 liquid-cooled V12 engine. The Yak-1's rounds had killed his Messerschmitt.

The Bf 109G was on fire when Erwin Meier popped his slab-sided canopy and abandoned ship. As he pulled the ripcord, he realized that the dogfight had taken him across the Volga from friendly territory, and that there would be no mugs of beer at the officer's club tonight.

As the Yak-1 that had claimed his Ace of Spades Messerschmitt flashed by, he noticed the white "02" painted on the side, but not the feminine face of its pilot.

When he had landed, and surrendered to Soviet troops, he reportedly requested to be taken to meet the "man" whose skills as a pilot had brought down the ace with the Iron Cross. As the story goes, they were reasonably close to the 437th IAP airfield at Verkhnaia Akhtuba, so his guards decided to humor the German and honor his request before throwing him into the cattle car that would take him to the Gulag that would be his new home.

They took him to the airfield to meet the "man" who had shot him down, but instead, they introduced him to a small, attractive, blonde woman who still looked like a teenage girl—and who was, in fact, barely a year out of her teens.

Meier took umbrage at the insult of such a ridiculous practical joke— that is, until Lilya Litvyak proceeded to describe, in meticulous detail, the dogfight in which the decorated German had come out second best.

Because German had been part of the curriculum when she was in school, Lilya was able to make herself understood by the astonished Luftwaffe pilot in his own language.

"Those who were there said that it was a masterly performance," Bruce Myles relates as having been told by Inna Pasportnikova. "The German's whole attitude, even his physical appearance changed. He was forced to concede in the end that no one except the pilot who had beaten him could possibly have known, move by move, exactly how the fight had gone. There was no question of his saluting the victor. He could not even meet her eyes. To have been shot down by a woman was more than he could bear. The others had never seen Lilya like that before. Her eyes were flashing like a tiger. She was enjoying herself … The German had made the mistake of showing contempt for her both as a pilot and as a woman. Now her victory was complete."

The amazing encounter between Lilya Litvyak and Erwin Meier became one of the most happily repeated tales from the collective memory of the women fighter pilots and their ground crews.

Lilya Litvyak had quickly revealed herself as an extraordinary fighter pilot. It was as though she had required no learning curve. It is hard to say whether it was the target-rich environment, a burning fire of innate aggressiveness, extraordinary flying skills, or a combination of all three. She was, as is the case with a tiny few in every form of human skilled endeavor, a natural.

On what was probably her first day over Stalingrad, she had shot down a Ju 88, and when a Messerschmitt had threatened her wingman, Lilya attacked Erwin Meier and shot him down.

Lilya also reportedly shot down another Bf 109 on the following day, September 14. Hans Seidl, in his book *Stalin's Eagles*, writes that she and Katya Budanova collaborated on shooting down this Messerschmitt, making it a shared kill.

While German records, which are regarded as meticulous, do not show a corresponding loss on this date, this was the day on which the Germans launched their big ground assault against Stalingrad, so things were more than a bit hectic, and certain data could have been lost in the shuffle.

Three days later, on September 17, the four young women who had been assigned to the 434th IAP, and who had then been in combat for just twenty-four hours, found themselves in the midst of intense fighting. According to the official records of the Soviet 16th Air Army, the regiment had flown sixty-five sorties in that short time, an average of three for each pilot, and downed seven Luftwaffe aircraft.

Meanwhile, in that period of time, the women had suffered one loss. Klavdya Nechayeva had become the first woman fighter pilot killed in action over Stalingrad. As was to be common practice, she was flying as wingman to a more experienced combat pilot, in this case Captain I. I. Izbinsky. Also common practice was for the wingman to fly cover while the lead lands. Just as Izbinsky lowered his landing gear on final approach and his fighter became most vulnerable, he was jumped by a pair of Messerschmitts.

As reported in the 16th Air Army's official history, Klavdya immediately went to his aid by racing between the Germans and her captain and drawing their fire. In this, she was successful, but in defending herself in a two-on-one dogfight, she was doomed.

Meanwhile, back with the 586th IAP, Lieutenant Valeria Khomiakova did shoot down a Ju 88 over Saratov on September 24. She was not the first, but the propaganda machine at the Stavka said she was. Granted, she was the first woman ever to shoot down an enemy plane at night.

The Stavka brought Valeria to Moscow. As a former aerobatic performer, Khomiakova was used to media attention, and there is no indication that she knew that Lilya had two victories that preceded hers, or that Lilya and Katya may have shared a third kill.

After several days in Moscow, Khomiakova returned to Saratov and went back to work. She never scored a second victory. On October 5, she crashed while taking off for a nighttime intercept mission. In separate postwar accounts about the women pilots, published four decades and six decades later, respectively, Raisa Aronova and Ekaterina Polunina, both of whom knew her at Engels and who later served in the 588th BAP, have suggested that there were questionable circumstances surrounding

Khomiakova's death. The theory centers around Khomiakova having been put on alert duty when she was still exhausted after her train trip back from Moscow. When ordered to take off, she woke up disoriented from a nap, her eyes unaccustomed to the dark. The crash was never fully investigated, and the facts never fully discerned, and they probably never will be.

It is believed that Tamara Kazarinova came under official PVO scrutiny for having lost Khomiakova. Shortly thereafter, she was relieved as commander of the 586th IAP and given a desk job at PVO headquarters in Moscow. In *In the Sky Above the Front*, Alexandra Makunina wrote that she was reassigned for health reasons. The leg injury she had suffered in Grozny nearly a year earlier had still not healed completely.

She was the last and only woman to command the all-women 586th IAP. She was replaced on an interim basis by a major named Beliakov and permanently by Major Aleksandr Gridnev, formerly of the 82nd IAP, who assumed command on October 14.

Meanwhile, the fact that Lilya, and possibly both she and Katya, had scored ahead of Valeria Khomiakova, seemed to have been overlooked, and it remained so even after the war. Why had it happened that such a milestone—or series of milestones—went unheralded for so long?

If one were looking for a convenient conspiracy theory, one might say that it was because Khomiakova's prewar aerobatic prominence better fit the propaganda narrative. Cited as evidence of such a conspiracy might be that both the state and the state-run media supported the inaccuracy. After Khomiakova was flown to Moscow on September 29 to meet the press, there would, of course, have been no backtracking. *Ogonek*'s initial report, though flawed, would have to stand.

However, the reason that Lilya was overlooked is probably more mundane than the conspiracy theorists would want to believe. Victories credited to a pilot with the 437th IAP would not obviously be a woman's victories. The compartmentalized Soviet media would have missed this, unless the journalists were keeping on top of the blizzard of transfers and reassignments that were taking place against the backdrop of wartime confusion. Indeed, such transfers were highly classified, and tantamount to state secrets, so it is improbable that the media would have reported it unless an official press release had been issued, and apparently it was not.

Meanwhile, on September 27, a major Soviet ground attack against the Germans inside Stalingrad had been met by a renewed Wehrmacht offensive inside the city. Overhead, as air activity also intensified, Lilya Litvyak continued her streak by helping to relieve the Luftwaffe of two more of its aircraft.

The first was a Ju 88 of Kampfgeschwader 76, which she badly damaged. The aircraft survived, but was written off. According to Hans Seidl, Lilya attacked the Junkers after it had badly damaged the LaGG-3 flown by the regimental commander Major Khostnikov, who had just two weeks earlier taunted the four young women in his unit as not being "real pilots," but merely a "bunch of girls."

The follow-up conversation back at Verkhnaia Akhtuba on the evening of September 27 can only be imagined.

Almost shot down by a bomber, and then saved by a girl?

The part of Khostnikov's anatomy not saved was his reddening face.

Lilya's second kill on September 27 was shared with Raisa Beliaeva as the two "girls" ganged up on a Bf 109 of Jagdgeschwader 52, flown by Horst Loose. JG 52, like Erwin Meier's JG 53, was a combat-hardened unit which would go on to the distinction of being the most successful fighter wing in history, with a claimed total of more than 10,000 victories over enemy aircraft.

The "home of the aces," JG 52 boasted the three top-scoring aces of all time, Erich Hartmann, Gerhard Barkhorn, and Günther Rall, who had nearly a thousand kills between them by the end of the war. Horst Loose was not among the aces however, nor would he have another chance to become one. Nor, like Erwin Meier, did he live to face the diminutive "girl" with eyes like a falcon.

In the meantime, Katya Budanova was proving herself to be another of Khostnikov's "girls" who was serious menace to the Luftwaffe. Some sources say that she scored her first solo victory on October 2, but Inna

Pasportnikova notes that Katya and Raisa Beliaeva merely engaged a group of twelve Ju 88s and forced them to abort a strike mission.

"We'll be damned if you'll get through," Pasportnikova imagines Katya or Raisa saying, as the two Yak-1s began dodging defensive fire from the machine guns in the bombers. "Not for the world!"

As the bombers tightened their formation and altered course, the women screamed "So, you've lost your nerve, vile creatures!"

All sources agree that Katya Budanova scored a kill on October 6. She and Raisa were sitting in their cockpits, squinting into the clear skies, waiting for word that German bombers were incoming. Unlike all those endless days of waiting at Anisovka, in the skies over Stalingrad, it was not a matter of "if" but "when," and "when" translated as "often."

Soon, there was a flare on the horizon: the signal had been given to scramble. Katya kicked the dozen cylinders of her Klimov into life and looked at Raisa Beliaeva, who had an expression of exasperation on her face. Her engine would not start.

Someone had to intercept the flight of German bombers that the forward observers had detected. The decision was made that Katya would fly alone.

She spotted the formation of Ju 88s, possibly from Kampfgeschwader 76, whose numbers had been reduced by Lilya Litvyak on September 27. Katya climbed through their altitude and slashed back into them from above, guns blazing.

As the formation took evasive action, she picked one Ju 88, put her sights on one of its two Junkers Jumo 211 engines, and opened fire. Clouds of black smoke were already billowing from the stricken aircraft when the woman in the Yak-1 sailed past. It tumbled from the sky.

Katya had scored.

As Inna Pasportnikova recalls, the excitement of the successful hunt was further amplified by the arrival of news that Katya's mother and sister, reported to have been killed earlier in the year, had been located unharmed.

Though there is no definitive accounting of Katya's early victories, some sources also credit her with a shared kill against a Bf 109 in October. In any case, by this time, she and Lilya were already the most watched and highest-scoring woman fighter pilots in the Soviet Union—or even anywhere across all of the world's bloody battlefronts.

Whatever their scores, they were not destined to continue long as Khostnikov's "girls." Officers farther up the chain of command than Khostnikov soon had their eyes on these two falcons.

*Chapter 14*

# STALINGRAD, THE VERY HELL OF THE WAR

I n October 1942, the short-lived women's contingent within the 437th IAP was discontinued. Though it would be easy to leap to the conclusion that it was because they were women, the probable reason was the dissimilarity in equipment. The women were equipped with Yak-1s, while the other pilots in the regiment flew the obsolescent LaGG-3s.

When any unit operates dissimilar equipment, two parallel stocks of routine parts must be maintained, and mechanics trained on one cannot readily adapt to the other. In the air, pilots flying together must learn to adapt to the different performance characteristics of one another's aircraft. In a war zone, especially one so enormously intense as at Stalingrad, this is demanding and distracting.

As most of the women returned to their previous home with the 586th IAP defending Saratov, Lilya Litvyak and Katya Budanova were sent to join the elite 9th Guards Fighter Aviation Regiment (*Gvardeiskii Istrebitel'nyi Aviatsionnyi Polk*, GvIAP). A unit bearing a "Guards" prefix was one that had particularly distinguished itself in battle and that was created by redesignating existing units. The designation was first authorized by the Stavka in September 1941, and the Commissar of Defense officially renamed the 100th, 127th, 153rd, and 161st Rifle Divisions as the 1st, 2nd, 3rd, and 4th Guards Rifle Divisions. Subsequently, selected units in all branches of the armed forces, and at every level from regiment to army were redesignated at various points throughout the Great Patriotic War.

The 9th GvIAP had originally been activated in 1939 as the 69th IAP, and had been redesignated as a Guards regiment early in 1942. It had distinguished itself in combat over Odessa and had recently been one of the units brought in to help defend Stalingrad. It had also just transitioned from LaGG-3s to Yak-1s, so the equipment and ground personnel that were transferred along with the women pilots were compatible.

In his book *Yakovlev Aces of World War II*, George Mellinger writes that Raisa Beliaeva was also briefly transferred to the 9th GvIAP, but that she was transferred back to the 586th IAP after her aircraft was shot down while on a training flight. Some reports also suggest that Mariya Kuznetsova also had been assigned briefly to the 9th GvIAP before going back to the 586th IAP.

By October 1942, the 9th GvIAP was in the midst of being reorganized as an elite unit composed entirely of skilled, aggressive pilots who were already aces or had the perceived potential to become aces. As Hans Seidl puts it, the unit was to be a "regiment of aces capable of defeating the enemy and establishing air supremacy."

Some sources say that the idea for the "regiment of aces" was conceived by Lieutenant Colonel Lev Lvovich Shestakov, the regimental commander, who had been with the regiment since the beginning of the war when it was still the 69th IAP. However, Hans Seidl nuances this slightly, writing that the project actually originated with the Stavka, who picked the 9th GvIAP because of Shestakov's proven abilities as a combat commander.

In any case, Shestakov was an ace in his own right, having been one of the top-scoring Soviet aces in the Spanish Civil War, and being in the process of adding more than two dozen shared and solo victories to his score in the Great Patriotic War.

Among the other aces in the 9th GvIAP at the time were Yevgenii Dranishchev, Arkadii Kovachevich, and Boris Yeremin, each of whom would ultimately be aces more than twice over. Also included were Vladimir Lavrinenkov, a 69th IAP veteran already with two dozen victories, and the colorful Sultan Amet-Khan, the son of a Dagestani Lak father and a Crimean Tatar mother, who had earned a peerless reputation in the fighting over Stalingrad. Both he and Lavrinenkov exceeded a total of forty kills, including shared victories, by the end of the war.

Some historians, including George Mellinger in *Yakovlev Aces of World War II*, maintain that Shestakov was cool on the idea of women in his regiment. However, it seems more likely that given his prerogative to pick and choose, he deliberately chose the women—or at least agreed to orders from higher up to take them on.

Indeed, he apparently made a point of declining an opportunity to send Lilya and Katya back to the 586th IAP along with Raisa Beliaeva and Mariya Kuznetsova. When Major Aleksandr Gridnev, who assumed command of the 586th IAP when Tamara Kazarinova left, requested that they be returned, Lilya and Katya lobbied hard against going back to the static defense mission over Saratov, and Shestakov supported them. They would never go back.

This marked the milestone of recognizing women as elite fighter pilots for the first time. Many men served in Guards units in the Soviet armed forces during the Great Patriotic War, but there were thousands of competent male pilots who never received an invitation to transfer into one.

Shestakov's having recognized the promise of Lilya Litvyak and Katya Budanova as ace material was the key turning point in their careers and in the history of women in combat aviation.

Lavrinenkov remembers Lilya and Katya in his postwar biography of Shestakov, entitled *His Call Code: Sokol 1*. He writes that when he first met the two women in the 9th GvIAP barracks, he was startled, thinking that he had gone to the wrong place. He also goes on to recognize them both as outstanding aviators.

He also lends credence to the notion that Shestakov wanted the women in his unit, recalling the regimental commander's welcoming speech, in which he admonishes the male pilots not to sell them short, saying "watch out for the girls, and don't offend them. [They] fly excellently and they have already killed some Fritzes."

Killing Fritzes was now the number one mission on everyone's mind. The ground troops within Stalingrad had seen the relentless wall of German troops, always there, always replenished no matter how many were killed. Those who fought in the air had seen the vast and endless tide of German troops and vehicles that spread below them, westward from the gates of Stalingrad.

Indeed, "Kill" was the title of a widely published article about the Fritzes by Ilya Ehrenberg, the popular Soviet war correspondent, which had been turned into a propaganda leaflet. By the onset of winter in 1942, nearly everyone had read it, even at the front.

"Germans are not human beings," Ehrenberg had written. Just as Hitler's worldview had denigrated the Slavic people as subhuman, the correspondent's taxonomy removed Germans from humanity. "Henceforth the word German means to us the most terrible curse. From now on the word German will trigger your rifle. We shall not speak any more. We shall not get excited. We shall kill. If you have not killed at least one German a day, you have wasted that day. If you think that instead of you, the man next to you will kill him, you have not understood the threat. If you do not kill the German, he will kill you. If you cannot kill your German with a bullet, kill him with your bayonet. If there is calm on your part of the front, if you are waiting for the fighting, kill a German before combat. If you leave a German alive, the German will hang a Russian and rape a Russian woman. If you kill one German, kill another—there is nothing more amusing for us than a heap of German corpses. Do not count days; do not count miles. Count only the number of Germans you have killed. Kill the German—this is your old mother's prayer. Kill the German—this is what your children beseech you to do. Kill the German—this is the cry of your Russian earth. Do not waver. Do not let up. Kill."

Killing Fritzes.

That's why Lilya and Katya had become fighter pilots, and this is what they aimed to do.

The reassignment of Lilya and Katya to the 9th GvIAP coincided with a critical juncture in the Battle of Stalingrad. The German 6th Army under General Paulus, supported by General Hoth's 4th Panzer Army, had punched though the gates of Stalingrad on September 14, finding it a decimated lunar landscape of a place that had already been blown to smithereens by relentless artillery shelling and aerial bombardment.

However, they also found it a city that was about to be resolutely defended, inch by bloody inch, by an amalgam of Soviet ground forces, mainly under the 62nd Army commanded by General Vasily Chuikov.

Having studied the Germans' use of integrated air and ground forces, Chuikov had decided to meet the Germans at close range. This meant that the Germans could not use Luftwaffe air power to support their ground troops for fear of hitting the troops they were trying to support. This has proven to be a major dilemma for commanders operating at close quarters in urban environments ever since, and it certainly confounded the German battle plan. Indeed, blitzkrieg tactics went out the window the moment that the Germans stepped into Stalingrad. Just as ground support from above impractical, so too was the use of great sweeping maneuvers by tanks. The coming winter months would be a nightmare of close, often hand-to-hand, combat. German forces used to advancing dozens of kilometers in a day, were now measuring progress in meters.

Paulus had predicted a swift capture of the city, but it took nine days to pass from the city limits to the Volga and declare the southern part of Stalingrad to have been captured. Chuikov's troops had suffered mightily, but they had made Paulus's men pay for every meter, and they still held much of northern Stalingrad.

On September 27, the same day that Lilya had scored her double victory in the skies above, Paulus had made those skies target rich by launching his second major push to take the city. Coincidentally, this was just as Chuikov was launching a narrow counterattack in the city center. The sky full of Luftwaffe aircraft encountered by Lilya and her fellow pilots were part of the vast air cover effort supporting this operation. The Luftwaffe bombers were especially active in their efforts to strike the vessels with which the Red Army ferried troops and supplies across the Volga from their positions on the eastern bank.

Chuikov responded with a counterattack on September 28, and the battle seesawed back and forth in bloody small-unit fighting, especially in the vicinity of the Krasny Oktyabr steel mill and the Dzerzhinsky tractor factory, until October 7.

During the second week of October, both sides halted their advances to catch their breath and lick their wounds, but this intermission was broken on October 12 by a 62nd Army surprise attack. Caught off guard, the Germans were pushed back 300 yards, a considerable distance by the standards of the fighting inside Stalingrad. Two days later, Paulus countered with his largest scale concentrated attack since the beginning of the campaign, throwing 90,000 troops, heavily supported by tanks and air power, against the center of the Soviet line.

By October 23, the Germans had succeeded in capturing most of the fortified Red Army positions in and around the Krasny Oktyabr and the Dzerzhinsky tractor factory, while repulsing Chuikov's attempts at counterattacks at various places on the line. October 29 saw the Germans in control of roughly nine tenths of Stalingrad. They had destroyed more than half a dozen Red Army divisions, but Chuikov was still running reinforcements across the river from the east.

Conditions grew miserable. Lieutenant Galina Chapligina-Nikitina, formerly the adjutant to Marina Raskova, was now a pilot with the 587th BAP. "At the front we were stationed near Stalingrad, and we were bombing the German positions there," she explained later to Anne Noggle. "The living conditions were grave at that time. We were living in the trenches with no water to drink except when we melted snow; and when we had meals in the canteen, which was an old wooden building, we saw the water dripping from the ceiling onto the tables. We joked that we were eating, and the soup was still in our bowls!"

As the late autumn days grew short, the pilots often returned from their multiple daily missions in the dark, and took off before daybreak. This created unique challenges. "When we took off at night I knew that the only way to survive was to be ice inside, to feel absolutely nothing, to concentrate, to focus only on the mission," Klavdiya Pankratova explained to Anne Noggle. She was a fighter pilot who continued to fly with the 586th IAP, but the conditions under which she flew that winter mirrored those experienced by Lilya and Katya in the 9th GvIAP. "To fight at night had to be by intuition, because we could actually see very little. The takeoffs and landings were extremely difficult—no lights, no guidance. When we returned to our field we were allowed for a short time to turn on one landing light."

On the ground, and in the air, these were the most difficult weeks of the terrible Stalingrad campaign. Katya Budanova wrote to her sister Olya that she now found herself "in the midst of the very hell of the war."

This was no overstatement.

As November arrived, the weather was growing colder and snowflakes were in the air. The German 6th Army had taken a beating, but it had delivered a worse beating to the Red Army. Paulus controlled nearly all of Stalingrad, having nearly satisfied Hitler's orders, but it was a city wrecked almost beyond recognition. Paulus and his men faced the prospect of spending the winter occupying a sea of rubble that had once been a city.

It was that ominous time of year when a commander looks around and starts thinking as much about logistics as he does about hammering the enemy. The Soviet supply line was a tenuous and vulnerable boat ride across the Volga. The German supply line stretched for hundreds of miles across the windswept steppes. Only a single rail line crossed that distance, and the parallel roads would soon be difficult or impossible for truck traffic.

On November 19, everything about the Battle of Stalingrad changed abruptly.

While Chuikov had been receiving reinforcements in dribs and drabs, and shuttling them across the Volga to fight a delaying action, the Red Army had been preparing for a massive offensive to the north and south that would change the course of the war.

Operation Uranus, commanded by Marshal Georgi Konstantinovich Zhukov, started on November 19 as a pincer on a colossal scale. A million-man Red Army force broke through the thinly spread German and Romanian forces guarding Paulus's flanks at points on the line roughly 60 miles south of Stalingrad and 80 miles to the northwest. The flanks collapsed and by November 30, the pincer maneuver had completed its encirclement.

Paulus still controlled nearly all of Stalingrad, but the 250,000 men of the 6th Army and what was left of the 4th Panzer Army were completely surrounded and cut off from the rest of the German armies by a distance that grew greater with each passing day.

The strength and momentum of the massive force Zhukov had been assembling since September made it impossible for a German relief force to counterattack and reestablish a link between German lines and the Stalingrad garrison.

The only hope of saving the 6th Army in November or early December would be for Paulus to forsake Stalingrad, break out, and allow the 6th Army to fight their way to German lines. Paulus prepared for this action and requested the necessary authorization from Wehrmacht headquarters. However, Adolf Hitler, the highest authority, strictly forbade any abandonment of the city he had demanded to be captured and had been (at least for the most part) captured.

His supply line cut, Paulus dug in his troops, who prepared for a difficult winter none of them had anticipated. The Germans still had several airfields within the pocket they controlled, and a Herculean effort by the Luftwaffe to resupply the beleaguered Stalingrad garrison by air was undertaken. Though hundreds of transport aircraft, mainly the trimotor Junkers Ju 52s, were pressed into service to build the air bridge to Stalingrad, they were barely able to supply half of the 6th Army's requirements.

At the same time, large-scale airlift activities were also an increasingly important part of VVS doctrine. Even as the Luftwaffe was undertaking to establish an air bridge to resupply the troops surrounded at Stalingrad, the VVS was undertaking similar efforts to support the partisans who were conducting an organized resistance movement behind German lines in the western areas of the Soviet Union, which had been occupied for more than a year.

In the forefront of these efforts was the 101st *Aviatsiya Dalnego Deystviya Polk* (Long-Range Air Regiment), commanded by Marina Raskova's old comrade from the flight of the *Rodina*, Valentina Grizodubova. She and the 101st ADD had also been active in flying supplies into the besieged city of Leningrad in an analog to the Luftwaffe's efforts at Stalingrad.

December brought the turning point to Stalingrad. It was not just the turning point in that campaign, but, through the lens of 20-20 hindsight, in the war itself.

As Von Hardesty and others have written, the period after Operation Uranus began on November 19 also marked a major reversal of fortune for Soviet air power.

Just as enormous ground forces were being prepared for Operation Uranus, so too were large numbers of newly manufactured modern aircraft. These included variants of Yakovlev and Lavochkin fighters, as well as American Lend Lease aircraft such as Bell P-39s and Curtiss P-40s. Even before the United States entered the war, aircraft flowed to Great Britain through Lend Lease to fight Hitler, and after December 1941, the Soviet Union also became a beneficiary of America's mighty "arsenal of democracy."

Lend Lease had become an important source of aircraft for the VVS and PVO. The PVO's 283rd IAD, for example, possessed 125 fighters, of which only nine had been manufactured in the Soviet Union.

Modern bomber types were coming on line in very large numbers as well. These included Soviet-made Pe-2s, and Il-2 Sturmoviks, as well as American Lend Lease Douglas A-20s. In the list of aircraft of American origin, one should also mention the Lisunov Li-2 flown by Valentina Grizodubova's 101st ADD, which was essentially a copy of the Douglas DC-3.

The VVS, outnumbered four-to-one when the Battle of Stalingrad was joined in September, finally surpassed the Luftwaffe in available tactical aircraft. General S. I. Rudenko, commander of the 16th Air Army, noted in his memoirs that his command, along with the 8th and 17th Air Armies, matched the Luftwaffe's 1,200 with 1,350 aircraft. Limited by weather in the first days of Operation Uranus, offensive air operations began in earnest on November 24.

Among those units earmarked to be part of the Operation Uranus offensive was the 587th BAP. On the first day of December 1942, one year after the darkest days of the defense of Moscow, the regiment had finally completed its transition to the twin-engined Pe-2 bomber and was declared operational.

Marina Raskova assumed command personally, as the 587th BAP received their assignment to the VVS 8th Air Army. Having fulfilled its mandate of training the women for three operational regiments, the 122nd Aviation Group, the first all-women military aviation unit of its kind, was formally disbanded.

However, the regiment was off to a rocky start. As they took off to report to their battle station, they ran into severe weather and were grounded at an intermediary landing field between Engels and Stalingrad. Meanwhile, their final destination near Stalingrad had been changed. As Ekaterina Migunova, the regiment's deputy chief of staff, recalled in a postwar journal article, it was not until the end of December that most of the 587th BAP's Pe-2s had finally reached the regiment's assigned duty station.

Indeed, this was a time of shuffling VVS and PVO units to new airfields as the Red Army captured ground west of an encircled Stalingrad. The idea was to establish a ring of bases surrounding the city. The Luftwaffe was, meanwhile, placed in a correspondingly disadvantageous predicament. As the Soviet advance completed the encirclement, Stalingrad was left an island within a Red sea sweeping westward, washing over German lines. This meant that the Luftwaffe had to relocate to airfields farther and farther west, away from Stalingrad.

As Von Hardesty points out, the Bf 109s were now being equipped with external fuel tanks, and these single-engine fighters were being augmented by larger, longer-range Messerschmitt Bf 110 fighters. Their mandate now included escorting the vulnerable transport aircraft that were flying supplies in to the German pocket at Stalingrad.

Though the range of the Bf 110 was a positive attribute, the larger aircraft was not nearly as maneuverable in a dogfight as the Bf 109 or a Yak-1. Two Bf 110 pilots found this out the hard way on December 10, when Katya Budanova shot down both of them on the approaches to Stalingrad.

Though her friend scored this pair of victories in December, Lilya Litvyak apparently shot down no German aircraft during the three months that she was with the 9th GvIAP. In retrospect, this is difficult to imagine, given that the massive Luftwaffe airlift to the 6th Army forces at Stalingrad presented Soviet fight pilots with numerous slow and vulnerable Ju 52 transports as targets. Indeed, they were a veritable shooting gallery. Estimates of the number of Ju 52s shot down during the airlift range from 266 estimated by Richard Suchenwirth to 676 claimed in a postwar Soviet analysis by I. V. Timokhovich.

Either way or in between, it is obvious that there were tremendous opportunities to score victories in December, and it is mystifying that Lilya scored none during this period.

Some have suggested that continued gender bias played a part in this, but if Lilya and Katya were truly unwanted in the 9th GvIAP, it would have been easy enough for Shestakov to have had them transferred them back to the 586th IAP.

Another, more plausible, explanation might be that as lesser experienced pilots, Lilya and Katya would have been assigned by their new regiment to fly as wingmen for more seasoned veteran fighter pilots.

In a unit comprised of a disproportional number of aces, there would have been a lot of men with more combat missions under their belts.

Then, too, was the fact that the 9th GvIAP was a PVO air defense regiment, and as such it would have been held back as part of the defensive umbrella over Stalingrad, rather than flying far to the west to shoot down Ju 52s. With the Red Army on the attack, most Soviet air activity would have involved VVS regiments flying in support of an offensive that was taking place at a considerable distance from the city. At the same time, most Luftwaffe fighter activity in December was related to escorting the transports and not in engaging PVO fighters over the city.

There were other factors as well. With the worsening weather in late November and through December, there would have been fewer days in which the 9th GvIAP took to the air. For example, the 587th BAP were stranded for most of December at an intermediary airfield, and they were flying a routine, noncombat, ferry mission.

It was shortly after the turn of the new year, that the "very hell" of the Stalingrad winter weather caught up with the most well-known and well-loved woman aviator in the Soviet Union. On January 4, 1943, Marina Raskova was still halfway from Engels to Stalingrad. She was shepherding the last of the 587th BAP's Pe-2s, which had been grounded for engine trouble, which had now been repaired.

She and the other aircraft took off, having been assured—erroneously, as it turned out—of good flying weather all the way to Stalingrad. However, as it grew dark, the ceiling closed in to the point where Raskova had to order them to make emergency landings in whatever open ground they could find. Her Pe-2 was the only one that did not make it.

The worsening weather delayed the search for the crash site for two days.

As he recalls in his memoirs, I. S. Levin of Saratov joined that search and was the one who found the wreckage. Far below, on the cliffs overlooking the Volga River, was the aircraft that had become the tomb of the charismatic woman whom he had known since the flight of the *Rodina* in 1938.

Even *The New York Times* covered the death of Marina Raskova, and her funeral on January 12. The paper noted that her ashes were placed in the Kremlin Wall during an "impressive ceremony" with full military honors. The paper noted that General A. V. Nikitin wrote her obituary in the official Commissariat of Defense newspaper, *Krasnaya Zvezda* (*Red Star*) and that the funeral oration was delivered by Lieutenant General Aleksandr Sergueyevich Shcherbakov who was the head of the political department of the Red Army. The *Times* also pointed out, significantly, that the thirty-three-year-old aviator received the first state funeral to be held in Moscow in the nineteen months since the Soviet Union had entered the war.

"Throughout yesterday crowds filed past the urn in which her remains rested in the domed hall of the Civil Aviation Club," the *Times* reported on January 13. "Before massively banked commemorative wreaths a guard of honor stood. Major Raskova's mother was present, but her 12-year-old daughter was not … General Shcherbakov's oration was broadcast throughout Russia, as were Chopin's Funeral March and the Internationale. Banners were dipped and officers stood at salute as an airplane flew low over Red Square."

As Diane Sheean wrote in the magazine *Soviet Russia Today* seven months later, the famous aviator had indeed made a big impression on the Americans. In June, during "Tribute to Russia Week," sponsored by the lobbying group Russian War Relief, a Liberty Ship launched in Los Angeles was christened *Marina Raskova*, making it "the first American ship to be named for a Russian."

The people and the media had just traded a heroine for a martyr.

Meanwhile, those women who idolized her, and who became military pilots because of her, had lost a friend and a mentor. There was fear in their ranks that the Stavka would disband the women's regiments. Yevegeniya Timofeyeva, an eskadrilya commander who served as interim regimental commander, recalls in *In the Sky Above the Front*, that the women "couldn't come to terms with Major Raskova's death and worried about the fate of our orphaned regiment."

This fear was unfounded, but the new commander of Marina's own 587th BAP was a man, Major Valentin Markov. As with Aleksandr

Gridnev at the 586th IAP, a second all-women regiment now had a male commanding officer, though Markov did not join the regiment until after the women had begun combat operations on January 28. Yevegeniya Timofeyeva reports that he had initially resented his assignment to the 587th, but that he soon mellowed and was eventually well-liked by the women as their leader.

As Valentina Savitskaya, the regimental navigator, told Anne Noggle in an interview half a century later, the women had secretly nicknamed him "Bayonet," but "after we had been flying with him for some time, we called him not 'bayonet,' but 'Daddy.' I was 25 and he was 33."

When they learned that Marina Raskova had been killed, many of the women in her regiments had recalled her own words upon the loss of fellow pilots during their training at Engels a year earlier. As Klavdiya Terekhova-Kasatkina told Anne Noggle, the women were sobbing beside the coffins of their dead comrades when Marina turned and said, "My darlings, my girls, squeeze your heart, stop crying, you shouldn't be sobbing, because in the future you have to face so many of them that you will ruin yourselves completely."

Indeed, there would be many coffins to come, and one of them had now been Marina's.

The hell of Stalingrad would soon be over. On February 2, a month after Marina's death, Friedrich Paulus, now promoted to the rank of field marshal, surrendered the entire German 6th Army, nearly 100,000 troops. The Germans secretly offered to trade Stalin's son Yakov, captured in 1941, for Paulus, but Stalin personally turned them down. The field marshal remained in Soviet custody until 1953.

Von Hardesty notes in his appropriately titled book, *Red Phoenix*, that it was at Stalingrad that Soviet air power, both the VVS and the PVO, would finally begin to emerge, phoenix-like from the fires of humiliation. He writes that "no longer did the VVS view the Luftwaffe as invincible. This shift in attitude alone signaled a turning point in the war."

*Chapter 15*

# A TIME OF HEROINES

In January 1943, as the Battle of Stalingrad was winding toward its bitter end, Lilya Litvyak and Katya Budanova were transferred once again. This time, their move took them to the 296th IAP, the regiment that would be their professional home for the rest of their careers.

Their transfer came just as Soviet air power, rebuilt in 1942 after the terrible devastation of 1941, was reawakening. Soviet airmen—and airwomen—would find the red sun shining ever more brightly as 1943 unfolded. The tactical situation had shifted from an era of Luftwaffe dominance to one of Red ascendancy. The Soviet aviators had yet to seize complete control of the skies, but the days when the Luftwaffe had air superiority anywhere they wanted it were over.

Lilya and Katya departed the 9th GvIAP as it was beginning the transition to American-built Bell P-39 Airacobras. It had been decided somewhere in the labyrinth of the PVO hierarchy to transfer the women to a regiment that was still flying Yak-1s. This unit was based at

Kotelnokovo (also spelled Kotelnokov), one of the new airfields southwest of Stalingrad, which was located in an area recaptured by the Red Army during Operation Uranus. Commanded by Colonel Nikolai Baranov, the 296th IAP was not yet redesignated as a Guards regiment as the 9th GvIAP had been, but the wheels were already in motion for this upgrade.

Baranov greeted the women with respect, and with none of the chauvinism that had confronted women pilots earlier in the war. The thesis that Soviet military men generally welcomed women into their ranks once the women had proven themselves was being borne out here. As with Valentin Markov at the 587th BAP, the women came to playfully refer to Baranov as "Daddy" or "Father." Both Lilya and Katya would occasionally fly as Baranov's wingman—or, rather, his "wingwoman."

More often that not, though, Lilya would fly with Alexei Frolovich Solomatin, who was the commander of one of the 296th IAP eskadrilya. An established ace whose total score would eventually reach to at least a dozen German planes, he become a legend among Soviet pilots for his heroism in leading seven Yak-1s in a battle against nearly thirty Messerschmitts over Stalingrad late in 1942.

On February 11, 1943, the weather cleared and warring airplanes filled the skies over the snow-covered plains which surrounded Stalingrad and which seemed to stretch infinitely into the distance on all horizons. Lilya was flying that day in a zveno with Baranov and Solomatin. Some sources, including Hans Seidl, say there was a fourth aircraft in the zveno, and it was being flown by Katya Budanova. It was around this time that Soviet fighter aviation was making the transition from three-ship to four-ship zvenos, so the number could have been either. Many accounts have this foursome flying together on numerous occasions during the coming months, and they might well have been on February 11.

At the same moment, a Luftwaffe strike force of more than two dozen aircraft was over Soviet-held territory west of the Stalingrad. It consisted of Junkers Ju 88s, as well as some Ju 87 Stuka dive-bombers assigned to *Sturzkampfgeschwader 77* (Dive Bomber Wing 77), all escorted by fighters.

For the dive-bombers, it was a target-rich environment on the ground as they prepared to attack the large numbers of Red Army T34 tanks that were part of Marshal Zhukov's grand strategy to push the Wehrmacht westward.

For the Soviet pilots, it was the sky that was rich in targets, and they started to pick them.

Some Ju 87s carried forward-firing 37-mm antitank guns beneath their wings, but for rearward protection, to defend against air attacks from behind, the gunner had only his 7.92-mm MG 15 machine gun. In a duel with a Yak-1's 20-mm ShVAK cannon, depending on the MG 15 was like bringing a knife to a gunfight. The pilot of the fighter with the red number "32" had brought her ShVAK to the gunfight.

She scanned the herd of Stukas and randomly picked Weber's.

Just as it had been six years earlier when Lazar Kaganovich had decided to purge "every second man" from his bureaucracy, it was a cold, arbitrary choice.

The Stuka's gunner aimed his MG 15 into the blizzard of 20-mm shells, hurtling toward him like fiery snowballs, and squeezed his trigger.

The time that it took for the Yak-1 to close in for the kill was less than it takes to tell about it.

Broken by the cannon shells, Weber's Stuka crumbled and cartwheeled across the winter sky. Someone said that they thought the two crewmen got out, but they never turned up on any POW list and were listed as missing in action and presumed dead.

Red 32 was seen to waggle its wings as it tore across the sky. Inside, Lilya Litvyak was back in combat—and tasting blood.

Lilya rejoined her zveno, and the hunting continued. It was, after all, a target-rich environment.

In the sky that day, there was a relative newcomer. The Luftwaffe had recently upgraded some of their *Jagdgeschwadern* (fighter wings) with the new Focke-Wulf Fw 190. Lighter and more maneuverable than the Bf 109, the Fw 190 had made its debut in the West in 1941, where it proved to be more than a match for the great Supermarine Spitfire fighter of the Royal Air Force.

The Luftwaffe had first started using the Fw 190s in the East against the Soviets only a couple of months earlier in late 1942, so few among the pilots of the 296th IAP had yet to see one. On February 11, 1943, the pilots in Lilya's zveno saw one, or, perhaps more accurately, were seen by one.

What happened next melts into the confusion of a rolling, tumbling brawl. They don't call aerial battles "dogfights" for nothing.

What seems to have happened is that Lilya Litvyak, her adrenalin rushing after her Stuka kill, locked onto the German pilot and pumped 20-mm shells into his Focke-Wulf until he maneuvered out of her sights. In turn, either Solomatin, or possibly Baranov, picked up where Lilya left off, and the Fw 190 tumbled as a burning, stricken artifact of war toward the snow-covered battlefield far below.

Luftwaffe records don't corroborate an aircraft of this type lost to a pair of Yak-1s west of Stalingrad that day, but most sources, including those referenced by Hans Seidl, Reina Pennington, Tomas Polak, and Christopher Shores credit Lilya Litvyak with a shared victory against an Fw 190 that day.

Lilya's successes on February 11, her first victories since September, clearly gave her the confidence and credibility that may have ebbed during her long dry spell with the 9th GvIAP.

Both she and her friend Katya Budanova had now earned themselves a place among their colleagues in the 296th IAP. Indeed, one day earlier, on February 10, Katya is said to have downed an Fw 190 herself.

In a speech she gave to women workers in April at the Moscow airplane factory where she once worked as a carpenter, Katya described another battle. In this fight, she scored against another Focke-Wulf product, an Fw 189 "Uhu" (Owl), a twin-engine, high-altitude armed reconnaissance aircraft. It is probable that the two accounts describe the same incident, and that references to her February 10 victory confuse an Fw 190 for the Fw 189 of which she later spoke.

"I attacked it, and then I saw that it was slipping away from me," she told the workers, according to the recollection of Inna Pasportnikova in *In the Sky Above the Front*, later translated by Dr. Kazimiera Jean Cottam.

"The pilot had done his evil deed [photoreconnaissance of Red Army ground positions], and now he wanted to escape, scot-free. I became furious. 'I won't let you go, come what may, you bandit! Was it for nothing that I've expended ammunition on you?' I rushed at him. He was trying to draw me on – he descended to a lower level and kept going deep into his territory. I went down, too, diving, but a further descent would have been dangerous to me. I thought: 'Since you're trying to outwit me, I'll be the one to outwit you.' I decelerated … A furious gunfire came from the ground. I approached the Focke-Wulf to a distance of some 30 meters; then I moved still closer to it and opened fire. Behold, the enemy plunged to the ground. They were firing at me from the ground, but I stayed longer on purpose, to turn a few times above the Germans; then I accelerated and flew home."

It was in the middle of the month—Seidl puts the date at February 19—that Lilya Litvyak and Katya Budanova were both commissioned as officers, as they were promoted from serzhant to *mladshii leitenant* (junior lieutenant). They also were authorized to lead patrols on their own, whose sole purpose was to engage and destroy enemy aircraft.

They were also permitted to fly with a wingman of their own choosing; most accounts have them still flying frequently with Baranov and Solomatin. Of course, many missions were flown, as the pilots frequently flew three or more times nearly every day when weather permitted, and therefore many wingman combinations.

Lilya was beginning to assert her individuality. Comfortable in her new home with the regiment, now a Guards regiment, the small girl with the white-blonde hair saw no reason to hold back the headstrong streak of self-determination which had first manifested itself in her military life at the barber chair in Engels.

Just as she had once altered her boots and coat, she sewed together various lengths of different color parachute fabric to create long scarves to wear. She also personalized her aircraft. "Lilya" means "lily," so she painted one on the side of her Yak-1. Unfortunately, no known photograph survives today of her aircraft decorated in this manner.

To some of those who saw it, especially among the Luftwaffe pilots, the flower looked like a rose, so Lilya Litvyak soon became known as the "White Rose of Stalingrad." In the making of myths, factual details can be an intrusive nuisance. The misnomer, though, wasn't completely off base. Lilya did like to fly with the picture postcard of yellow roses in her cockpit.

Once considered shy, Lilya had grown confident to the point of cockiness. Fully self-assured after having found herself in possession of uncanny flying skills, she routinely engaged in aerobatics when returning from a mission. A few low-level passes or a low-altitude roll would become Lilya's trademarks for celebrating a successful mission.

"When Lilya approached the airdrome after a victory, it was impossible to watch her," Inna Pasportnikova recalled. "She would fly at a very low altitude and start doing aerobatics over the field … She flew over the field so low the covers of the aircraft would flap and fly around, she created such a wind!"

Of course, such showboating was strictly forbidden by regulations, but this did not deter an enthusiastic response from ground crews and fellow pilots when her Yak-1 came over so low that they could make out every detail of each delicate petal on the white lily painted on her aircraft. But the enthusiasm wasn't universal.

"I will destroy her for what she is doing," Inna heard Nikolai Baranov shout as she came in low and fast across the field. "I will teach her a lesson!"

"Did our Father shout at me?" Lilya asked Inna after she had landed and taxied to her waiting mechanic.

As Inna recalled, Baranov "did shout at her, and then he admired what she had done."

Writing in 1968, in the magazine *Aviatsiya i kosmonavtika* (*Aviation and Cosmonautics*), the journalist S. Gribanov colorfully envisioned Baranov and fellow pilots watching this spectacle.

"Both hugging the ground and accelerating, a swift machine with a bright lily painted on its cowling and visible from afar, passed over the pilots' heads," he waxed lyrically. "In a second, and in an exactly calculated place, the fighter sharply broke its flight path and shot up vertically. In the next moment, it dove toward the men, as if testing their nerves, and then again transitioned to a pitch-up, ending the recovery with a semi-loop. Having reappeared over the forest looking like a tiny cross, it grew in front of the spectators' eyes, and unceremoniously flew upside-down over the heads of the enthusiastic airfield fans."

Gribanov imagined that Baranov "by nature a merry and cheerful person, notwithstanding his strictness, couldn't help but admire true airmanship and the faultless landing of the 'reckless' pilot, and in the end involuntarily broke out into a rumbling laughter: 'What a devil this Lil'ka is!'"

By all accounts, Gribanov's manufactured dialogue represents "Father's" reaction to the young woman with reasonable accuracy.

Having flown the aircraft marked with the red "32" in early February, Lilya is said to have switched to a Yak-1 marked in yellow with a "44." It was in this aircraft that she may have shot down a second Fw 190 on March 1. Meanwhile, about a week later, on March 9, Katya shared a victory over a Bf 109 with another pilot from the regiment.

At this point, if all of the reports associated with them to date were true, both women were now confirmed aces, the only such women in the world. Counting all their possible claims, Katya had scored five solo victories and had shared in two more, while Lilya had scored five solos and shared three.

Two heroines at the peak of their enthusiasm had honed their skills to the peak of perfection. To paraphrase the old pop song, "March of the Happy-Go-Lucky Guys," which they remembered from teenage years, their country had commanded them to be heroines, and heroines they had become.

If only Marina Mikhailovna Raskova had lived to see this moment! Every airwoman flying for the Rodina that winter felt the pain of her loss.

On February 23, both Lilya and Katya were awarded the Order of the Red Star medal, which was presented to military personnel for "exceptional service in the cause of the defense of the Soviet Union in both war and peace."

It was also around this time (Reina Pennington puts the date as early as March 8, other sources a bit later) that the 296th IAP officially received its anticipated Guards designation, formally becoming the 73rd GvIAP.

In addition to their Orders of the Red Star, both Lilya and Katya also received, during their short careers, an Order of the Red Banner for valor during combat, and two Orders of the Patriotic War. For fighter pilots— for aces—it was customary to receive the latter decoration for shooting down three enemy aircraft and a second medal for another three victories, or ace status plus one. Lilya and Katya were both aware that there would not be a third Order of the Patriotic War for nine victories, but that ten usually brought a recommendation for the ultimate decoration, the red star of the Hero of the Soviet Union.

Standing on the tarmac that winter day as Baranov pinned on their medals, the two women were a contrasting pair. Katya was tall, while Lilya was small.

While Lilya was aloof, an extrovert in her personal style and in her flying, Katya was described as exuding personal warmth. Inna Pasportnikova wrote in *In the Sky Above the Front* that Katya was "the life and soul of our group. She was noted for her courage, persistence, and inexhaustible energy, which she successfully combined with plain dealing, sensitivity, and a caring manner of treating others. Willingly passing her flying skills and sharing her experience with younger pilots, she trained her subordinates for combat using personal example and wise counsel."

Katya kept her hair cut short, though not as short as the haircuts inflicted on the women as recruits. Lilya, meanwhile, took pride in her long, curly hair and went to great lengths to keep it just as she liked it. She even went so far as to use hydrogen peroxide, purloined from the field hospital, to bleach it out to the almost-white color that she liked.

"Often at the end of the last sortie of the day I would bring Lilya a large bucket and a towel and a piece of soap," Inna Pasportnikova reportedly told Bruce Myles. "She would open the radiator cap on her Yak and drain the scalding water into the bucket, and then top off the bucket with cold. Then she'd fling off her flying helmet and tuck the towel around her neck, and would pour the hot water over her head as she worked up a lather with the soap. Then she'd mix more hot water from the radiator and do it again, then rinse it thoroughly with cold. The men couldn't believe it when they first saw her doing it. Neither could Katya Budanova. But the idea soon caught on. Lilya would stride off to our bunker with the towel wrapped around her head and a few minutes later she'd emerge with her hair shining and bouncy."

When spring came, the steppes became a profusion of wildflowers. As Inna recalled in a conversation with Anne Noggle, "Lilya was very fond of flowers, and whenever she saw them she picked them. She would arrive at the airfield early in the morning in the summer, pick a bucket of flowers, and spread them on the wings of her plane."

Lilya also picked them in bouquets with which she decorated the cockpit of her Yak-1. The men teased her about this, and she teased them back by leaving bouquets if she knew a man was going to fly the same aircraft after her. In turn, they teased her back by holding their noses at the sight of flowers in the cockpit.

It was now the time of heroines.

The term described not only the pair of Marina's *equitissae* who were flying the fighters of the 73rd GvIAP against the Luftwaffe, but those heroines who were flying bombers against the German troops on the ground.

In February, the 588th NBAP had become the first of Marina Raskova's three all-women regiments to be honored with a Guards redesignation. The regiment was now the 46th *Gvardeiskii Nochnoi Bombardirovochnyi Aviatsionnyi Polk* (GvBAP), but to posterity, they will always be known by another name. For the Germans and in the annals of myth and legend, the women in their night-flying Polikarpov Po-2 biplanes were, and are, the *Nachthexen*, the "Night Witches."

Just as Lilya Litvyak would long be remembered by the erroneous epithet "White Rose of Stalingrad," so too would the term "Night Witches" come to describe this cadre, not of supernatural sorceresses, but of young, flesh-and-blood, hard-working women. Though not as the nickname suggests at its most contemptuous, Lilya and her fellow airwomen did deal death by night to the trespassers in the Rodina.

One of the women, Lina Yegorova-Arefieva, later told Anne Noggle, "The Germans called the crews night witches. They liked to sleep at night, and our aircraft made the Germans' life not so easy; they disturbed their sleep. Sometimes, when our planes were throttled back gliding over the target, the Germans would cry out, 'Night witches!' and our crews could hear them."

Zheka Zhigulenko, who flew with the 46th GvNBAP and produced the 1981 documentary film *Night Witches in the Sky*, later explained to Soviet journalist Vladimir Pozner that "You have to understand the German mentality: if there is no offensive going on, you are supposed to sleep at night; this is *Ordnung*, order, something sacred for the Germans. But we Russians didn't follow the rules. And suddenly in the middle of the night, we would disrupt their sleep with the sound of our propellers: tak-tak-tak, and then bombs would erupt. We flew at intervals of three to five minutes, so someone was always over the target dropping bombs. The Germans went straight out of their minds. It got to the point where the German command announced that whoever shot down one of those miserable U-2s would receive the Iron Cross. They were terribly afraid of us."

It was hellish for the Germans to have to endure the slow-flying, low-flying, death-dealing shadows, which often appeared suddenly in the night sky, often coming in unseen in the darkness, and often unheard, because the women often throttled back their engines for their bomb runs.

It was hellish for the women who flew the machines and sat in the cold and darkness, flying low and vulnerable, below tree-top level, over enemy lines. As Captain Larisa Litvinova-Rozanova later told Anne Noggle, "Each mission was a constant overstrain. We inhaled the gunpowder, choking and coughing, unable to breathe, from the antiaircraft gunfire bursting around us. It sometimes lasted fifteen minutes until we completely escaped the searchlights. When you leave behind the area of the target, the sea of antiaircraft fire, and the searchlights, the next instant you start shivering—your feet and knees start jumping—and you cannot talk at all because you are wheezing in your throat … When we flew five nights with maximum missions, we lost appetites and sleep in our reaction to the overstrain … pilots sometimes fell asleep during a mission. We even had a kind of agreement between the pilot and the navigator that one of us would sleep going to the target and the other returning to the airfield. I have a feeling that there were times when both the pilot and navigator dozed off for a minute or so because of exhaustion."

"The youngest was 17, the commander was 27," Zheka Zhigulenko recalls of the women with whom she flew. "These girls flew every night. Sometimes, in the winter nights we had to fly ten to fifteen combat missions. And each time you flew, you thought, 'that's all, I'm not going to return, it's the last one, it's over.' And suddenly you see your girls are burning, and you can do nothing to help them. And so it was, for 1,100 nights … I saw one of our planes burning, saw the right wing torn off, saw the face of my friend Galka in the cabin. Her mouth was wide open— probably, in the last seconds she was calling for her mother."

She also remembered the obvious disdain with which they had been greeted by General Konstantin Vershinin, the commander of the 4th Air Army, when they had become operational in 1942. On a repeat inspection tour in early 1943, around the time they became a Guards regiment, Vershinin personally awarded decorations to the women, with the words, "I was wrong, I repent."

To this, Zheka reports that the women answered, "We did some wrong, too, but we're not repenting." She doesn't mention whether they said it within earshot of the general.

The strategic situation across the entire Southwest Front had changed greatly as the winter began to fade and the heavy snows faded to flurries. By March 1943, the spring was bringing great changes to the battlefield beneath the wings of the battling airplanes—and these changes were not symbolized by the fields of wildflowers which Lilya Litvyak so enjoyed, but by the metallic hoofbeats of the riders in black who were returning to the steppes.

The great Soviet winter offensive that had driven the Wehrmacht from Stalingrad's threshold had swept westward, recapturing such major Russian cities as Kursk and Rostov. Armies under General Nikolai Vatutin succeeded in recapturing the great city of Kharkov on February 16, after it had been controlled by the Germans for sixteen months.

However, this great Soviet offensive, which had secured Stalingrad, ran out of steam and was halted by the Germans. Stalingrad may have been a milestone, but the men in black were far from defeated. The Red Army's overextended southern flank invited attack, and on February 21, German Field Marshal Erich von Manstein's Army Group Don (later Army Group South) launched a massive counterattack against Vatutin's Southwest Front.

By March 15, Manstein's legions had succeeded in recapturing Kharkov. At the same time, the Germans surrounded and captured large numbers of Red Army troops in tactical operations reminiscent of the great encirclements of 1941. Essentially, the Germans had once again swept the Red Army from eastern Ukraine. This marked a serious setback for the Soviets, whose armed forces had only just begun to come into their own offensively.

The Red Army, which had taken two steps forward after Stalingrad, had been compelled by Manstein to take a step back. With March, things no longer looked so good for the men in red. There was a lot of work to do, in the air as on the ground. There were still dangerous and difficult days to come.

While many aviation regiments which had been active over Stalingrad had moved north toward Kursk, to help prevent it, too, from being retaken by the Germans, other regiments, including the 73rd GvIAP, were moved south and west in support of the Southwest Front operations in eastern Ukraine.

By now, the 73rd GvIAP had evolved into a tight-knit family. There were the daughters, of whom the often-teasing brothers were justifiably proud, and there was Baranov, the father with the stern countenance and the soft, understanding heart.

There was no shorter road to Baranov's soft side than when Katya Budanova, with her exceptional voice, would start to sing his favorite song, "O Dnipro, Dnipro."

It was the same popular, tear-jerking song about returning one day to happier times that Marina Raskova had liked to sing. Perhaps that is part of the reason that the women in his regiment gravitated to their "Father."

Just as the 73rd GvIAP had recently been honored with the title "Guards," cast opposite them across the line was the Luftwaffe's elite Jagdgeschwader 3, which had been honored with the official nickname, "Udet," after the famous aviator Ernst Udet. One of Germany's greatest aces of World War I, his score of sixty-two victories was second only to that of his commander, Manfred von Richthofen, the legendary "Red Baron."

Having fought in the Battle of Britain and Operation Barbarossa, JG 3 served for a time in the Mediterranean Theater before going back to the Soviet Union in May 1942 to support the Wehrmacht's summer offensive. Along with JG 52 and JG 53, the Geschwader's Messerschmitts were among the fighters most frequently encountered by Soviet aircraft during the assaults on Stalingrad in September and October.

With the encirclement of the 6th Army, JG 3 was relocated to the encircled Pitomnik Airfield on the outskirts of the city, from which it flew *Platzschutzstaffel* (Point Defense) missions through the end of the year. Despite having just a handful of serviceable Bf 109G fighters, JG 3 had claimed 130 Soviet planes from November through the end of 1942.

During January and February, as the German armies were pushed back, and as they then stabilized their line against Marshal Zhukov's great offensive, JG 3 remained in action, harassing bomber formations such as the 587th BAP's Pe-2s and dodging fighters, such as the 73rd GvIAP's Yakovlevs.

As the great air battle over the eastern Ukraine continued, JG 3's numbers were periodically refreshed by newly arriving pilots. As with the Soviet units on land and in the air, as old blood was spilled, new blood was thrown into the fire.

On March 22, two of these young men were Lieutenant Franz Müller and Unteroffizier Karl-Otto Harloff, flying as a part of a half dozen Bf 109s escorting a large flight of Ju 88 bombers.

Suddenly, the bombers came under attack by as many as seven Yak-1s.

Müller and Harloff saw Ju 88s starting to fall, fatally hit, and they both turned in pursuit of a Yak-1 that had just claimed a Ju 88. Just as Lilya Litvyak and Alexei Solomatin had double-teamed to kill a Messerschmitt on February 11, the two Germans now set their sights on the Yak-1 with the lily on the side.

They had seen the white flower on her aircraft, and they had probably heard of the "White Rose of Stalingrad." Ganging up to kill a woman was hardly a chivalrous thing for these young knights of the Luftwaffe to be doing, but the White Rose of Stalingrad had a reputation—wildly inflated by rumor and hyperbole, of course—as a she-devil in a dark green killing machine.

The White Rose of Stalingrad had earned a reputation as a killer that was blown out of proportion. Just as the species of her flower was mishandled in the myth, so too was her reputation. Nevertheless, it should not be forgotten that the importance of myth is on par with the importance of facts, because myths govern perceptions, and perceptions govern actions.

The White Rose of Stalingrad was an excellent pilot. She was an ace. But she was no more a cold, heartless killing machine than anyone else in the sky that day. Perhaps it was because of her flower, or perhaps it was because she was a woman in a dogfight fueled by testosterone, that Lilya was of singular significance to the German pilots that day.

An aerial victory in the skies west of Stalingrad on March 22, 1943, would have given any Luftwaffe pilot cause for celebration and another kill mark painted on the fuselage of his Messerschmitt. However, to kill the White Rose of Stalingrad would be something else, something more.

Anthropologists have often written that throughout the mythology of cultures, across time and across the globe, it is axiomatic that to kill an enemy imbued with exceptional magic, or power, or mojo, is to take and possess some of that indescribable and unquantifiable power. In killing a legend, one becomes a legend.

This is probably why the Yak-1 with the yellow "44" and the white flower soon had, not just two, but six Messerschmitts chasing it across the sky.

Inside that aircraft, it was neither an legendary Amazon warrior nor a mythical she-beast, but a twenty-one-year-old woman, hardly old enough not to be called a schoolgirl, who felt the pain of shrapnel in her leg. She snap-rolled the Yak-1, a maneuver with which she was intimately familiar, and side-slipped the stream of tracers.

The earlier Bf 109 variants were armed with a 20-mm MG 151 cannon firing through the center of the propeller spinner. The Bf 109G-6 variant, which JG 3 "Udet" was flying, carried a 30-mm MK 108 cannon. A 30-mm cannon shell is an enormous and deadly thing, almost the same size as the forearm of a small woman such as Lilya Litvyak.

Lilya's Yak-1, because of the difficulty in processing aluminum under wartime conditions, was constructed largely of plywood. It takes little stretch of the imagination to understand what was going through Lilya's mind as the 30-mm shells pummeled her fragile aircraft.

As she rolled and outmaneuvered the heavier, more powerful Messerschmitts, Lilya realized that to escape one might be easy for someone with her skill, and even to escape two was probable—but six?

What she did next was not the act of a timid woman hardly old enough not to be called a girl, but of a fighter pilot for whom flying and fighting had intuitively evolved far beyond second nature.

She slipped away and stood the Yak-1 on its tail, straining the thousand horses that lived inside her Klimov M-105 V-12 engine, forcing the engine to give her as much of its 50 feet per second of vertical climb capability as it could manage. She then rolled over and, as experienced fighter pilots do in circumstances such as this, dove. The Soviet pilots colorfully described the diving attack as the *sokoliny udar*, the "falcon blow."

Assisted by gravity and the power of the Klimov, Lilya rapidly converted her altitude into speed and dove straight into the swirling mass of predatory Messerschmitts, straight at Franz Müller and Karl-Otto Harloff.

They reacted as instinct demands when three tons of machine are hurtling at you and gaining speed. They ducked.

To a pilot on the receiving end, a *sokoliny udar* looks a great deal like another Soviet fighter tactic, the *taran*, the "ramming attack." Soviet pilots had begun using the taran in the desperate days of 1941, when their aircraft were mostly inferior to those of the Luftwaffe. In those days, a taran was the equivalent of suicide. When Ekaterina Zelenko had become the first woman to use a taran against a Messerschmitt Bf 109 in September 1941, pilots who used the tactic did not expect to walk away. She didn't.

Over time, however, Soviet pilots developed techniques for making the tactic survivable, such as clipping the control surfaces of the target aircraft with one's propeller or wingtip in an effort to knock it out of control. Still exceptionally dangerous, a taran was used only when guns were jammed or out of ammunition. Though rarely used, the taran nevertheless loomed large in the Luftwaffe mythology of what to expect from those maniacal Reds.

The threat of such an attack was terrifying. As Franz Müller and Karl-Otto Harloff had just done, a pilot threatened by a taran usually ducked. Discretion was the better—and safer—part of valor.

Cool and in control, not the least bit maniacal, Lilya Litvyak jerked her control stick, rolled out of her dive, and thumbed the trigger on her ShVAK cannon, sending a deadly stream of 20-mm shells into the nearest Messerschmitt.

Both Müller and Harloff went down that day. As clearly witnessed by the other members of her zveno, Lilya was definitely responsible for at least one of them, and probably both. She likely also nailed one of the Ju 88s that had fallen to Soviet guns before the Messerschmitts had attacked.

The Luftwaffe pilots escaped their stricken Messerschmitts and lived to fight another day. Harloff returned to Germany later in the year, along with elements of JG 3 that were sent home to fly *Reichsverteidigung* (Defense of the Reich) missions against American bombers striking German industrial targets. He was killed in action in a fight with an 8th Air Force escort fighter almost exactly one year later, on March 18, 1944.

Lilya escaped the Messerschmitts, almost certainly with the aid of other members of her flight, but she was critically injured, and bleeding badly. Inna Pasportnikova told Anne Noggle that somehow Lilya "managed to land the aircraft, but she couldn't taxi or get out of the cockpit because of her wound."

The young woman with the wildflowers in her cockpit, whom the Luftwaffe had turned into a metaphor of fierce malevolence, bled real blood, which trickled from her battered and punctured airplane and soaked into the black earth of her Rodina.

## Chapter 16

# SPRINGTIME IN MOSCOW

Lifted gently from the cockpit of her battered "Yellow 44," the frail and ashen Lilya Litvyak received emergency medical care at a frontline medical facility after her heroic struggle with the Udet Jagdgeschwader. They removed the shrapnel, bandaged the ugly lacerations in her leg, and replaced the blood that had ebbed from her body while she fought so bravely in the skies over the battlefield on March 22, 1943.

They did what they could at the field hospital, but her wounds demanded further attention, and it was decided that she should be sent to a better hospital in Moscow. In the context of the titanic struggle then taking place on the largest battlefront in world history, it is hard to imagine that the wounds suffered by a junior lieutenant would justify the effort made to send her all the way to Moscow for treatment, but she was.

She reached the once-beleaguered capital at the beginning of April. When she had left the city of her birth eighteen months before, on that mad and confusing night of October 17, 1941, she had been herded into a dark, cramped freight car with dozens of others. She returned riding in a railway passenger car, her dozing head resting against window glass. Lilya, and her life, had been altered immeasurably during those months.

Just as Lilya was barely recognizable as the same person as the frightened twenty-year-old of 1941, so too had Moscow changed. The city had been in chaos on that awful night back then, as tens of thousands sought to flee the Hitlerite hoards whose imminent arrival in Red Square was considered inevitable.

Now, in the spring of 1943, it was still a city at war, and a yet-to-be-decided war at that. However, it was no longer a city with the enemy at its gates, it was the capital of the country which had erased the German 6th Army and denied Stalingrad to the Hitlerite hoards.

Richard Lauterbach, the occasional correspondent for *Time* magazine, who had repeated the innuendos about Marina Raskova before the war, had returned to the Soviet Union himself around this time, and he also noticed the refreshed mood in the country.

"Finally in the spring of 1943 things changed," he wrote in his book *These Are the Russians*. "The buds that formed that spring were somehow bigger, and the grass that sprouted was stronger. Stalingrad had been the storm of blood which soaked the Soviet soil with new strength and life and singing determination and confidence."

Arriving in Moscow that April, Lauterbach compared the city to what he had experienced on a previous visit. When he had first set foot in Moscow, Lilya had been in her early teens, and she never would have crossed paths with this young and impressionable American writer, enamored at a distance, like so many young people in his country, with the fantasy world of Stalinism.

"I found great changes in Moscow in 1943 when I returned there after eight years," he wrote of his impressions of the same city which now greeted the wounded Lilya. "The greatest change was nothing you could see. It wasn't the streets full of Red Army men, the splashy war posters, the unfinished buildings, the bomb damage, or the hollow cheeks. The difference was a difference of spirit. In 1935, these Russians were outcasts battling for the existence of a new social and economic order that, by its revolutionary nature, had set them apart from the outside world. Today they are not only battling for their own survival, they are struggling for the continued existence of that outside world, or part of it; they are fighting together with great nations that once frowned on them. They have done well, and they know it. They have killed millions of Germans."

Lilya had killed more than the share which Lauterbach would have apportioned to this young woman who had been just one of thousands of Muscovite Young Pioneers when he was last in town.

Lauterbach arrived barely conscious of the contribution being made to the winning of the Great Patriotic War by the women of the Rodina. By the time he left Moscow to go home to write his book, however, he would be fully aware.

Lilya was taken for surgery to a Moscow hospital. It might have been a military hospital, or perhaps it was originally a civilian hospital, but those distinctions had long since faded away. Except for the clinics that served those who were very much "more equal than others" among the Party elite, every hospital in the Soviet Union served the war effort, patching up the battered bodies of young men and women who had placed themselves in harm's way for their Rodina.

The battle with Müller and Harloff of JG 3 had taken a mammoth toll on Lilya's small body. Even after the Moscow doctors, who were presumably among the best, had finished their best work, her injuries left her with a limp. Ever since the surgery, she was still in pain, and this persisted for weeks, if not months.

Lilya Litvyak was scheduled to be sent to a convalescent facility, but she requested and was granted permission to recuperate at her own home at 88 Novoslobodskaya Street.

Her younger brother, Yuriy, was ecstatic, and Lilya's beloved "mamochka" was overjoyed to see and to hold her daughter again after a year and a half, which seemed to both like an eternity.

For the article which he wrote about Lilya in the journal *Aviatsiya i kosmonavtika* (*Aviation and Cosmonautics*), Gribanov interviewed Anna Vasil'yevna Litvyak in the mid-1960s, gleaning intimate details about the visit by the young ace to the apartment now shared by her mother and brother.

Gribanov wrote of her awakening not to the jarring scream of a Klaxon ordering her into the cockpit to intercept a strike force of Ju 88s, but to the "homey smell of her favorite pies" and "the rhythmic din of streetcars." As her mother told Gribanov, Lilya awoke, "not in a cold dugout but a cozy room at home, where every object was familiar to her since childhood."

He wrote appealingly of Anna Vasil'yevna bustling about in the apartment's tiny kitchen, getting out "the jars of jam specially prepared and kept for Lily." But he also told of how her mother saw the changes in the young woman's face, writing that Lilya seemed to her mother to have "become more mature, somewhat more severe looking, yet at the same time calmer and softer. So Anna Vasil'yevna understood that her Lilya had already experienced things which, very likely, others would never experience in their entire lifetimes."

For Lilya, the apartment was not entirely about jam jars and favorite pies, nor about artifacts of a childhood filled with sweet memories. It was also about what was missing: her father.

The absence of Vladimir Litvyak haunted the daughter who now wore the uniform of the state that had imprisoned and killed him. Part of what drove her, what impelled her to strike and kill the Fritzes, was to atone for whatever crimes made Vladimir an enemy to the people and to rehabilitate the Litvyak name, so that she, her mother, and little Yuriy could once again hold high their heads.

During April 1943, as a recuperating Lilya Vladimirovna closed her eyes at night in the apartment that once rang with the voice and laughter of her father, dark thoughts haunted her. What indeed happened with her father? Had he died a terrible death because his heart really had turned black with betrayal? Or had he simply been an unlucky victim of circumstance, a "second man" when "every second man" was arbitrarily marked for arrest?

If the dark and impersonal hand of the state had fallen upon her father, Lilya feared it could fall upon anyone. It could fall upon Lilya herself.

She knew about Order No. 227 and Order No. 270. Everyone knew about them. She knew what could happen. Everyone knew. Under Order No. 270, anyone who was captured would be considered a malicious deserter. They would be subject to being shot on the spot, and their family members would be subject to arrest.

This line of conversation came up from time to time back at the airfields, but only among the closest of friends, and only in hushed and whispered tones, because, just as every regiment had its quartermaster, every regiment had its political officer, its *politruki*, to make sure that no one dared express incorrect opinions, nor think incorrect thoughts.

Just as her father suffered when "every second man" was marked for arrest, could there not be a time when every second woman could be marked?

"What if I am shot down behind the German lines?" Lilya had asked rhetorically of herself. She thought of this on the day back in September when she faced Erwin Meier. She had laughed, and laughed often, about this strutting Nazi, a head taller than she was, and of how she had bested him. What if that had been her, surrounded by Germans? It could have been. They were just a few miles to the west.

She then thought of March 22, and of the shells exploding within her Yak-1. She had not fallen behind German lines, but she might have, and very easily. With the airspeed of her aircraft, it would have been just a matter of a very few minutes.

On par with the fear of a Nazi prison, or of some brutish Hitlerite having his way with her, Lilya feared what the political officers on her own side would do to her if she was ever captured and repatriated—and what might happen to her mother and her little brother under Order No. 270.

Walking the streets of Moscow that month, she almost choked with panic one day when a pretentious army officer halted her and angrily denounced her for wearing a flower in her uniform cap. The flashbacks of the day her father went away for good nearly stopped her heart. He demanded her papers, which was the normal course of affairs. Compared to a mere lieutenant, senior officers were omnipotent.

When he saw her limp, though, and when he read in her papers the circumstances of her being injured, it was his turn for an awkward sputter. He proceeded to escort the young heroine to her metro stop. He even insisted on personally finding her a seat on a car.

So much had changed since 1941, not only to her city, but to Lilya herself.

When the red sun rose, and the red man rode into the brilliant day, the dark thoughts of her father retreated into their dark recesses. In the spring sunshine, it did seem that things were growing ever better—as Stalin had promised since Lilya had been a Little Oktoberist. Indeed, the Hitlerite forces of darkness had never come to Red Square. The banners, and the posters of Stalin were still there, brilliant as ever, and Lilya wore his uniform, and his medals. As part of that generation born of the Revolution, she was part of its defense, and she was part of its glory—and an increasingly big part.

As she walked those streets in those warm days of a spring filled with bigger buds and an atmosphere of new strength and singing determination, Lilya wore her newly minted Order of the Red Star and imagined her future.

She passed a newsstand and noticed on the front page of *Pravda* a face that any Soviet fighter pilot would have immediately recognized. It was the smiling face of everyone's hero, Stalin's Falcon of Falcons, the Soviet Union's ace of aces. Sasha Pokryshkin was coming to town to be awarded the red star of the Hero of the Soviet Union.

Lilya had never met Aleksandr Ivanovich "Sasha" Pokryshkin, the chestnut-haired Siberian peasant boy turned fighter pilot, but she knew him well. Every Soviet aviator, and especially every Soviet fighter pilot, did. Though he had not yet received his Hero of the Soviet Union medal, he already was among the heroes of the Soviet Union.

The newspapers were filled with news of the most prominent of Stalin's Falcons, the man who had emerged as the Soviet Union's greatest ace. He had downed a Bf 109 on the first day of the war, and never stopped. By the beginning of 1943, his number of aerial victories was climbing toward twenty. He was the fighter pilot equivalent of Alexei Stakhanov, a simple man who had become the quintessential Soviet aerial warrior. As noted previously, had Stakhanov not existed, the Soviet state would have had to invent him, and to a certain extent, they did.

But Sasha Pokryshkin had no need of being invented. He was the real deal.

Though he would not receive his first until May 1943, Pokryshkin would go on to be one of only three men ever to be awarded the Hero of the Soviet Union three times.

In *Pravda*, the Soviet people read that once he had been shot down, but he survived and was picked up by a Red Army battalion. The captain of this unit welcomed him, and told the pilot that they were about to attack a German position.

"You fought in the sky," said the captain, "try it on earth. Not being accustomed to it, maybe it will be bad. Then stand in the second row and acclimatize yourself."

"It's not nice for me, in the second row," Pokryshkin had replied. "I am always at the forefront. Thus is my business."

Though the attack was successful, the captain was mortally wounded.

"You fought well, flier, fought well," the captain said before he died in Pokryshkin's arms. "A falcon's bravery you have."

"I'll take revenge," Pokryshkin replied sternly, as reported in the Soviet media, "believe me."

Such were the stories that fired the imagination and the fighting spirit of the Soviet people—and especially Soviet pilots.

Fighter pilots from throughout the VVS and the PVO studied Pokryshkin's tactics. He went on to fifty-nine solo victories and is still remembered as perhaps the premier Soviet air combat tactician of the Great Patriotic War. Lilya Litvyak and Katya Budanova studied his tactics, and like their male counterparts all across the vast battlefront, they asked themselves the technical question, "What would Sasha do?"

What Sasha did was to master the *sokoliny udar*. As she had on March 22, and again and again, Lilya Litvyak would do as the Falcon of Falcons did.

"Already they speak of him: in the stilted slogan language of yesterday's *Pravda* and tomorrow's textbook," Richard Lauterbach wrote adoringly of the Soviet media obsession with Pokryshkin. "To the Russians he is already three times life-size and all of him one dimensional: strong. That is his greatness and theirs, too … A Foreign Office official agreed that no man, with the exception of Lenin, had received such personal publicity during the entire existence of the Soviet press. Since almost nothing is ever printed concerning generals and marshals, and even less about ranking members of the party or the government, the significance of this organized build-up for one solitary air hero is difficult to understand without a close examination not only of Pokryshkin's record and background but of what he symbolizes in the present Soviet struggle."

Lilya saw the headlines and thought it very nice that an aviator so excited the media, but she asked the rhetorical question, "Why not a woman?"

Sasha Pokryshkin wore the Order of the Red Star, but so too did Lilya. Sasha Pokryshkin wore the Order of the Patriotic War, but so too did Lilya.

A month later, Pokryshkin would walk into the Kremlin, and into the imposing reception hall of the Council of People's Commissars to be awarded the red star of the Hero of the Soviet Union. The bright and self-confident Lilya saw the headlines, and she asked the rhetorical question, "Why not me?"

Meanwhile, women were beginning to receive the coveted red star. As a great many young Soviet women of Lilya's generation were playing an increasingly important role in the fight against the Hitlerites, they were starting to get the recognition that they deserved. Just as Soviet women workers had been celebrated in the Stakhanovite 1930s, the Soviet women warriors, whom the state had reluctantly, then timidly, sent into combat eighteen months before, were accomplishing things that were worthy of celebration.

At the time Lilya arrived in Moscow, there was a great deal of talk around town about two young women her own age who had just been awarded posthumous Hero of the Soviet Union medals on February 14. Natalya Kovshova and Mariya Polivanova were two friends from just west of the Urals who joined the Red Army together and became a sniper team with the 528th Rifle Regiment.

Renowned for their marksmanship, the pair had "canceled" more than 300 Fritzes by August 1942, when their position near Sutoki-Byakovo in Novgorod Oblast was overrun by German troops. Natalya pulled the pin of a hand grenade at the precise moment when she knew it would kill a maximum number of the Germans who were closing in on the two young women. She also knew the grenade would kill her and her comrade.

In later years it was written that the Soviet media largely ignored women combat pilots during the Great Patriotic War, but that seems not to be the case for Lilya Litvyak in the spring of 1943. *Ogonek*, the Moscow-based illustrated magazine which had, seven months earlier, erroneously acclaimed Valeria Khomiakova as the first woman fighter pilot to down a German aircraft, now made amends—of a sort—and published an article about Lilya and her fellow woman fighter pilots. Meanwhile, a newspaper published for military flyers carried a picture of Lilya on its front page along with headlines that shouted exuberantly, "The Glory of the Girl Hero! Feats of Destruction! Lilya Litvyak."

If the women pilots were largely ignored after the war, at least until Gribanov "rediscovered" them in the 1960s, they were certainly in the news in 1943. The tragic and unnecessary death of Marina Raskova was well covered, and after April 1943, so too was the news surrounding the young Lilya. With her Order of the Red Star and her ace status, she seemed tailor-made for the hero-hungry Soviet media to transform into a folk heroine for younger Russian girls who would put her picture in their school bags as she once carried pictures of Marina Raskova.

Lauterbach may have passed Lilya on the street near Red Square, or perhaps even at the metro station at the head of Novoslobodskaya Street. He may have noticed the smile of the attractive young woman with the blonde hair, the piercing gray eyes, and the pea-green uniform of the Soviet armed forces decorated with the Order of the Red Star.

He certainly did notice the headlines, and just as he was aware of Sasha Pokryshkin, he was aware of, and later wrote about, Lilya Litvyak.

Albert Parry, another American journalist who was in Moscow at the same time as Lilya and Lauterbach, was aware of the article and of Lilya's growing celebrity. He had even gotten the impression that both Lilya and Katya Budanova had come to Moscow in April 1943 on "special furloughs" to make media appearances and to be officially "praised for their fight in the air."

In fact, Katya was also in Moscow at this time, and she did make at least one public appearance, at the aircraft factory where she once worked, where she told of shooting down the Focke-Wulf reconnaissance aircraft. Even if Lilya had originally been sent to Moscow for surgery and a family visit, it is evident that both she and Katya did meet the press during April.

As he wrote in his book, *Russian Cavalcade*, published in the United States at the end of 1943, Parry had learned that between them, Lilya and Katya "had 'cancelled' 11 Nazi planes in a year of service, which included some stout battling above Stalingrad … On March 22, 1943, four Messerschmitts surrounded Lilya's machine, but she continued to fire and dive, shooting down one foe; and finally, having run out of fuel and ammunition, she picked her way to safety notwithstanding a leg wound."

In fact, the two women had been in combat for only half a year.

The total of "11 Nazi planes," including Lilya's on March 22, was taken from reports Parry read in the Soviet press, which were, in turn, probably taken from official sources. The latter may or may not have been accurate and up to date, given the inefficiencies of Soviet record keeping. At least this number provides a baseline minimum number and confirms the ace status of the two women.

The maximum number of possible victories for Lilya and Katya at this point, assuming that they each had five solo victories on February 23 when they received their Orders of the Red Star, would have been six for Katya and eight for Lilya. The latter assumes that Lilya downed a Ju 88 and only one Bf 109 on March 22.

In any case, the women fighter pilots were now getting the publicity they deserved. Indeed, their exploits were known beyond the Soviet Union. When Parry's book was discussed in *The New York Times* in January 1944, Lilya and Katya were both mentioned and pictured.

In a touching vignette relayed to Gribanov by Lilya's mother, he writes of Lilya walking through the courtyard of the apartment building on Novoslobodskaya Street, where she herself had played as a carefree child.

Anna Vasil'yevna looked out at the window of the apartment at the yard, covered with chalk lines. Here little girls, noisy like sparrows, were playing hopscotch, Gribanov relates. "A slender pilot, with a ruby-red star pinned to his chest, for awhile observed the skinny legs of the girls, their stockings held up by rubber bands, as they negotiated imaginary obstacles. Then he suddenly approached the white line and adroitly jumped into all of the squares crosswise, there and back. Afterwards, slightly limping with his left leg, he walked away, disappearing in the building's entrance. Their mouths open from amazement, only then did the little girls notice the beautiful blonde locks escaping from under the field-service cap of the decorated pilot."

Lilya was no longer a little girl playing hopscotch, but a hardened warrior in what one might take for a man's uniform—even though the women had long since gotten properly tailored uniforms—playing a man's game.

She knew and accepted this, and sought eagerly to return to the world where the game was not hopscotch, but an aerial duel in which the loser's fate was often death.

*Chapter 17*

# ROMANCE AND TRAGEDY

Lilya Litvyak returned to the 73rd GvIAP around the first of May in 1943 after spending a month in Moscow. By now, her regiment was more of a home to the "more mature, more severe" Lilya than was the apartment at 88 Novoslobodskaya Street.

It was also during this time that she was promoted from *mladshii* to *starshii leitenant* (junior to senior lieutenant), though the exact date is unclear.

When she had returned to the 73rd GvIAP, Lilya returned to her familiar comrades. Her eyes met those of Alexei Frolovich Solomatin, her customary wingman, a man who had come to idolize her. By all accounts, Solomatin was not alone among those who recognized and were extremely impressed with—even amazed by—Lilya's flying skills. Major (later General) Boris Eremin, who had once been Solomatin's flight leader and who was now a regimental commander in the same air defense division, called her a "born fighter pilot." Solomatin called her a "miracle."

Years later, Eremin told Reina Pennington that "Solomatin had a very high opinion of [her] as a pilot … they fought well. Such friendship. They had a special friendship." Eremin went on to say that Solomatin had once told him that "she's a great pilot. She understands me perfectly."

It is generally believed that this "understanding" carried over into their personal lives, but probably not as far as the folklore yearns to believe.

"Lil'ka" and "Lyosha," as they called one another, have always been linked romantically in the mythology of that time and place, but the evidence of their being lovers is more imagined that verifiable. Some extremely apocryphal tales about their relationship still circulate. In some of these untraceable fabrications, they are even said to have been married.

In fact, their story is more likely a classic unconsummated romance than a torrid love affair. It was the sort of tragic romance about which they once wrote operas. He was a farm boy from a village in the Kaluga Oblast, near the Oka River, about 100 miles southwest of Moscow. She was a city girl from the capital. He was an example of a man for whom the Soviet classless system worked, a peasant lad who became a decorated fighter pilot. She was one who had to fight the system just for the opportunity to attain the greatness she had achieved—and who never would have found herself in the cockpit of a Yak-1 if not for good fortune and Marina Raskova.

At last, in the cold, dark bleakness of the Stalingrad winter, they had found one another.

They had been comrades in arms, thrown together by war, each respecting the other's skills as a consummate warrior. Had this been an opera, the audience would have been on the edge of their seats, watching a professional relationship become a friendship, and yearning for the friendship to blossom into love.

Had these comrades in arms been comrades in one another's arms?

The folklore demands with tearful eyes that the answer be that they were.

Though Bruce Myles writes that Inna Pasportnikova had told him that there had been much more to the friendship than merely the comradeship of fellow pilots, she was more circumspect when she discussed this relationship between Lilya and Alexei with Reina

Pennington many years later. As Inna explained, Lilya "understood that Solomatin was an exceptional pilot and she appreciated him. Everyone knew that he loved her, everyone knew. But she never told me she was in love with him."

She was, but she kept it to herself.

Perhaps she kept it from herself.

Lilya fought her feelings for Solomatin. Even though their commanders and their fellow pilots thought they flew well and worked well together, she is said to have impulsively asked for a transfer to the other eskadrilya within the 73rd GvIAP so that she would no longer have the distraction of being a wingman to someone whom she knew to be so deeply in love with her.

"When you've recovered," the doctors had replied noncommittally when she asked how soon she could leave Moscow and return to her unit. By so doing, they seemed to have left the decision in her hands. With this choice open to her own interpretation, Lilya made the decision to go back sooner rather than later. By most accounts, she left Moscow before her recovery was truly complete. She was still in pain and had yet to recover her full strength. Nevertheless, she was determined to get back into the cockpit, and back into the skies over the Southwest Front.

Lilya quickly proved that she had lost none of that miraculous talent which earned her the Order of the Red Star, as well as the admiration of superiors and fellow pilots alike. On May 5, her zveno was escorting a flight of Pe-2 bombers when Messerschmitt Bf 109Gs slashed into the bomber formation. A Yak-1 with a lily painted on the side, and a pilot in the cockpit with uncanny skill and much to prove, leapt upon one of the Messerschmitts with great ferocity.

In the old folk tale, Vasilisa returned to her stepmother's house carrying a human skull with fire glowing ethereally its eye sockets.

In May 1943, Lilya Litvyak returned to the 73rd GvIAP, to the house of Nikolai Baranov, her stepfather, with fire glowing metaphorically in her own eye sockets.

She hammered the Messerschmitt like an exorcist hammering all the demons that could have been conjured up by Baba Yaga.

When Vasilisa returned with the skull, the wicked stepsisters ran away frightened, but the skull pursued them, its burning, vindictive eyes locked upon them until they caught fire and burned to ash.

When Lilya returned to the sky over the Southwest Front and locked onto the tail of a Messerschmitt, the maneuvering, twisting, slithering German fighter tried to evade her. But the Yak-1 pursued it with aggressive vengeance. The bright, burning tracer rounds from the ShVAK cannon locked upon the Messerschmitt like burning, vindictive eyes, until it caught fire, tumbled from the sky, and burned to ash.

She landed to rearm and refuel and go back into that burning sky, but Nikolai Baranov ran out to take stock of his White Lily. Her face was as white as her bleached hair. The fact of her having failed to fully convalesce was starkly apparent. He forbade her to fly again without a rest.

On May 6, one day after Baranov had grounded Lilya, he was leading his flight against the Luftwaffe, when he was hit. As he wrestled his Yak-1 back toward friendly lines, the fire in its Klimov engine was spreading. At last, as tongues of flame licked at his cockpit, he could see his own airfield far below. Home at last!

He jettisoned his canopy and leaped from the stricken aircraft. As he pulled the ripcord, smoldering embers that had made their way into his parachute pack burst into flame, consuming his parachute.

The helpless pilots and ground crew of the 73rd GvIAP watched him fall. The grounded Lilya watched the flailing Baranov hit the hard black earth with a crack, ash from the burning parachute falling around him. If not for Baranov's own stern and fatherly compassion, Lilya would have been up there that day.

The next day, she was.

Again, a woman with angry, vindictive fire glowing in her eye sockets chased one of the Luftwaffe's finest—or most unlucky—just like the she-devil from the myths they told about the White Rose of Stalingrad.

Again, as in the old folktales of Vasilisa and the newer folktales of the White Rose, a Messerschmitt caught fire and burned to ash.

According to the *Khronika Boevykh Pobed Gvardeiskii* (*Chronicle of Guards Combat Victories*) and other sources, including Hans Seidl, Tomas Polak, and Christopher Shores, it was thanks to Lilya that the Luftwaffe was compelled to write off another Bf 109G on May 7. Counting all of her reported victories, her score now stood at ten solo kills, plus four shared, making her an ace twice over.

The sun shone also for Alexei Solomatin, for it was during that same week that he was awarded the most coveted medal of them all, Hero of the Soviet Union. Counting all his victories, he now had at least fifteen, and possibly seventeen, solo kills, and as many as twenty-two shared victories. Lilya felt great pride for her friend, and yearned to hug him, but she was a twenty-one-year-old woman anxious to hide her feelings.

Solomatin, hero of the Soviet Union, had a red star, which proclaimed his status as an ace. But that which he truly desired—Lilya's love—was beyond his grasp.

Had this been an opera, this would have been the moment where they came together, perhaps embracing against a blood-red sunset of the kind one sees on the steppes when there are countless fires burning beyond the western horizon. But this was not an opera, it was war, and the countless fires were only too real.

Through the coming weeks, as the air war intensified, new pilots, all men, came to join the 73rd GvIAP to make up for the losses. Experienced pilots generally took them up for frontline familiarization flights. If these newcomers were startled to find a woman cast in the role of the experienced pilot, her comrades would be swift to explain that this little blonde was the pilot to whom the Fritzes referred—with trepidation as well as amazement—as the "White Rose of Stalingrad."

On May 21, it was Alexei Solomatin who was flying one of these routine flights. After having flown into combat against the Germans many dozens of times, a flight with a new pilot within sight of the field was hardly a flight worthy of more than a couple of quick scratches in the log book, but this day was different.

Anyone on the ground would not have noticed the familiar, routine growl of the Klimovs in the sky, but every man—and woman—below would have looked skyward at the sound of an out of place cough or sputter. At the moment of that sputter and cough, Lilya was in her cockpit, waiting for takeoff clearance, chatting with her mechanic, Inna Pasportnikova, who was sitting on the wing of her Yak-1.

"One of the aircraft started coming down with a roar, crashed, and exploded.," Inna later told Anne Noggle. "Everyone thought it was the new pilot, but no, it was the squadron commander, it was Alexei."

Alexei Frolovich Solomatin never had a chance. He was too low to bail out. The fireball and the gut-wrenching sound of the Yak-1 impacting the ground stopped hearts.

"We buried him, and after this happened, Lilya didn't want to stay on the ground, she only wanted to fly and fight, and she flew combat desperately," Inna Pasportnikova recalled.

According to Reina Pennington, Lilya's letters reveal that "she did not realize she loved Solomatin until after his death."

In a poignant and eloquent letter to her mother, preserved by Inna Pasportnikova and quoted by Reina Pennington in her book, Lilya wrote "Fate has snatched away my best friend Lyosha Solomatin … He was everyone's favorite and he loved me very much, but at that time he was not my ideal. Because of this there was a lot of unpleasantness."

Lilya also wrote of a dream in which Solomatin was standing on the far side of a river, asking her to come across. To this, she replied "If they let me." If this was an opera, the river would be the Dnieper, and the chorus would be "O Dnipro, Dnipro."

At last, she finally revealed a glimpse into her feelings for Lyosha, writing "I confide, mamochka, that I valued this friendship only in the moment of his death. If he had remained alive, then it seems this friendship would have become exceptionally beautiful and strong. You see, he was a fellow not to my taste, but his persistence and his love for me compelled me to love him, and now … it seems to me that I will never again meet such a person."

Overcome by melancholy so dark that it matched the shadows cast by the dark clouds of spring thunderstorms across the wildflowers on the hillsides—a sadness that she could not admit, even to herself—Lilya Litvyak continued to fly and fight.

She became a driven woman, driven to defeat the enemy of her Rodina, which had taken the lives of those so dear to her.

*Chapter 18*

# THE WHITE LILY OF
# THE DONBASS

Ever since Lilya Litvyak had come home to the 73rd GvIAP at the beginning of May, the key focus of the air war on the Southwest Front had been in the Donbass region (also referred to as the Donets Basin) of eastern Ukraine, a strategically significant coal-mining area south and east of Kharkov and south and west of Stalingrad. The Donbass had been captured by the Germans in fall 1941 and liberated very briefly by the Red Army early in 1943, just after Stalingrad. It was quickly recaptured by the Germans. Now both sides were preparing for the next round of bitter fighting here.

The importance of the Donbass and the surrounding area to the Soviet economy was immense. Prior to Barbarossa, its coal mines had produced half of the Soviet Union's coal, while its industry provided 60 percent of the nation's pig iron, 40 percent of its aluminum, 20 percent of its chemicals, and 20 percent of the machinery manufactured in the Soviet Union.

At the center of the Donbass lay the symbolically important city of Stalino (now known as Donetsk). While the pivotal battle of the Great Patriotic War had been fought for one Russian city named for Josef Stalin, this Ukrainian city named for the Man of Steel also became the scene of terrible fighting as it changed hands several times before the war was over.

The men and women of the 73rd GvIAP were deeply affected by the loss of both Nikolai Baranov and Alexei Solomatin in the space of just two weeks, especially because the losses came from flukes rather than enemy action.

However, the regiment had but a quick moment to mourn, and no choice but to carry on. Now based at the eastern Ukrainian city of Krasny (or Krasnyy) Luch in Voroshilovgrad Oblast (now the Luhansk Oblast, also called Luhanska), the 73rd GvIAP would be an important part of the impending battle for the Donbass.

For Lilya Litvyak, the loss of the two men, especially that of the man who had lived for and longed to be her lover, transformed a young woman, already serious beyond her years, into the single-minded killing machine that the Germans had long believed her to be. She now had little desire for anything in life but to fly and fight.

Soon, a new regimental commander, Major Ivan Golyshev, was assigned to replace Baranov. By all accounts, he arrived in a frame of mind to give Lilya the respect as a fighter pilot which she deserved—and which she had earned. Like his predecessor, he did have, and did express, a concern for the residual effects of the injuries that she had suffered at the end of March, and which still troubled her.

It was at the end of May, probably the last day of the month, that Lilya volunteered to take on a particularly perplexing problem. Near a village called Troitskoye, the Germans had run up an observation balloon. The steppes being devoid of hills and high ground that could be used by artillery spotters, this balloon afforded them an enviable eye in the sky. Located about 10 miles behind the lines, it could snoop on Soviet positions, but was out of range of Soviet guns and heavily protected from air attack.

"Many Soviet airmen tried to shoot it down but turned back, because there was a wall of fire from the guns," Inna Pasportnikova recalled to Anne Noggle. "She went to the regimental commander and said, 'Let me shoot down the balloon.' He said she could not, for she was still ill … She told him that if he did not let her do it she would do it without his permission, and he told her in that case she should tell him how she was going to do it."

Lilya's approach was not a frontal attack, which had been tried several times without success by others, but deception. She crossed the front lines some distance from Troitskoye and flew westward, deep into enemy-held territory. She then reversed course and flew eastward at an altitude so low that her three-bladed prop almost clipped the tall sunflowers. She hit the balloon from behind, at the moment when her Yak-1 was approaching directly out of the sun and therefore virtually impossible to see. Lilya caught the Germans by surprise and sent the balloon down in flames before they had a chance to respond. Their antiaircraft artillery was still pointed the opposite direction, anticipating another frontal attack.

Because the Germans used hydrogen rather than helium, the firestorm of the exploding "sausage" could be seen for miles, eliciting a grand round of applause from those ground troops who had suffered under the artillery directed by the insidious gasbag. When she landed, a smiling Lilya was greeted by comrades with enthusiastic congratulations and pats on the back for her ingenious sneak attack.

It was not just the ground troops and fellow pilots who now celebrated Lilya's skill and bravery. The male hierarchy that once had ridiculed her as a girl doing a man's job now saw her as an accomplished fighter pilot with great leadership potential. According to the *Khronika Boevykh Pobed Gvardeiskii*, it was on June 13, not long after he came aboard that Major Golyshev assigned Lilya as the squadron commander for the 73rd GvIAP's 3rd Eskadrilya, though occasionally, he would ask her to fly as his own wingman. In so doing, he paid her the most practical of compliments.

A short time later, while on a mission in which Lilya was flying wing for Golyshev, the two Yak-1s came under attack by four Bf 109s. Recognizing by the markings on his aircraft that the regimental commander was in the lead, the Messerschmitts tore into Golyshev. The shells ripped into his plane, injuring him, but not seriously. The attack had lasted but for a few seconds before the attackers came under fire themselves.

As the regimental commander's wingman, Lilya knew that it was her job to protect Golyshev. She set her sights on his attackers, shooting and maneuvering in an effort to peel them away from Golyshev. This gave him the split-second window of opportunity that he needed to sideslip, bank, turn, and get away.

Unfortunately for Lilya, she was now in the line of fire herself.

Unfortunately for the Germans, the airplane with the lily painted on the side was an extraordinarily slippery target. Though they managed to hit the Yak-1 repeatedly, the skill of an experienced pilot in a highly maneuverable airplane with which she was intimately familiar prevented any of them from making a kill that day.

Had it not been for the necessity of escorting her damaged flight leader back to safety, Lilya might well have turned her miraculous skills, and her mounting aggressiveness in battle, against the Messerschmitts and added a victory mark or two to her own tally.

She touched down as soon as Golyshev was safely on the ground, and the ground crews took stock of severe battle damage done to both of the Yak-1s.

As these and other Yak-1s were being written off, the regiment started to receive the newer Yak-1B fighters. Lilya Litvyak traded in her battered Yak-1 with the yellow "44" for a Yak-1B with a white "23" to match her white lily.

Unlike the Yak-7 and Yak-9, or the later Yak-3, which were improved generations of fighters based on the Yak-1, the Yak-1B was an improved Yak-1, having the same dimensions and many of the same features. The obvious difference was a lowered rear fuselage and a bubble canopy—like those of the Yak-9 and Yak-3—which gave the pilot vastly improved rearward visibility. It was much better in this regard than the German Bf 109. The Yak-1B also had an improved gunsight and control system, as well as a Klimov M-105PF engine, which was optimized for lower-altitude operations where most of the combat was taking place.

Though the Yak-1Bs were first available around the time of the Stalingrad campaign, many units, even Guards regiments such as the 73rd GvIAP, did not receive their aircraft until the middle of 1943. It was just in time. By June, there had come an ominous sense that the Germans were about to launch their third massive summer offensive in as many years.

After the great Soviet offensive that had saved Stalingrad was halted—and in Ukraine, reversed—by von Manstein's counteroffensive in February and March, movements on the ground had slowed as both sides responded to the *rasutitsa*. A part of the annual routine of the steppes for as long as humans can remember, the rasutitsa, or "quagmire season," is the time when the vast flat plains of Russia and Ukraine become a sea of mud because of rain and melting snow and unpaved roads become impassable.

By summer, as the ground was drying out, there was a rumbling in across the western horizon. It was the sound of engines, the engines of Panzers and Messerschmitts.

German overall strategy for the summer of 1943 called for holding their gains in Ukraine and the south, while launching their third annual massive summer offensive against the center of the sprawling 2,000-mile front. It was aimed not at Moscow, as had been past offensives against the center—because the Germans had been pushed far away from the capital—but at the city of Kursk.

Located 280 miles southeast of Moscow, Kursk had marked the high-water point of the Red Army's counteroffensive of the previous winter. Now, the Wehrmacht wanted to retake it, as they had Kharkov and Stalino.

Because Kursk was precariously located in a bulge in the front line, it was already surrounded by German armies on three sides. It therefore appeared—at least on the maps—like the proverbial low-hanging fruit.

Mustering a quarter of a million men and nearly 3,000 tanks, including the remarkable PzKpfw V Panthers and PzKpfw VI Tigers, the Germans launched Operation Zitadelle (Citadel) on July 5.

The objective of Operation Zitadelle was to capture Kursk by pinching off the bulge with a two-pronged pincer. Elements of Field Marshal Erich von Manstein's Army Group South attacked from the south, while Field Marshal Günther von Kluge's Army Group Center attacked from the north and west. The Wehrmacht intended to turn the bulge into another great encirclement.

To support Zitadelle, the Luftwaffe concentrated 2,000 aircraft in the area, amounting to roughly seven of every ten combat aircraft that it had available on the entire front facing the Red Army. On the opposing side, the Stavka brought together a force of nearly 3,000 tactical aircraft, including the most up-to-date types, making it the largest concentration of Soviet air power since the VVS had been devastated by Barbarossa back in 1941.

As the battle began, the Luftwaffe immediately seized air superiority over Kursk. However, as the first week unfolded, the Soviet 2nd and 16th Air Armies, backed by substantial reserves, were able to hold their own. On the ground, the Battle of Kursk is remembered for being the largest tank battle in the history of warfare, but the battle overhead was also one of the largest yet in the Great Patriotic War.

While this campaign was underway, the Red Army also was preparing for its counterstrike, a renewed offensive 200 miles to the south of Kursk in Ukraine. This was the long-awaited move toward liberating Kharkov and the Donbass once and for all, pushing all the way to the beloved and storied Dnieper River. The air support for this immense operation would eventually include elements of the 5th, 17th, and 2nd Air Armies.

Opposing the Red Army were those armies from Field Marshal Erich von Manstein's Army Group South that were not directly involved in the Kursk operations. They were supported in the air by Luftflotte 4, which included elements of the recent nemesis of the 73rd GvIAP, Jagdgeschwader 3.

On July 5, the same morning that the Germans launched Zitadelle, the VVS launched a series of bombing raids against Luftwaffe bases around occupied Kharkov. While the Luftwaffe dominated the aerial battlefield over Kursk by a wide margin on that day, the VVS caught the Germans off guard at Kharkov.

On July 16, Lilya and her new "White 23" were leading the 3rd Eskadrilya into combat over Voroshilovgrad (now Luhansk) at the far eastern edge of Ukraine. According to the *Khronika Boevykh Pobed Gvardeiskii* (*Guards Chronicles*) in the TsAMO, the Central Military Archives, the 73rd GvIAP pilots intercepted and turned to attack 30 Ju 88s and were then attacked by four Messerschmitts. These belonged to JG 3.

German data, meanwhile, confirm that the Geschwader did see a great deal of action in the area that day. By the record of one JG 3 ace, Oberfeldwebel Hans Grünberg, it is evident that some pilots probably flew at least two sorties, which was not uncommon. Grünberg is credited with downing one Yak at 0615 hours that day and another at 0850. It is improbable that a single aerial battle would have lasted for more than two hours.

Grünberg was an ace many times over, who had scored his first kill in August 1942, a month before Lilya had her first aerial victory. His score now stood at fifty-three victories, including sixteen Il-2 Sturmoviks. Of these, he had killed seven in one day, on May 7, and he had added three more in just the past forty-eight hours.

Having tasted blood twice that day—and against Red fighters at that—Grünberg was hungry for more. As his Bf 109G-6 hurtled across the sky, the ace spied his likely third Yak of the day. It was marked with a white "23," and it had a white lily to match.

Hans Grünberg had been in action on the front west of Stalingrad with JG 3 for almost a year, so he had almost certainly heard of the fabled "White Rose of Stalingrad." Many a Messerschmitt ace had seen the white lily and imagined himself bragging about being the one who sent the Red she-devil to her grave.

The killing machine who had erased two Yaks since breakfast put the white lily in his gunsight. He thumbed the trigger and sent a stream of those 30-mm cannon shells the size of a small woman's forearm in her direction. But the airplane with the white lily on the side sideslipped, though not without taking some hits.

Grünberg licked his lips, jerked his stick to follow the evading Yak-1B, and put the she-devil back into his sight.

She was there, and then she wasn't.

Next, it was Hans Grünberg who was in the sights of the woman known to legend as the White Rose of Stalingrad, who might have been more accurately nicknamed the "White Lily of the Donbass."

Lilya, too, tasted blood that day. Henry Sakaida, Tomas Polak, and Christopher Shores write that she had downed one of the Ju 88s. Luftwaffe historian Jochen Prien, who wrote a three-volume history of JG 3, also mentions another Bf 109G-6 flown by one of the ace's JG 3 Geschwader-mates as having possibly been damaged by Lilya before escaping.

Lilya was not keen to let Grünberg get away, and like a cat with her paw on the tail of a mouse, she did not. She shot him up, and her comrades watched as she forced him down. It was an aerial victory without kill, but a victory nonetheless.

Hans Seidl, Tomas Polak, and Christopher Shores agree that at least one of Lilya's fellow pilots came to her aid after she was hit, also putting some rounds into Grünberg's Messerschmitt, and sharing the victory with her. The Luftwaffe records for Grünberg show that he was, in fact, forced down that day—one of four times he survived the loss of his aircraft—thus confirming the claim.

Meanwhile, records in the TsAMO indicate that Lilya was injured in this aerial battle, and that she was attacked again on her way home, suffering injuries to both her leg and her shoulder. Nevertheless, she guided her "White 23" back to base, landed safely, and was patched up by regimental medics.

Grünberg also went on to fly and fight again, ending his career flying Me 262 jets in *Reichsluftverteidigung* (Defense of the Reich) missions against American 8th Air Force bombers over Germany itself.

He later was awarded the Knight's Cross of the Iron Cross, and he eventually scored eighty-two aerial victories—but he never got the White Lily of the Donbass.

*Chapter 19*

# TWILIGHT OF THE FALCONS

O n July 19, 1943, three days after Lilya Litvyak was wounded during her aerial duel with Oberfeldwebel Hans Grünberg, the 73rd GvIAP was tasked with the same type of mission that Jagdgeschwader 3 had been flying on July 16: bomber escort.

Golyshev was hesitant about letting his White Lily fly again so soon after the injuries she had suffered, but she told the regimental commander that she was fine, that her wounds were no hindrance. They were just a scratch, she said, though they were probably more serious than she let on. By all accounts, she was anxious not to be grounded for medical reasons. She feared that if she was sent away again to recuperate, as she had been in April, she might be declared physically unfit for flight duty, and that she would never return to her unit.

Since the death of Alexei Solomatin, flying and fighting had become everything for Lilya. They were her life. Without them, she had no reason for being. In a letter to her mother, written in late July and shared with Reina Pennington by Inna Pasportnikova, she wrote "I am completely absorbed with combat life. I can't seem to think about anything but the fighting."

Golyshev allowed her to fly. He may have had second thoughts, but he let her go anyway. Just as Lilya had come to wrap Nikolai Baranov around her finger, so too did the new regimental commander bend to the aspirations of the White Lily of the Donbass.

July 19 dawned hot and sultry. This was typical for eastern Ukraine or southern Russia during the dog days of summer, and the heat seemed to suck the life out of the aircrews of the regiment. Because of the mounting losses that were being suffered, a somber mood prevailed. There was no laughing that day, no joking. In the anthology *In the Sky Above the Front*, Inna Pasportnikova writes that Katya Budanova, who was usually in good spirits, appeared more solemn than usual.

The pilots boarded a bus that took them to their aircraft, rocking and jostling along the dusty road to the airfield near Krasny Luch. Someone suggested that Katya sing Nikolai Baranov's favorite song, the mournful one by Dolmatovsky about returning to the Dnieper River, which was still 200 miles away at its closest. They liked her voice, and they all were fond of the song.

She started to sing, but broke off after a few bars. It made her sad. It also had been one of Marina Raskova's favorite songs.

Inside the cockpits, it was scorching hot, so different from the icy chill of the Stalingrad winter. Even as they took off, and were escorting the Il-2 Sturmoviks on their low-level ground attack mission, it was hot. The humidity made the pilots uncomfortable. Sweat dripped from foreheads and pooled in goggles. The aircrew longed for a high-altitude mission, where things would be cooler. Some even thought nostalgically of the winter.

Today, the bombers managed to get through to their targets without being harassed by German fighters. There was plenty of antiaircraft fire, but the 73rd GvIAP keeping watch above detected no air activity from the "Fritzes." On the return flight, the bombers spread out into a looser formation, and Katya took up a position at the rear of the flight.

Suddenly, the Yak-1Bs came under attack by three Bf 109G-6s of JG 3. Reacting instinctively, Katya pulled up to screen the bombers, trying to draw the Messerschmitts away from the Sturmoviks. As she succeeded, they turned to attack her aircraft instead. She urged her nimble steed into a turn, using its maneuverability and tight turning radius against the enemy's superior speed and power, and found a Messerschmitt in her sights.

She gave the Luftwaffe fighter a 20-mm burst from her ShVAK cannon, and as Pasportnikova recalls from what she heard from pilots who were there, "It dropped its nose, lost control, and went down."

Meanwhile, Katya's Yak-1B had taken some serious hits itself.

Below, though not far below, because the aircraft were operating at fairly low altitudes, people in the villages of Kal'chynivka, Ksenivka, Novoyanysol, and Novokrasnovka were watching the aerial battle with great interest.

They heard the snarl of the Daimler-Benzes and of the Klimovs and watched the fast airplanes streaking through the sky.

As recalled by Inna Pasportnikova in *In the Sky Above the Front*, Katya "rolled over one wing, and rushed at another enemy plane. She let out a long burst, and the second Messerschmitt began to fly away in a westerly direction, leaving a black trail of smoke behind it."

Though other sources are vague on the topic, Inna Pasportnikova relates the notion that Katya scored two victories during this engagement. Katya Budanova would never have the opportunity to make the claim herself.

The people in Novokrasnovka saw "the red-starred fighter turned upside down," Pasportnikova writes. "Out of control, it began to fall. Then it sideslipped and leveled off. Tongues of fire licked its wings. The plane began to glide onto a field adjacent to the village, all churned up with foxholes, trenches, and craters. After it had touched down, one of its wheels fell into a crater and the fighter nosed over."

Katya had written to her sister Olya from Stalingrad during the winter before, "though I don't want to die, I am not afraid of it. If and when I must die, my death will cost the enemy dearly. My dear winged 'Yak' is a good machine and our fates are indissolubly joined together; if we must perish, we are bound to die like heroes. Keep well ... and don't forget me."

Many years later, sometime in the 1950s or early 1960s, Inna Pasportnikova spoke with Tamara Pamyatnykh, a former comrade from the regiment who had traveled to Novokrasnovka after the war, looking for answers to what had happened to Katya Budanova. The people whom she met told her that some farm workers from a nearby kolkhoz had reached the aircraft shortly after it touched down. Before the flames spread, they managed to pull the pilot from the cockpit.

They discovered that she was a woman, and that she was still alive. As Pasportnikova writes, "an old woman wiped off the blood from Katya's face, loosened the collar of her flying suit, and took out her Party membership card which read: 'Yekaterina Vasil'yevna Budanova.'"

The people carried her to the nearest house, but Katya was dead by the time that they got her there. They buried her nearby. When Tamara Pamyatnykh visited Novokrasnovka, she was shown Katya's gravesite.

Katya Budanova died an ace and a heroine, though the often-proposed award of a posthumous Hero of the Soviet Union decoration would never come. She was beyond doubt an ace, but there is no definitive accounting of her exact score. Conservative estimates are usually in the range of six solo victories and five shared, although some authorities such as Allan Magnus give her eleven solo victories. Tomas Polak and Christopher Shores indicate that she had six through the end of June and had added five during the intense air combat of July, but some of the original six they cite might have been shared with other pilots.

Meanwhile, Lilya Litvyak was also in action on July 19, possibly on the same escort mission during which Katya Budanova was killed. By this time, each pilot was flying multiple missions every day. Tomas Polak and Christopher Shores credit Lilya with a Messerschmitt that day, while other sources suggest that the Bf 109 she had attacked was merely damaged. They do not associate this victory with the same aerial battle in which Katya Budanova fell.

The legendary White Rose of Stalingrad had taken off on that hot and sticky morning, just as she had three days before when she took off to cancel two Fritzes. Then as on this day, she was completely absorbed with combat life. When Lilya had told her mother that she couldn't "seem to think about anything but the fighting," had it been because she became single-minded in order to force the emotion of lost friends out of her mind?

Lilya may have been in the same patch of sky over Novokrasnovka as Katya on July 19. She may have seen her friend die, or she may have cursed herself for being so involved in her own dogfight that she did not see Katya's stricken Yak-1B beset by angry Messerschmitts.

One by one, Lilya had been losing the people who mattered in her life. First, there had been her father, and then Marina Raskova. In the past two months, Nikolai Baranov, whom everyone called "Daddy," and then her beloved Lyosha. Today, Katya fell.

The mature severity that Anna Vasil'yevna had seen in Lilya's face in April hardened even more. As she had begun doing with her vigorous denial of her love for Alexei Solomatin, Lilya exiled all sensitivity and compassion to a Gulag deep inside her being, sentencing it to an internal exile that would last until no more German airplanes prowled the skies above her beloved Rodina.

It is something warriors do to preserve their sanity.

Though Lilya probably didn't learn about it for a day or two, July 19 was also darkened by the death of Raisa Beliaeva. She was the prewar aerobat who was one the group of four women, including Lilya, Katya, and Mariya Kuznetsova, who had served with the 437th IAP back in fall 1942.

Raisa had returned to the 586th IAP late in 1942, around the time that Lilya and Katya transferred to the 296th IAP, which became the 73rd GvIAP. By July 1943, the 586th IAP was based at an airfield on the Voronezh River, about 200 miles east of Kursk and about 400 miles north of where Lilya and Katya were based.

Olga Yamshchikova, who had known Raisa since they were twelve-year-olds at the Krasnin School in Kirov, had been reunited with her in the 586th. Olga writes in *In the Sky Above the Front* that she had followed her friend's aerobatic career, and when the war started, Raisa pulled stings to get Olga transferred to the all-women regiment from an engineering position in an aircraft factory in Siberia. She goes on to write that Raisa, like Lilya, loved performing low-level aerobatics, upon which their commanders officially frowned but unofficially chuckled.

"She performed aerobatics just above the ground," Olga recalled. "She rolled, looped, and flew upside-down … [She] was scolded and punished, and finally her superior categorically forbade her to practice aerobatics over the airfield. Raisa gave in, but all along she had the urge to fool around in the sky … In addition to flying upside down, at altitudes of 300–500 meters, Raisa 'twirled' a variety of her favorite aerobatics; now a delayed triple roll, now a loop with a 'bow,' a roll in the upper part of the loop, and now a double half-roll."

Just like Lilya Litvyak.

In comments made to Reina Pennington in interviews half a century later, Aleksandr Gridnev, who had become commander of the 586th IAP in October, acknowledged a great admiration for Raisa Beliaeva's skills as a pilot. He added that he had never met anyone—male or female—who could withstand a greater G-force in the tight turns required for aerial combat.

On the morning of July 19, four of the 586th IAP fighter planes were scrambled for action over Kursk.

"I glanced at the sky, which was completely overcast," Olga Yamshchikova recalls of the long time she spent waiting for the aircraft to return that day. "It was quiet; there was not the slightest wind. Suddenly, a swelling engine roar was heard, and an aircraft fell out of the clouds at a high speed. Apparently, the pilot tried to effect a recovery by handling both throttle and controls, but the dive kept getting steeper and steeper. The fighter fell down between two barracks housing a field hospital and caught fire. We ran to the site of the crash. There was a hole in front of me, in which the remains of the fighter were burning. Those who stood around it kept throwing earth on the flames."

"Who is this?" Olga asked.

"Beliaeva!"

"Everything swam before my eyes," she recalled. "A wave of anger and indignation engulfed me. I couldn't imagine Raisa dead."

"What are you doing?" Olga demanded. "Dig her out, quickly! Dig her out!"

Olga had to be dragged away as others fought to control the fire.

The news of Raisa Beliaeva's death, occurring on the same day as Katya's, devastated Lilya. The long list of personal losses that included Vladimir Litvyak, Marina Raskova, Nikolai Baranov, Alexei, and Katya, now included Raisa.

One day, some day, Lilya thought, all the dying would be over. The skies would be quiet. The red sun would shine down upon the land. In Moscow, the banners would echo the promises of the Man of Steel, the Father of fathers, proclaiming that "Life has become better, comrades; life has become more cheerful," and it would be true.

But that day would not come in July 1943.

More than a year before, back in June 1942, Lilya had written to her mother about a dream. "We were walking together, rushing to visit someone or to see a play, so dressed up, so gay, and you are so young and merry," she wrote. "At such times I feel so joyful, for some reason. May God make this come true. In the past, my dreams have always come to pass."

One day, she hoped, this dream would come to pass.

But that day would not come in July 1943.

At Kursk, the biggest battle of the year between the Soviets and the Germans had seen nearly 3 million men—and no small number of Soviet women—clash mightily since July 5.

This great campaign had reached its crescendo on July 12 in an enormous clash of armor at Prokhorovka, a town southeast of the city of Kursk, where the German II SS Panzer Korps faced off with a large Soviet armored force that included the 1st Tank Army and the 5th Guards Tank Army. Though the Red Army suffered tremendous casualties, they succeeded in blunting the German advance, effectively turning the tide and stopping the German pincer from surrounding and capturing Kursk.

By the time Soviet armies finally blunted the German advance and Hitler called an end to Operation Zitadelle on July 16—the same day that Lilya had been wounded—a quarter of a million casualties had spilled their blood. However, this massive series of battles would not finally be over until the end of August, by which time the casualties had reached a million.

As Zitadelle sputtered to its ignominious finale, the Red Army prepared for their long-awaited counterstrike on the Southwest Front. The objectives for this offensive was retaking the Donbass and Kharkov, and finally pushing the Germans back to the Dnieper River, the subject of everyone's favorite bittersweet, tear-jerking song.

Scheduled for August 3, the operation would be code-named *Polkovodets Rumyantsev*, meaning "Rumyantsev's Regiment," named for the eighteenth-century Russian Field Marshal Pyotr Rumyantsev, a favorite of Catherine the Great, governor of Ukraine, and a hero of the Russo-Turkish Wars. In a sense, he was to the lore of Russian military memory what Frederick "Barbarossa" was to the Germans.

The intense air activity that had consumed the 73rd GvIAP throughout July was part of the preparation by the respective sides for the Donbass-Kharkov campaign that everyone could see coming.

It was an intense time for the pilots, not only because of the growing aggressiveness of their enemy, but also for the necessity of flying multiple missions every day. For the 73rd GvIAP, "multiple" did not always mean merely "two or three." It was an exhausting schedule of take off, fight, land, refuel, then take off, kill, land, refuel, and take off, survive, and hope to land to do it again tomorrow.

As part of the Luftwaffe's realignment in the wake of the failure of Operation Zitadelle, Jagdgeschwader 52, against whom Lilya Litvyak had fought in 1942 during the Stalingrad offensive, was brought back to replace JG 3, who were being rotated to Germany to defend against the Anglo-American bomber offensive. Having been operational in the Crimea during the intervening months, JG 52 came north as part of the Luftwaffe's air cover for Zitadelle, but was then reassigned to Ukraine.

An exhausted and hollow-eyed Lilya Litvyak was back on the bus heading to the airfield as the hot, red sun came up on July 21. Two days had passed since Katya Budanova had been asked for the last time, on this same bus, to sing "Father" Baranov's favorite song, "O Dnipro, Dnipro."

Of course, neither Baranov nor Katya lived to see the Dnieper again.

As Lilya crawled into her Yakovlev's cockpit, the metal of the canopy frame was already warm to the touch. Beads of sweat ran where tears had run two days before, stinging her eyes. It was, in the American vernacular, going to be a scorcher. The wildflowers she had gathered to adorn the cockpit would wilt quickly.

She kicked the Klimov into life and watched as Ivan Golyshev's aircraft began to roll. As usual since June 13, when she had saved his life, the regimental commander wanted Lilya as his "wingwoman."

This morning's mission, as was frequently the case these days, involved escorting Il-2 Sturmovik ground attack aircraft as they hammered German defenses in anticipation of Operation Polkovodets Rumyantsev. At their level in the chain of command, a major and a lieutenant were in no position to know that the operation would begin in exactly two weeks, but everyone on the Southwest Front knew that it was coming, and coming soon.

Across that entire front, especially after the enormous air battles around Kursk, both sides had come to fully appreciate the effectiveness of the Sturmoviks, as well as their vulnerability to air attack. Just as the Red Army had come to love them, the Luftwaffe had been directed to kill them. Of course, exploiting their vulnerability in order to make the kills meant having to break through the screen of fighters, such as the one with the white lily, which flew on this day in protection of the Sturmoviks.

In July, during the transition from JG 3 and JG 52, Lilya and the pilots of the 73rd GvIAP noticed that the Germans were employing the tactic of sending large concentrations of their fighters to overwhelm the Soviet fighters defending the Sturmoviks. It was a matter of bringing dogpile tactics to the dogfight.

Such would be the nature of the action the 73rd GvIAP pilots would face on July 21. Lilya and Ivan Golyshev suddenly found themselves more engulfed than merely attacked as they were jumped by as many as ten Messerschmitts.

As usual, the Germans focused the bulk of their attention on the lead plane, which was Golyshev's. As was her role, Lilya intervened in support of him, but this swarm of Bf 109s swept over her as well.

Both of the Soviet pilots were in a life-and-death struggle, and one lost. A plume of black smoke rising from the earth below marked the site of Ivan Golyshev's demise.

Lilya was lucky—or at least luckier—that day.

Some sources say that she bailed out of her stricken aircraft, but others, including Inna Pasportnikova, in her conversation with Anne Noggle, say that she was able to make a crash landing.

Lilya scrambled out of her plane, crumpled and useless in a Ukrainian farm field, scraps of metal and plywood scattered in a deep furrow cut through black earth. Just moments before, her ears were overpowered by the cacophonous clamor of howling aircraft engines and the hammer of cannon shells tearing at the Yakovlev. Now, Lilya found herself suddenly in a silent world. She stood in the quiet of a pastoral landscape, shimmering in the sweltering heat.

Off in the distance, framed against the billowing thunderheads, a tall column of smoke, as black as the dirt beneath her boots, marked the smoldering pyre of Golyshev's wreck.

From somewhere across the rolling hills, she heard them before she saw them. They were coming. There was the murmur of a vehicle engine and the sound of shouts in the German language. The men in black, who had ridden into and across her Motherland, and who had ravished it for the past twenty-five months, were coming—for her. She had escorted the Pe-2s behind enemy lines. She had battled Messerschmitts behind enemy lines. Now she was standing behind enemy lines.

The young aviator knew that she was in a precariously difficult position. She was between the rock of capture by the black riders of the Wehrmacht and the hard place of men in red who were tasked with enforcement of Order 270. As she knew, anyone who surrendered would be considered a malicious deserter. They would be subject to being shot on the spot, but so, too, would anyone whom the political officers perceived as being a malicious deserter.

The Soviet pilots had a way of taking care of their own. Generations before the air forces of the world started prepositioning rescue helicopters to retrieve pilots downed behind enemy lines, they themselves landed to rescue their own.

At some point before the Germans arrived, help came. It may have been moments before the Germans closed in or the better part of an hour.

Lilya heard the sound of a low-flying aircraft and saw the welcome sign of red stars, not black crosses, on its wings. Those wings waggled on the first pass and brought the friendly pilot in for a landing on the second.

The small woman with the long blonde hair ran toward the opened cockpit as fast as her limp could carry her.

"It happened that if you were shot down and landed, one of your aircraft would land next to you if they saw it," Inna Pasportnikova explained. "At that time another Soviet fighter pilot [some sources say that it was a Sturmovik] landed and picked up Lilya [as German troops were running toward her], and she escaped. There were two different airdromes in our area, and when the pilot flew back with Lilya, he landed on the other airfield so nobody knew who he was; she never found out."

In a letter to her mother, Lilya mentioned being shot down and wondered aloud whether it would have happened if she had still been flying on Alexei Solomatin's wing.

She still missed him—a lot.

She was still missing a lot of people.

The list of the lost was growing. The 73rd GvIAP had lost two commanders in less than three months. Somewhere, analysts were saying that the tide of the Great Patriotic War had turned in the favor of the Rodina after Kursk. Out here on the edge of the Donbass, though, it sure didn't look that way to a young woman standing in a dusty field with triumphant Messerschmitts swarming above her.

Within a few days, Lilya was back on the flightline at the airfield near Krasny Luch, back with the falcons whom she knew, back with the new faces of the rising number of replacements who had come to fill the slots of friends who could never be replaced.

Heroes faded away, and so too the heroines with whom they flew. Nikolai. Alexei. Katya. Raisa. Now, Ivan, whom she had barely gotten to know.

On July 28, while she was sitting in her cockpit on alert for takeoff, Lilya dictated a letter to a regimental adjutant, which was to be sent to her mother. It rang with the same homesickness as her letters from monotonous Anisovka when she was yearning for the combat action which she now had in abundance.

"It has been a long time since I heard the noises of Moscow streets with their rumble of streetcars, and saw cars moving in all directions," she said wistfully. "I am completely absorbed in my army life. It is difficult for me to find a moment to write you a letter and tell you about myself, that I am safe and sound."

For the moment, she was, but moments are fleeting.

*Chapter 20*

# LOST LILY

The first day of August, like most of the latter days of July, dawned hot and muggy over the Donbass front. The hot, red sun began its slow, burning rise into a mainly clear sky. As was the typical weather pattern, clouds would gather by afternoon, sparking thunderstorms in the area.

At the airfield near Krasny Luch, the pilots of the 73rd GvIAP—nearly two dozen men and one woman—had awakened for another long and dangerous day in their cockpits.

According to Tomas Polak and Christopher Shores, the 73rd GvIAP was now making the transition from the Yak-1B to the Yak-1M. Lilya Litvyak may have been flying one when she was shot down on July 21, or she may have begun flying the new aircraft after she lost her previous aircraft that day. If she was flying the Yak-1M on July 21, her unfamiliarity with the new aircraft may well have played a role in her getting shot down. For a fighter pilot used to flying by feel or instinct, even the most subtle variations in performance characteristics in a new aircraft could result in over- or underhandling that aircraft.

The Yak-1M, in which the "M" stands for "*Moskit*," or "Mosquito," was the most advanced of the early generation of Yakovlev fighters. As such, it was the transition aircraft to the Yak-3, which is seen by many as having been the "ultimate" development of the Yak family during the Great Patriotic War. The Yak-3 would not reach squadron service until 1944, but the Yak-1M arrived in 1943 as an interim aircraft, incorporating various new features that were planned.

The objective of the Yak-1M program was to increase maneuverability and performance over those of the earlier Yak-1 family by reducing size and weight, and through an improved Klimov M-105PF engine with increased power. Indeed, the Moskit was one of the first Soviet fighters to be able to outperform a Bf 109 in a vertical climb, and it could hold its own with either a Bf 109 or an Fw 190 at lower altitudes.

Compared to the Yak-1 or Yak-1B, the wingspan of the Yak-1M was reduced by about 3 feet, wing area by about 14 percent, and weight by around 10 percent. The weight reduction was accomplished in part by substituting wooden wing spars for aluminum. Like the previous Yaks, the Moskit was skinned in plywood rather than aluminum. As with the Yak-1B, the Yak-1M had a cut-down rear fuselage and a canopy that afforded good rearward visibility, which fighter pilots greatly desired.

As the men and woman of the 73rd GvIAP climbed into the Yakovlevs that sticky morning, there was a mirror image of that scene only 45 miles due west at the big Luftwaffe fighter base near Kuteinikovo (Kuteinykove), about 20 miles southeast of Stalino, the major city of the Donbass.

Among the German pilots who prepared for battle was Feldwebel Hans-Jörg Merkle. He was a rising star in Jagdstaffel 1, the first squadron in Jagdgeschwader 52, which had recently returned from the Crimea to fight the Reds who would be trying to recapture the Ukraine. He was an aggressive pilot with twenty-nine victories, half of them scored since the first of July. Of these, fifteen were kills, eleven of which had been of fighters, mainly various Yakovlev variants.

At the nearby field that was home to JG 3, Lieutenant Hans Schleef pulled on his summer weight flight suit and walked toward his Messerschmitt. A young man from Gross-Börnecke, near Magdeburg in Saxony, Schleef had only just turned twenty-three on July 19, yet he was a highly experienced hunter. He had scored his first aerial victory against a Royal Air Force Hurricane fighter in February 1941 while flying with JG 3 in France, and had been awarded the Knight's Cross of the Iron Cross in May 1942.

Like Feldwebel Merkle, Schleef had been heavily involved in aerial combat during July. On the first day of Operation Zitadelle, June 5, he had shot down one Soviet fighter at 0630 hours, but was forced down himself. Undaunted, he returned to his base, borrowed another aircraft and shot down three more Soviet aircraft the same day. He scored his milestone eightieth victory the following day, and his score reached ninety by July 30. As he prepared for action with Jagdstaffel 8 of JG 3 on the hot and dusty morning of August 1, the tenacious Schleef had a record of ninety-two victories.

That same morning, the only woman ace across the thousands of square miles of battlefront that separated the Germans and the Soviets could claim around a dozen solo victories.

Lilya Litvyak took off early that morning on the first of her four sorties for the day. On one of the first missions, she and her fellow pilots escorted a group of Il-2 Sturmoviks against German positions. On her third, she engaged and destroyed a Messerschmitt Bf 109G and had a shared kill of a second one, according to Tomas Polak and Christopher Shores.

Around noon or shortly thereafter, Lilya and her Yak-1M touched down at their base to be refueled. There was probably a lunch break, either in the cockpit or nearby, before she took off again with fellow pilot Ivan Borisenko and four others. On this, her fourth sortie, they flew out to hunt German bombers coming eastward to do to Soviet positions what the Sturmoviks had done to the Germans on the ground that morning.

By now, the Yak-1Ms were flying through and around the cumulus that builds up in the summer afternoons across the steppes, just as it does on hot summer afternoons across the American Great Plains.

Hans Seidl writes that on this mission the six Yak-1Ms spotted thirty Ju 88s in the vicinity of Marynivka (also called Marinovka), which is about 25 miles southwest of Krasny Luch and 50 miles south by southeast from Stalino.

As the 73rd GvIAP pilots were sizing up the bomber formation, as many as a dozen Messerschmitts fell upon them from out of the clouds. It was the familiar vertical, layered aerial battlefield—a layer of bombers beset by a layer of fighters, who were in turn attacked by a layer of fighters protecting the bombers. The top layer melded into the middle layer, a superior number piling onto a smaller number. It was a ratio of air superiority that was designed to be overwhelming. The Luftwaffe tactic of ganging up on the red aviators was in play.

As the layers converged into one another, the dogpile of Messerschmitts became a dogfight of Messerschmitts and Yaks, a swirling, swarming mass of aerial machinery laced together by red-hot tracers.

Counting the bombers, four dozen airplanes littered this patch of sky, moving in and out and among the clouds at ferocious speed. The layer of German bombers was the first to escape, slipping out of the noose as the Soviet fighters, outnumbered two to one, now battled for their lives.

Operating with practiced precision, six Messerschmitt hunters each sought out and struck toward a red-starred target, while six Messerschmitt wingmen held back to cover their attacking leaders.

Outnumbered but not outmaneuvered, the Yakovlev fighters sideslipped and rolled, climbed and dove, turning the tables whenever and wherever they could.

As the swirling dogpile-turned-dogfight tumbled into the darkening clouds, it was hard to keep track of all the other aircraft. You just kept an eye toward your six-o'clock position—straight back—and hoped it stayed clear as you sought out the six o'clock of an enemy.

There were target-rich environments—and then there was this.

Battling to outmaneuver a Messerschmitt himself, Borisenko tried to keep an eye on Lilya, but it was nearly impossible as everyone was tumbling through the clouds at 200 mph.

He saw her through an opening in the clouds, and then he did not.

Lilya looked up. One moment, she was surrounded by a great dome of blue. The next moment, she plunged into darkness. A shimmering bolt of lightning, the color of her peroxide-bleached hair turned everything a pale, white hot.

Then there was darkness.

Then there was light.

Little Vasilisa of the old story represented the brightness of sunlight while her wicked stepsisters represented darkness. Lilya, a heroine of the new order, now slipped between these two worlds with blinding speed, slipping into light only to be pursued by the Messerschmitts of darkness.

There again was the dome above, the color of a robin's egg.

There was the dome below, the color of straw, splattered with the black of forest patches.

The below became the above, and above below. Dirty orange tracers ripped past the canopy of the Yak like the lightning bolt.

A 30-mm cannon shell hit the Yak. Lilya's aircraft shuddered a moment, then flew straight, and the line of hot, dirty orange tracers fell away.

For a split second, she saw Borisenko through an opening in the clouds. Then she did not.

"Lily just didn't see the Messerschmitt 109s flying cover for the German bombers," Ivan Borisenko told Bruce Myles many years later. "A pair of them dived on her and when she did see them she turned to meet them. Then they all disappeared behind a cloud."

He caught another brief glimpse of her. Then she was gone.

She saw one of the Messerschmitts, reaching and clawing to outmaneuver her aircraft, and she maneuvered to get away.

It was crunch time, and she did what she did instinctively. She was skilled enough after hundreds of missions to know exactly which snap of the wrist demanded this result or that from her aircraft. Like a musician who deftly fingers a note on her cello or a jockey nudging a thoroughbred, she had become one with her machine in the complex cause and effect of split-second demands made and split-second demands obeyed.

However, a Yak-1M was not a Yak-1B.

Just as a musician playing an instrument that is not her own discovers notes that are subtly too sharp or minutely too flat, so too did the warrior with the white lily on the side of her warplane find herself plunged into a cold bath of complex cause and effect in which split-second demands made were met with imprecision.

A Messerschmitt moved into alignment behind her. She deftly slipped to the right. With the excellent rear visibility afforded by the bubble canopy, she could see as he maneuvered to stay with her.

As she hit her left rudder pedal to dodge in the other direction, the pain from her left leg, injured in March and still troubling her, sent a lightning jolt through her body. Her leg faltered at the rudder pedal. Her body, crushed on March 22 and battered further on July 16, the day that Katya died, was slowly giving out.

She fought the pain. She fought her own body with the same tenacity that she battled the Messerschmitts. At least against the Messerschmitts, she still had some tricks left. She did as she so often she had done in times like these.

Lilya stood the Yak-1M on its tail, whipping and spurring the nearly 1,200 horses that lived inside this improved Klimov. If the touchy controls of this Moskit had not served her well on this day, at least she could use this much-touted rate of climb against the vile Fritzes who pursued her.

It will probably never be known who it was in that Messerschmitt which tried so hard to catch the legendary White Rose of Stalingrad that day. Based on Luftwaffe records, it seems to come down to either Hans-Jörg Merkle or Hans Schleef, both of whom were in that same time and place. Given that they were flying with separate Geschwaders, it is improbable that they both fought her that day.

Perhaps this pilot, whoever it was, knew that he was fighting the White Rose of Stalingrad—the only woman fighter pilot on the Southwest Front—or perhaps not. It is unknown whether Lilya, with everything else that had been vying for her attention over the past few weeks, had gotten around to painting her signature lily on the replacement aircraft she received after being forced down on July 21.

Having outclimbed her attacker, Lilya rolled out, probably to the right, favoring her injury, and dove. With gravity on her side, and with the improved Klimov at full throttle, she converted the altitude for which she had been clawing a moment ago into numbing acceleration.

In her sights, Hans-Jörg Merkle, or whoever it was, watched the Yakovlev hurtling toward him at a speed that he and his Daimler engine could not match.

In twenty-nine aerial battles, Merkle had fought the Reds and won. In all of what he had learned about the Reds and the way they fought, he knew that their falcon blow, their *sokoliny udar*, began the same way as their taran, their "ramming attack."

A split second before Lilya reached the Messerschmitt, Ivan Borisenko caught a fast glimpse of Lilya through a sliver of an opening in the clouds, but the sliver quickly closed.

Hans Schleef scored his ninety-third that day, but Luftwaffe records have it being in the early morning, not in the afternoon. It is listed as being a LaGG-3, not a Yakovlev fighter, although the two were occasionally confused for the other by observers during the heat of battle.

Meanwhile, Luftwaffe records indicate that Merkle engaged a Yak at an altitude of 3,500 meters and at 1435 hours, which would be consistent with the afternoon engagement reported by the Soviet pilots. He is credited with a kill, although he was reported to have been rammed by that same Soviet pilot, and he, too, was killed in action.

As Inna Pasportnikova, who was on the ground that day awaiting Lilya's return, told Anne Noggle, "She tried to escape by diving into the clouds, and at this point another Soviet pilot, Ivan Borisenko, saw this scene and tried to find her after she dove. He looked everywhere but couldn't find her. He never saw an aircraft explode or a pilot jump with a parachute. She never returned from that mission."

Lilya was gone.

The small woman with the long blonde hair and the airplane with the cockpit filled with wildflowers had vanished without a trace. Borisenko had seen her one minute, but she was gone the next, as though into a wrinkle in the fabric of space in time as narrow as a sliver of an opening in a cumulus cloud.

On the ground, her comrades waited until the red sun had set over the battlefield. They waited into the night for their Lilya to return from her 168th operational mission. She never did.

At that same moment, far, far away in the apartment house at 88 Novoslobodskaya Street, Anna Vasil'yevna Litvyak was opening a letter, the one her daughter had dictated from that same flower-bedecked cockpit four days earlier. The wistful words written in someone else's hand spoke of how, in the Ukraine, the "meadows and the rarely encountered forests remind me now of our dear environs of Moscow where I grew up, and where I spent many a happy day."

The letter closed with an expression of yearning for "a happy and peaceful life, after I've returned to you and told you about everything I have lived through and felt during the time when we were apart. Well, good-bye for now. Your Lily."

The young woman who had become a legend had disappeared into the ether like a legendary heroine in some ancient mythic epic.

Stalino and the surrounding area were finally recaptured during the first week of September, and a search was made for the missing Yakovlev and its young pilot. Hundreds of crashed aircraft were scattered across the length and breadth of the Donbass, and though there were many Yakovlev skeletons here, nothing matching the description of Lilya's aircraft was found.

Among the pilots in the 73rd GvIAP, there was a groundswell of support for recommending that Lilya Litvyak be awarded a posthumous Hero of the Soviet Union, and the paperwork was prepared. Eventually, thirty-one woman aviators would be awarded the medal for actions during the Great Patriotic War, but the majority of these would be awarded in 1944–46. As of August 1943, the only woman pilot to have received the award was Yevdokiya Nosal of the 46th Guards Night Bomber Regiment.

In retrospect, one could say with no reasonable chance of contradiction that no woman aviator serving in the Great Patriotic War was more deserving of the HSU than Lilya Litvyak. Even by the strictest regulations, she deserved the highest award for valor. She had received her Order of the Patriotic War medal for three victories, and a second for three more. For ten victories, the HSU was authorized. Lilya had achieved ten, and more.

Most sources credit Lilya Litvyak with twelve solo victories, although there is some variation as to which of her specific victories are included. Some even include the observation balloon that she shot down in May as being among her victories. Official sources, such as the *Khronika Boevykh Pobed Gvardeiskii* (*Chronicle of Guards Combat Victories*), often cited among the sources for her number of victories, are probably accurate with respect to those she scored with the 73rd GvIAP, but not necessarily for earlier victories.

In going through the checklist of her probable victories, she had a total of ten solo victories by May 7. Working forward, she had added three soloes, plus one shared through the end of July, not including the balloon. If she had, as Tomas Polak and Christopher Shores write, gotten one solo and one shared during her early missions on August 1, this would bring her total to fourteen solo and six shared.

If it had been Lilya who rammed Merkle, and if she had remained in level flight longer than he, then he would have been her victory, not vice versa as claimed by the Luftwaffe. He would have been her fifteenth solo, and she would not have been his thirtieth. Early photographs of the monument erected to her memory in Krasny Luch many years later show it marked with twelve stars. Later photos show it with fifteen stars.

In Soviet practice, solo victories are listed separately from shared victories. In American practice, shared victories are added to the overall total as fractions. By this measure, which makes sense mathematically, Lilya Litvyak's shared victories would add three to fifteen, giving her a final maximum tally of eighteen plus the balloon, for nineteen total (see appendix).

The paperwork recommending Lilya Litvyak for the HSU was submitted through proper channels—but the request was denied. A posthumous award was certainly permissible. Indeed, that of Yevdokiya Nosal had been posthumous. With Lilya Litvyak, however, there was no proof that she had died.

The highest scoring woman ace of all time, certainly a heroine by any definition, had fallen in battle—but she also had fallen into oblivion.

The same paranoid dread which had driven Stalin and his henchmen to distrust and imprison Soviet soldiers who had been captured would not allow for the award of an HSU to someone who was neither alive nor dead, but missing in action.

In the weeks and months after Lilya's disappearance, there were rumors that she had been captured and that she was still alive. Over the years, a persistent report of a Soviet woman pilot being led away from a crash site by German troops was linked to Lilya. There was also a report that a Soviet woman whose voice sounded like Lilya's had been heard on German radio.

On one hand, Lilya's having survived would have been great news, but on the other, terrible news. Given the suspicious and accusatory tone of Stalin's insidious Order No. 270, it was counterintuitively possible that the state would have been more likely to arrest her upon her being repatriated than to proclaim the brave young woman as a Hero of the Soviet Union.

To paraphrase Aleksandr Solzhenitsyn's quoting Stalin, "the Motherland could not forgive Lilya for the shame she would have caused the Rodina."

Like Amelia Earhart, Lilya Litvyak disappeared without a trace. But Lilya disappeared into the cauldron of mankind's most terrible war, at a time when many, many young warriors were dying and disappearing every day.

The Amelia Earhart riddle remained iconic, while the mystery of the White Rose of Stalingrad gradually faded from institutional memory, submerged in the vast tide of events that surged across the land as part of the Great Patriotic War.

As part of this vast tide of events, the other women in the regiments that fulfilled Marina Raskova's vision would fight on.

The all-women 586th IAP, which was near Voronezh at the time of the Battle of Kursk in the summer of 1943, later flew top cover in the Red Army campaign to recapture the Ukrainian capital of Kiev in November 1943. The end of the war in May 1945 found them operating out of a base near Budapest in Hungary, supporting the drive by the 3rd Ukrainian Front—formed from the armies of the Southwest Front—against the southern part of Hitler's doomed Third Reich.

Official documents indicate that the pilots of the 586th IAP flew 4,419 combat missions and shot down thirty-eight enemy aircraft, including a dozen fighters. This victory count seems low, given the target-rich environment over the battlefront and the caliber of the women who flew with the regiment. The latter is certainly illustrated by the story of how Tamara Pamyatnykh and Raisa Surnachevskaya bravely engaged forty-two German bombers near Voronezh on March 19, 1943.

Nevertheless, no woman who spent her Great Patriotic War career with the 586th IAP is credited with having achieved "ace" status, which is surprising, given the intensity of the combat that was going on in the last two years of the war. Indeed, Ivan Kozhedub, the highest-scoring Soviet male ace of the war, scored all of his sixty-four victories—five more than Sasha Pokryshkin—after the beginning of the Battle of Kursk. Perhaps the lack of victories by the women can be explained by the 586th IAP having been kept in a defensive role some distance from the action.

Unlike the other two originally all-women regiments, a sizable number of male pilots were assigned to the 586th IAP, though the integration seems to have gone rather smoothly. Alone among the three regiments, the 586th IAP was never given a Guards designation, nor were any of the women ever awarded the Hero of the Soviet Union decoration.

It is hard to believe that the regiment's Tamara Pamyatnykh and Raisa Surnachevskaya did not deserve the decoration for heroically attacking a formation of forty-two German bombers one day during April 1943 and shooting down two each. Ironically, the incident was reported by a British observer, and the women did receive engraved gold watches from King George VI.

In a conversation with Reina Pennington in the 1990s, Aleksandr Gridnev, who commanded the 586th IAP after the departure of Tamara Kazarinova, suggested that the regiment was deliberately blacklisted by the PVO hierarchy. He specifically blamed Kazarinova, who was now at

PVO headquarters, and General Aleksandr Osipenko, whose late wife, Polina Osipenko, had flown with Marina Raskova in the flight of the *Rodina* in 1938.

According to Gridnev, Osipenko and Kazarinova also seemed to have a vendetta against Raisa Beliaeva, the prewar aerobat who was killed in a suspicious crash on July 19, 1943, the same day Katya Budanova died. Apparently, the general had seen Beliaeva doing some aerobatics over the airfield during an earlier inspection tour and ordered her arrested for insubordination.

Gridnev said that a Guards redesignation for the 586th IAP was all but official by autumn 1943 after the Battle of Voronezh. The necessary paperwork had been approved by field commanders and was submitted to PVO headquarters, where it was deliberately sidetracked by Kazarinova.

And then there were the women bomber pilots, who would also continue the fight against the "Fritzes" until they no longer darkened the door of the Rodina. The former 588th Night Bomber Regiment (NBAP), which had become the 46th Guards NBAP in February 1943 at Stalingrad, chased the retreating Germans all the way to Berlin. The regiment whom the Germans called "Night Witches" became honored with the term "Taman" for their heroism in defeating the Germans in the Taman Peninsula, part of the Crimea situated between the Sea of Azov and the Black Sea.

As Polina Gelman, a veteran of the regiment, underscored in a 1993 letter quoted by Reina Pennington, the 46th GvNBAP was the only one of the three original regiments that "remained purely female until the end of the war." Indeed, Yevdokya Bershanskaya remained as commander of the regiment from the time it first went into action until it was disbanded in October 1945.

These women also deserve immense credit for flying more than 20,000 missions at night, often alone over enemy territory and in open-cockpit biplanes. As often as not, the women flew multiple missions every night, and often there were heavy casualties inflicted against the slow, low-flying Polikarpov Po-2 bombers.

A significant number of women in the 46th GvNBAP were awarded the HSU. Reina Pennington writes that there were twenty-four; Henry Sakaida lists twenty-one. Among them was Nina Raspopova, the pilot who told Anne Noggle that she had "sang, cried, and sobbed with happiness" on her first solo fight, and who had briefly been swept up in the Great Purge of 1937.

Zheka Zhigulenko, who flew with the 46th GvNBAP and later made the 1981 documentary film *Night Witches in the Sky*, reflected many years later that "We were not crucial to winning the war. They could have gotten by without us. They couldn't have gotten by without the nurses and the switchboard operators. I only later understood why I joined the air force. I apparently thought then, I must get there quickly, quickly, in order to finish everything all the more quickly. And only several years later, when my son was born, did I understand certain things. You see, for a man the important things are courage, heroism, being tough. But a woman is motivated by the feeling of motherhood. I am sure of this. Nature made woman this way. The desire to save one's future children was what apparently moved me and all the women who left the universities to serve in aviation."

Meanwhile, the 587th Bomber Regiment (BAP), the regiment originally commanded by Marina Raskova herself, received its Guards designation in September 1943, becoming the 125th GvBAP. It was also later honored with the name "Marina Raskova."

Initially disgruntled by his assignment to the regiment, Marina's male replacement, Major Valentin Markov, gradually came to trust and respect the women he commanded, as they did him, and the unit performed well.

After participating in the Battle of Kursk and being honored as a Guards regiment, the regiment was assigned to the 1st Air Army of the VVS, and with it, supported the Soviet westward advance, ending the war at Königsberg in East Prussia (now Kaliningrad in Russia). They flew more than a thousand missions, far fewer than the 46th GvNBAP, but because of the longer range of their Petlyakov Pe-2s, the missions were longer, and therefore deeper inside enemy territory.

After participating in the victory flyby over Moscow on June 24, 1945, the 125th GvBAP remained active for a year and a half, and was not disbanded until February 1947. Both Pennington and Sakaida note that five women from the regiment, three pilots and a pair of navigators, were awarded the HSU, and that the medals were all officially bestowed on August 18, 1945. To indicate how important the women's regiments were to the VVS, this award was part of the official observance of the twelfth Soviet Air Fleet Day.

August 18, 1945, also would have been the twenty-fourth birthday of Lilya Vladimirovna Litvyak.

# Epilogue

I n the summer of 1979, as the white cumulus of the afternoon billowed against a deep blue sky over the slightly rolling hills ablaze with wild flowers, some people discovered human skeleton. It was buried in the rich black earth of eastern Ukraine, near the meandering streams flowing gently through the woods on the outskirts the village of Dmytrivka.

It was peaceful that day, as it had been for most days in the thirty-six years since the greatest war in human history swept through this land—as it had been for all those years since Lilya Litvyak vanished without a trace.

Things had been quiet here in all those years since the black riders and their black horses had trampled this land and since the red riders on their red horses had swept them from the Rodina.

The remains of the small woman with the gold filling in her teeth which were taken from the rich black earth that day were identified as Lilya's. They might have been hers, or perhaps they were those of another young woman who gave her life for her Rodina during the Great Patriotic War.

The rumors that Lilya had not died in that field near Dmytrivka continued even after she was declared to have been killed in action. As with Amelia Earhart, there have been various rumors and theories, as well as a great deal of wishful thinking, surrounding her final flight. As with so much about her life, the facts surrounding Lilya's demise are intertwined with the myths.

In 2004, Ekaterina Polunina, who had been a chief mechanic with the 586th IAP during the Great Patriotic War, published her memoirs. In them, she gave credence to the reports that Lilya had been captured by German troops.

Dr. Kazimiera Jean Cottam, a recognized academic authority on Soviet women in combat during the Great Patriotic War, spoke to Polunina in 2005 and was convinced that Lilya Litvyak had not died during the war. Cottam believes that, contrary to the Soviet Ministry of Defense announcement, a body matching Lilya's description was never actually recovered and identified.

In a piece she posted online in 2006, Cottam cites several pieces of evidence that contradict the official conclusion. She mentions the story of a person who sounded like Lilya speaking on German radio and references a report by fighter pilot Vladimir Lavrinenkov, who flew with her and believes that he later saw Lilya in a German prisoner of war camp.

Cottam also writes that in about 2000, "Russian television featured a broadcast from Switzerland, during which a correspondent introduced a former Soviet woman World War II pilot, a mother of three children who was twice wounded during the war and resided abroad since the war." Though the name of the woman was not given, Cottam reports that Nina Raspopova, a veteran of the 46th GvNBAP "assumed that this must be Lidiya Litvyak."

Had this been the case, it is deeply lamentable that Lilya felt that she could never return home after the war ended to visit her mother and brother. Even in its final days, the Soviet Union was harsh and uncompromising when it came to its perceived enemies and those who had the temerity to turn their backs on the regime.

As with the Amelia Earhart story, that of Lilya Litvyak has many layers of complexity. On August 1, 1943, Lilya Litvyak had fallen into oblivion, and that is where she would remain. As with Amelia Earhart, she slipped through a wrinkle in the fabric of time and space, and she never returned.

The important thing about the remains of the young woman found on that day in 1979 is not so much whose they were, although that would have been very meaningful, but what they meant.

In March 1986, the slow-moving bureaucracy of the Soviet Ministry of Defense officially removed Lilya Litvyak from the "missing" list, declaring her to have been "killed in action."

As the clouds of obscurity parted, they even erected the monument to her in Krasny Luch, near the airfield that was her last duty station, and topped it with a bust of Lilya, complete with her goggles pushed back over her flying helmet.

On May 5, 1990, four long years after the bureaucracy had spoken, Lilya's name was spoken in the Kremlin. It had been forty-seven long years since Lilya had limped the streets of Moscow on a leg injured in combat. She had stared up at the imposing walls of the Kremlin and breathed the air of a spring filled with bigger buds and an atmosphere of new strength and singing determination. She had seen the headlines that trumpeted the triumphs of Stalin's falcon of falcons, the Soviet Union's ace of aces. She had known that Sasha Pokryshkin was due to walk into the reception hall of the Council of People's Commissars to be awarded the red star of the Hero of the Soviet Union. Lilya had asked the rhetorical questions, "Why not a woman? Why not me?"

At last, it was to come to pass. Here in the Kremlin, in a hall not far from the hallway where Marina Raskova had argued personally with Josef Stalin about the creation of the all-women regiments, in the discussion which opened the door for Lilya Litvyak to achieve the ultimate in heroism, Lilya would at last be recognized for that ultimate in heroism.

On May 5, 1990, the Soviet Union was in its final days, but celebrating its finest moment. Mikhail Gorbachev, the last of Stalin's successors, was in the midst of a round of commemorations of the forty-fifth anniversary of the Soviet Union's victory in the Great Patriotic War, and medal ceremonies were part of the agenda. In same building where Pokryshkin had received his own award, Lilya Litvyak, now officially recognized as having been killed in action, was finally and posthumously awarded the decades-overdue red star of a Hero of the Soviet Union.

Her gold star was presented to her brother, Yuriy, who had long since changed his surname to Kunavin, their mother's maiden name, to get out from beneath the cloud of a purged father. Even though nearly four decades had passed since Josef Stalin had gone to his grave, the paranoid official stigma attached to the "missing" of the Great Patriotic War still prevailed, and the dark shadow of the Man of Steel was still felt in the land. Yuriy's sister had fought and died, in part, for the redemption of the family honor, and it had taken this long to secure that redemption.

Lilya's HSU was among the last to be issued before the Soviet Union ceased to exist in 1991. While a number of women who had earned the HSU during the Great Patriotic War received their medals after the war, only two women earned the decoration after the war. Both of them, Valentina Tereshkova and Svetlana Savitskaya, were Soviet cosmonauts. The first and second women ever to fly in space, they were the ultimate evolution of what began with Marina Raskova's young falcons and reached its wartime apogee with the likes of Lilya Litvyak and Katya Budanova.

Katya, like Lilya, had been proposed for the HSU, but like Lilya, she was written off as "missing," and so she never did receive one. However, in October 1993, Russian President Boris Yeltsin authorized her to be posthumously awarded the medal considered to be the successor decoration to the HSU, the Hero of the Russian Federation.

The two friends, the two woman aces of a long-ago Great Patriotic War, both now had the highest of decorations their Rodina could give them. Though small by comparison to the sacrifices that they had made, the medals were long deserved.

To paraphrase Leo Tolstoy, each of these women had gone cheerfully and proudly to meet her death, and both died with firmness and composure, and with the noble spark which made of her a hero; a spark which flashed into a flame and which illuminated great deeds.

Great literature is filled with the tragedy of great warriors who die young, yet in this they never age. They remain "forever young," always remembered as they were in their prime. Lilya Litvyak, the young woman who loved to fly and who learned to fight, is but one of those to remain forever young. She never lived to see her twenty-second birthday. We still remember her as a young woman, barely old enough to no longer be called a schoolgirl, who became the scourge of the Luftwaffe.

We still remember a life cut short and dreams never fulfilled. We remember the golden hair, the shy and occasionally sly smile, the white lily painted on a dark green cowling, and a cockpit overflowing with wildflowers.

*Appendix*

# AERIAL VICTORIES CREDITED TO LILYA LITVYAK

## SEPTEMBER 13, 1942–AUGUST 1, 1943

| | |
|---|---|
| September 13, 1942 | Junkers Ju 88 |
| September 13, 1942 | Messerschmitt Bf 109G |
| September 14, 1942 | Messerschmitt Bf 109G (shared) |
| September 27, 1942 | Junkers Ju 88 (shared?) |
| September 27, 1942 | Messerschmitt Bf 109 (shared) |
| February 11, 1943 | Junkers Ju 87 |
| February 11, 1943 | Focke-Wulf Fw 190 (shared) |
| March 1, 1943 | Focke-Wulf Fw 190 |
| March 22, 1943 | Messerschmitt Bf 109G |
| March 22, 1943 | Junkers Ju 88 |
| May 5, 1943 | Messerschmitt Bf 109 |
| May 7, 1943 | Messerschmitt Bf 109 |
| May 31, 1943 | Observation balloon |

| July 16, 1943 | Messerschmitt Bf 109G |
| July 16, 1943 | Messerschmitt Bf 109G (damaged) |
| July 16, 1943 | Junkers Ju 88 |
| July 19, 1943 | Messerschmitt Bf 109G |
| July 21, 1943 | Messerschmitt Bf 109 |
| August 1, 1943 | Messerschmitt Bf 109G |
| August 1, 1943 | Messerschmitt Bf 109G (shared) |
| August 1, 1943 | Messerschmitt Bf 109G (scored by ramming?) |

*Note:* This is a checklist of all the possible aerial victories which have been, in various sources, credited to Lilya Litvyak, all of which are described in this book. Most sources credit her with at least twelve solo victories, although the sources do not necessarily agree as to which twelve to include, and she may have had more than this number.

# About the Author

Bill Yenne's mother was a pilot during the 1940s, making her first solo flight at Helena, Montana on July 15, 1944.

Mr. Yenne is the author of more than three dozen nonfiction books, especially on aviation and military history. These have included histories of the Strategic Air Command, the U.S. Air Force, and histories of America's great aircraft manufacturers, including Boeing, Convair, Lockheed, and McDonnell Douglas. His recent dual biography of Dick Bong and Tommy McGuire, *Aces High: The Heroic Story of the Two Top-Scoring American Aces of World War II*, was described by pilot and best-selling author Dan Roam as "The greatest flying story of all time."

*The Wall Street Journal* calls Mr. Yenne's recent biography of Julius Caesar "excellent," while General (Ret.) Wesley Clark called his biography of Alexander the Great the "best yet." *The New Yorker* wrote of *Sitting Bull*, Mr. Yenne's biography of the great Lakota leader, that it "excels as a study in leadership."

A member of the American Aviation Historical Society, Mr. Yenne has contributed to encyclopedias of both world wars and has appeared in several History Channel programs. He lives in San Francisco, and on the web at www.BillYenne.com.

# Selected Recurring Acronyms

| | |
|---|---|
| ADD | Aviatsiya Dalnego Deystviya Polk (Long-Range Air Regiment) |
| ATS | Auxiliary Territorial Service |
| BAD | Bombardirovochnaia Aviatsionnaia Diviziia (Bomber Aviation Division) |
| BAP | Bombardirovochnyi Aviatsionnyi Polk (Bomber Aviation Regiment) |
| CCCP | Cyrillic alphabet acronym for SSSR, or Soyuz Sovetskikh Sotsialisticheskikh Respublik |
| Cheka Chrezvychaynaya Komissiya | (Extraordinary Commission for Combatting Counterrevolution and Sabotage) |
| GARF | Gosudarstvennyi Arkhiv Rossiiskoi Federatsii (Central State Archive of the Russian Republic, formerly the Central State Archive of the RSFSR). |
| GPU | Gosudarstvennoye Politicheskoye Upravlenie (State Political Directorate) |
| Gulag | Glavnoye Upravlyeniye Ispravityel'notrudovih Lagyeryey i Koloniy (Chief Administration of Corrective Labor Camps and Colonies) |

| | |
|---|---|
| Gv Gvardeiskii | meaning Guards, the prefix indicating that a specific unit had been honored with the redesignation as a "Guards" unit |
| HSU | Hero of the Soviet Union (Geroi Sovetskogo Soiuza) |
| IAD | Istrebitel'naia Aviatsionnaia Diviziia (Fighter Aviation Division) |
| IAP | Istrebitel'nyi Aviatsionnyi Polk (Fighter Aviation Regiment) |
| JG | Jagdgeschwader (Luftwaffe Fighter Group) |
| KG | Kampfgeschwader (Luftwaffe Bomber Group) |
| KGB | Komitet Gosudarstvennoy Bezopasnosti (Committee for State Security) |
| NBAD | Nochnoi Bombardirovochnaia Aviatsionnaia Diviziia (Night Bomber Aviation Division) |
| NBAP | Nochnoi Bombardirovochnyi Aviatsionnyi Polk (Night Bomber Aviation Regiment) |
| NEP | Novaya Ekonomicheskaya Politika (New Economic Policy) [1921] |
| NKO | Narodnyi Komissariat Oborony (People's Commissariat of Defense) |
| NKVD | Narodnyy Komissariat Vnutrennikh Del (People's Commissariat for Internal Affairs) |
| ODVF | Obshchestvo Druzei Vozdushnogo Flota (Society of Friends of the Air Fleet) |
| OGPU | Ob'edinennoe Gosudarstvennoe Politicheskoe Upravlenie (Joint State Political Directorate) |
| Osoaviakhim | (or OSoAviaKhim) Obschestvo Sodeistviya Aviatsii i Khimicheskomu Stroitel'stvu (The Society for Assistance to the Aviation and Chemical Industry) |
| PVO | Protivo Vozdushnoy Oborony (Air Defense Forces) |
| RKKF | Raboche-Krest'yansky Krasny Flot (Workers' and Peasants' Red Air Fleet) |

| | |
|---|---|
| RSFSR | Rossiiskoi Sovetskikh Sotsialisticheskikh Respublik (Russian Soviet Socialist Republic) |
| SchlG | Schlachtgeschwader (Luftwaffe Ground Attack Bomber Group) |
| ShVAK | Shpitalnyi-Vladimirov Aviatsionnyi Krupnokalibernyi (ShpitalnyVladimirov large-caliber aircraft cannon) |
| SSSR | Soyuz Sovetskikh Sotsialisticheskikh Respublik (Russian for Union of Soviet Socialist Republics, USSR) |
| StG | Sturzkampfgeschwader (Luftwaffe Dive Bomber Group) |
| TsAGI | Tsentralniy Aerogidrodinamicheskiy Institut (Central Aerohydrodynamic Institute) |
| TsAMO | Tsentral'nyi Arkhiv Ministerstva Oborony (Central Archive of the Ministry of Defence) |
| USAAF | US Army Air Forces |
| USMCWR | US Marine Corps Women's Reserve |
| USSR | Union of Soviet Socialist Republics (English for Soyuz Sovetskikh Sotsialisticheskikh Respublik, SSSR) |
| VA | Vozdushnaya Armiya (Air Army) |
| VVS | VoennoVozdushnye Sily (Military Air Force) |
| WAAC | Women's Army Auxiliary Corps |
| WAAF | Royal Air Force's Women's Auxiliary Air Force |
| WAC | Women's Army Corps |
| WASP | Women Airforce Service Pilots |
| WAVE | Women Accepted for Volunteer Emergency Service |
| WRNS | Women's Royal Naval Service (the "Wrens") |

# Bibliography

_____. "I Remember: Soviet WWII-veteran Memoirs." Retrieved March 26, 2012, from http://english.iremember.ru/home.html.

Aleksievich, Svetlana. *War's Unwomanly Face*. Moscow: Progress Publishers, 1988.

Anthony, David W. *The Horse, the Wheel, and Language: How Bronze-Age Riders from the Eurasian Steppes Shaped the Modern World*. Princeton, NJ: Princeton University Press, 2007.

Bailes, Kendall E. *Technology and Society Under Lenin and Stalin: Origins of the Soviet Technical Intelligentsia, 1917–1941*. Princeton, NJ: Princeton University Press, 1978.

Barber, John, and Mark Harrison. *The Soviet Home Front 1941–1945: A Social and Economic History of the USSR in World War II*. London: Longman, 1991.

Barber, John. "Popular Reactions in Moscow to the German Invasion of June 22, 1941," *Operation Barbarossa: The German Attack on the Soviet Union, June 22, 1941*, edited by Joseph L. Wieczynski. Salt Lake City, UT: Charles Schlacks, 1993.

Berg, Raissa L'vovna. *Acquired Traits: Memoirs of a Geneticist from the Soviet Union*. New York: Viking, 1988.

Bergström, Christer, Andrey Dikov, and Vlad Antipov. *Black Cross-Red Star. Air War over the Eastern Front. Volume 3. Everything for Stalingrad.* Hamilton, MT: Eagle Editions Ltd., 2006.

Bergström, Christer. Barbarossa: *The Air Battle: July–December 1941.* Kent Science Park, Sittingbourne, England: Ian Allan, Classic Publications, 2007.

Bergström, Christer. *Stalingrad: The Air Battle: 1942 Through January 1943.* Hinckley, England: Midland, 2007.

Bonner, Elena. *Mothers and Daughters.* New York: Random House Value Publishing, 1994.

Boym, Svetlana. *Common Places: Mythologies of Everyday Life in Russia.* Cambridge, MA: Harvard, 1994.

Brontman, Lazar and Khvat. *The Heroic Flight of the Rodina.* Moscow: Foreign Languages Press, 1938.

Brüggemann, Karsten. *Motive Does Sowjetischen Mythos im Massenlied der 1930er Jahre.* (*The Myth of the "Great Soviet Family" in the Mass Songs of the 1930s*). Hamburg, Germany: Kovac, 2002.

Campbell, D'Ann. "Women in Combat: The World War Two Experience in the United States, Great Britain, Germany, and the Soviet Union." *Journal of Military History*, 1993.

Carswell, J. P. *The Exile: A Memoir of Ivy Litvinov.* Manchester, NH: Olympic Marketing Corporation, 1983.

Casey, Heather Gollmar. *Babushka, Feministka or Housewife? Women in the Russian Transition.* (Ph.D. dissertation, HQ1665.15.C384 2000 Regenstein stacks). University Park, PA: Pennsylvania State University, 2000.

Chatterjee, Choi. *Celebrating Women: Gender, Festival Culture, and Bolshevik Ideology, 1910–1939.* Pittsburgh, PA: University of Pittsburgh Press, 2002.

Colton, Timothy. *Moscow: Governing the Socialist Metropolis* (Russian Research Center Studies). Cambridge, MA: Belknap Press of Harvard University Press, 1996.

Conquest, Robert. *The Great Terror: A Reassessment.* New York: Oxford University Press, 1990.

Conquest, Robert. *The Great Terror: Stalin's Purge of the Thirties.* New York: Macmillan, 1968.

Cottam, Kazimiera Janina (Jean), (Ed.). *The Golden-Tressed Soldier.* Manhattan, KS: Military Affairs/Aerospace Historian Publishing, 1983.

Cottam, Kazimiera Janina (Jean). *Soviet Airwomen in Combat in World War II.* Manhattan, KS: Military Affairs/Aerospace Historian Publishing, 1983.

Cottam, Kazimiera Janina (Jean). "Soviet Women in Combat in World War II: The Ground Forces and the Navy." *International Journal of Women's Studies,* 1980.

Cottam, Kazimiera Janina (Jean). *Women in Air War: The Eastern Front of World War II.* Newburyport, MA: Focus Publishing/R. Pullins Company, 2006.

Cottam, Kazimiera Janina (Jean). *Women in War and Resistance— Selected Biographies of Soviet Women Soldiers.* Newburyport, MA: Focus Publishing/R. Pullins Co., 1998.

Cottam, Kazimiera Jean. *Lidya (Lily) Vladimirovna Litvyak (b. 1921).* 2006. Retrieved March 26, 2012, from http://www.redarmyonline.org/FI_Article_by_KJ_Cottam.html

Davies, Sarah. *Popular Opinion in Stalin's Russia: Terror, Propaganda and Dissent 1934–1941.* Cambridge and New York: Cambridge University Press, 1997.

Davis-Kimball, Jeannine. *Warrior Women: An Archaeologist's Search for History's Hidden Heroines.* New York: Warner Books, 2001.

Dunham, Vera. *In Stalin's Time: Middleclass Values in Soviet Fiction* (Studies of the Harriman Institute). Durham, NC: Duke University Press Books, 1990.

Durova, Nadezhda (translated by Mary Fleming Zirin). *The Cavalry Maiden: Journals of a Russian Officer in the Napoleonic Wars.* Bloomington, IN: Indiana University Press, 1989.

Erickson, John. *The Soviet High Command: A Military Political History, 1918–1941.* New York: St. Martin's Press, 1962.

Feuchtwanger, Lion (translated by Irene Josephy). *Moscow 1937: My Visit Described for My Friends*. New York: The Viking Press, 1937.

Figes, Orlando. *The Whisperers: Private Life in Stalin's Russia*. New York: Picador, an imprint of Macmillan Publishing, 2008.

Fischer, Louis. *Russia's Road from Peace to War: Soviet Foreign Relations 1917–1941*. New York: Harper and Row, 1969.

Fischer, Louis. *The Soviets in World Affairs: A History of the Relations Between the Soviet Union and the Rest of the World 1917–1929* (two volumes). Princeton, NJ: Princeton University Press, 1951.

Fischer, Marjorie. *Palaces on Monday*. London: Penguin Books, 1944.

Fitzpatrick, Sheila and Yuri Slezkine (Eds.). *In the Shadow of the Revolution: Life Stories of Russian Women from 1917 to the Second World War*. Princeton, NJ: Princeton University Press, 2000.

Fitzpatrick, Sheila. *Everyday Stalinism: Ordinary Life in Extraordinary Times: Soviet Russia in the 1930s*. New York: Oxford University Press, 2000.

Fitzpatrick, Sheila. *Stalin's Peasants: Resistance and Survival in the Russian Village after Collectivization*. New York: Oxford University Press, 1994.

Fitzpatrick, Sheila. *The Commissariat of Enlightenment*. Cambridge, England: Cambridge University Press, 1970.

Gal, Susan and Gail Kligman. *The Politics of Gender After Socialism: A Comparative Historical Essay*. Princeton, NJ: Princeton University Press, 2000.

Garder, Michel. *A History of the Soviet Army*. New York: Praeger, 1966.

Garros, Veronique, Natalia Korenevskaya, Thomas Lahusen, and Carol A. Flath. *Intimacy and Terror: Soviet Diaries of the 1930s*. New York: New Press, 1997.

Goldman, Wendy Z. *Women at the Gates: Gender and Industry in Stalin's Russia*. Cambridge, MA; New York: Cambridge University Press, 2002.

Goodpaster-Strebe, Amy. *Flying for Her Country: The American and Soviet Women Military Pilots of World War II*. London: Greenwood Publishing Group, 2007.

Gorky, Maxim, Leopold Averbakh, and Semen Georgievich Firin (translated by Anabel Williams-Ellis). *The White Sea Canal: Being an Account of the Construction of the New Canal Between the White Sea and the Baltic Sea*. London: John Lane, 1935.

Gregory, Paul R., Valery Lazarev, and V. V. Lazarev. *Economics of Forced Labor: The Soviet Gulag*. Stanford, CA: Hoover Institute Press, 2003.

Griese, Ann Eliot, and Richard Stites. "Russia: Revolution and War," in *Female Soldiers: Combatants or Noncombatants? Historical and Contemporary Perspectives*, edited by Nancy Loring Goldman. Westport, CT: Greenwood Press, 1982.

Gunston, Bill. *Aircraft of the Soviet Union*. London: Osprey, 1983.

Hardesty, Von. *Red Phoenix: The Rise of Soviet Air Power, 1941–1945*. Washington, DC: Smithsonian Institution, 1982.

Hessler, Julie. *Culture of Shortages: A Social History of Soviet Trade, 1917–1953*. Chicago: University of Chicago, 1996.

Hillyar, Anna and Jane McDermid. *Revolutionary Women in Russia, 1870–1917: A Study in Collective Biography*. Manchester and New York: Manchester University Press, 2000.

Ilic, Melanie (Ed.). *Women in the Stalin Era* (Studies in Russian and East European History). New York: Palgrave Macmillan, 2002.

Inness, Sherrie A. (Ed.). *Action Chicks: New Images of Tough Women in Popular Culture*. New York: Palgrave Macmillan, 2004.

Inness, Sherrie A. *Tough Girls: Women Warriors and Wonder Women in Popular Culture*. Philadelphia: University of Pennsylvania Press, 1999.

Jackson, Robert. *Air Aces of World War II*. Ramsbury, Marlborough: Vital Guide, Airlife Crowood Press, 2003.

Kazarinova, Militsa Aleksandrovna with Natalya Meklin Kravtsova and A. A. Polyantseva. *V Nebe Frontovom: Sbornik Vospominanly Sovetskikh Letchits, Uchastnits Velikoy Otechestvennoy Voyny* (*In the Sky Above the Front: A Collection of Memoirs of Soviet Airwomen, Participants in the Great Patriotic War*). Moscow: Molodaya Gvardiya, 1962, 1971.

Kenez, Peter. *The Birth of the Propaganda State: Soviet Methods of Mass Mobilization, 1917–1929*. New York: Cambridge University Press, 1985.

Keyssar, Helene and Vladimir Pozner. *Remembering War: A U.S.-Soviet Dialogue*. New York: Oxford University Press, 1990.

Khrushchev, Sergei. *Nikita Khrushchev and the Creation of a Superpower*. University Park, PA: Pennsylvania State University Press, 2001.

Koenker, Diane P. and Library of Congress. *Revelations from the Russian Archives: Documents in English Translation*. New York: Madison Gallery, Library of Congress, 2011.

Kosterina, Nina (Mirra Ginsburg, translator). *The Diary of Nina Kosterina*. New York: Crown Publishers, 1969.

Kotkin, Stephen. *Magnetic Mountain: Stalinism As a Civilization*. Berkeley, CA: University of California Press, 1997.

Kovalevskaia, Sof'ia Vasil'evna (translated by Natasha Kolchevska with Mary Zirin; introduction by Natasha Kolchevska). *Nihilist Girl*. New York: MLA, 2001.

Krivosheyev, Grigoriy Fedotovich, Prof. John Erickson (Foreword). *Soviet Casualties and Combat Losses in the Twentieth Century*. London, Greenhill Books, 1997.

Krylova, Anna. *Soviet Women in Combat: A History of Violence on the Eastern Front*. Cambridge, MA: Cambridge University Press, 2010.

Lauterbach, Richard E. *These Are the Russians*. New York: G. Braziller, 1945.

Lenin, Vladimir. *Lenin's Collected Works*, Volume 28. Moscow: Progress Publishers, 1965.

Levin, I. S. *Groznye Gody* (*Terrible Years*). Saratov, Russia: Privolzhskoe, 1984.

Leyda, Jay. *Kino: History of the Russian and Soviet Film*. New York: Allen and Unwin, 1960.

Markova (Dzhunkovskaia), Galina. *Rasskazhi, Bereza*. (*Tell Us, Birch Tree*). Moscow: Voenizdat, 1983.

Markova (Dzhunkovskaia), Galina. *Vzlet: O Geroe Sovetskogo Soiuza M. M. Raskovoi* (*Takeoff: About Hero of the Soviet Union M. M. Raskova*). Moscow: Politizdat, 1986.

McCannon, John. *Red Arctic: Polar Exploration and the Myth of the North in the Soviet Union, 1932–1939*. New York: Oxford University Press, 1998.

Medvedev, Roy and George Shriver. *Let History Judge*. New York: Columbia University Press, 1989.

Mellinger, George and Jim Laurier. *Yakovlev Aces of World War 2* (Aircraft of the Aces). Botley, Oxford, England: Osprey Publishing, 2005.

Messana, Paola. *Soviet Communal Living: An Oral History of the Kommunalka*. New York: Palgrave Macmillan, 2011.

Milanetti, Gian Piero. *Le Streghe Della Notte: La Storia non Detta Delle Eroiche Ragazze-pilota dell'Unione Sovietica Nella Grande Guerra Patriottica*. Rome: Istituto Bibliografico Napoleone, 2011.

Miller, Frank J. *Folklore for Stalin: Russian Folklore and Pseudofolklore of the Stalin Era*. Armonk, NY: M. E. Sharpe, 1990.

Morgan, Hugh and John Weal. *Soviet Aces of World War 2* (Aircraft of the Aces). Botley, Oxford, England: Osprey Publishing, 1997.

Muggeridge, Malcolm. *Winter in Moscow*. Grand Rapids, MI: Eerdmans Publishing Company, 1987.

Myles, Bruce. *Night Witches: The Amazing Story of Russia's Women Pilots in World War II*. Novato, CA: Presidio, 1981.

National Archives and Records Administration. "Correspondence of the Military Intelligence Division Relating to General, Political, Economic, and Military Conditions in Russia and the Soviet Union, 1918–1941" (Microfilm Publication M 1443, MID 2090, roll 20, frame 188). Washington, DC: Author.

Neuberger, Joan. *Hooliganism: Crime, Culture, and Power in St. Petersburg, 1900–1914*. Berkeley, CA: University of California Press, 1993.

Noggle, Anne: *For God, Country; and the Thrill of It: Women Airforce Service Pilots in World War II*. College Station, TX: Texas A&M University Press, 1990.

Noggle, Anne, and Christine A. White. *A Dance With Death: Soviet Airwomen in World War II*. College Station, TX: Texas A&M University Press, 1994.

Orlava, Raisa (translated by Samuel Cioran). *Memoirs*. New York: Random House, 1983.

Osokina, Elena, Kate S. Transchel, and Greta Bucher. *Our Daily Bread: Socialist Distribution and the Art of Survival in Stalin's Russia, 1927–1941* (New Russian History). Armonk, NY: M. E. Sharpe, 2001.

Osokina, Elena. *Zoloto dlia Industrializatsii: "Torgsin" (Gold for Industrialization: "Torgsin")*. Moscow: Rosspen, 2009.

Parry, Albert. *Russian Cavalcade: A Military Record*. New York: Ives Washburn, Inc., 1944.

Payson, William Farquhar (Ed.). *Russia USSR: A Complete Handbook*. New York: William Farquhar Payson. 1933.

Pennington, Reina (Ed.). *Amazons to Fighter Pilots: A Biographical Dictionary of Military Women*. Westport, CT and London: Greenwood Press, 2003.

Pennington, Reina (Foreword by John Erickson). *Wings, Women, and War: Soviet Airwomen in World War II Combat*. Lawrence, KS: University Press of Kansas, 2001.

Pipes, Richard. *Communism: A History* (Modern Library Chronicles). New York: Modern Library, 2003.

Polak, Tomas with Christopher Shores. *Stalin's Falcons: The Aces of the Red Star*. London: Grub Street, 1999.

Polunina, Ekaterina K. *Devconki, Podruzki, Letcicy (Girls, Girlfriends, Serving Pilots)*. Moscow: The House Journal of the Air Fleet, 2005.

Prien, Jochen, Gerhard Stemmer, Peter Rodeike, and Winfried Bock. *Die Jagdfliegerverbände der Deutschen Luftwaffe 1934 bis 1945—Teil 9 Tielband II Wom Sommerfeldzug 1942 bis zur Niederlage von Stalingrad 1.5.1942 bis 3.2.1943*. Eutin, Germany: Struve Druck, 2006.

Prien, Jochen, Gerhard Stemmer, Peter Rodeike, and Winfried Bock. *Die Jagdfliegerverbände der Deutschen Luftwaffe 1934 bis 1945*. Eutin, Germany: Struve Druck, 2003.

Pyatnitskaya, Yulia (Iuliia Piatnitskaia). *Dnevnik Zheny Bofshevika*. Benson, VT: Chalidze Publications, 1987.

Raack, Richard C. *Stalin's Drive to the West, 1938–1945: The Origins of the Cold War*. Stanford, CA: Stanford University Press, 1995.

Raskova, Marina. *Zapiski Shturmana* (*Notes of a Navigator*). Moscow: Molodaia Gvardiia, 1939.

Reese, Roger R. *Stalin's Reluctant Soldiers: A Social History of the Red Army, 1925–1941* (Modern War Studies). Lawrence, KS: University Press of Kansas, 1996.

Reese, Roger R. *Why Stalin's Soldiers Fought: The Red Army's Military Effectiveness in World War II* (Modern War Studies). Lawrence, KS: University Press of Kansas, 2011.

Sakaida, Henry. *Heroines of the Soviet Union: 1941–45*. Botley, Oxford, England: Osprey Publishing, 2003.

Salmonson, Jessica Amanda. *The Encyclopedia of Amazons: Women Warriors from Antiquity to the Modern Era*. New York: Paragon House, 1991.

Saywell, Shelley. *Women in War*. New York: Viking, 1995.

Scheffer, Paul. *Seven Years in Soviet Russia: With a Retrospect*. New York: Macmillan, 1932.

Scott, John. *Behind the Urals: An American Worker in Russia's City of Steel*. Boston: Houghton Mifflin, 1941.

Seidl, Hans D. *Stalin's Eagles: An Illustrated Study of the Soviet Aces of World War II and Korea*. Atglen, PA: Schiffer Military History, 1998.

Smith, Gregory Malloy. *The Impact of World War II on Women, Family Life, and Mores in Moscow, 1941–1945*. Stanford, CA: Stanford University Press, 1989.

Solzhenitsyn, Aleksandr Isaevich (Thomas P. Whitney, translator). *The Gulag Archipelago, 1918–1956: An Experiment in Literary Investigation*. New York: Harper and Row, 1974.

Spearman, M. L. *Scientific and Technical Training in the Soviet Union*. Hampton, VA: NASA Langley Research Center, 1983.

Spick, Mike. *The Complete Fighter Ace: All the World's Fighter Aces, 1914–2000*. London, Greenhill Books, 1999.

Stalin, Joseph Vissarionovich. *Sochineniya (Works)*. Moscow: Gosizdat, 1951.

Stalin. Joseph Vissarionovich. *O Velikoy Otechestvennoy voine Sovetskogo Soyuza. Istoriya Velikoy Otechestvennoy Voyny Sovetskogo Soyuza, 1941–1945 (The History of the Great Fatherland War of the Soviet Union, 1941–1945)*. Moscow: Gosizdat, 1951.

Stites, Richard. *Russian Popular Culture. Entertainment and Society Since 1900*. Cambridge, England: Cambridge, 1992.

Suchenwirth, Richard. *Historical Turning Points in the German Air Force War Effort* (USAF Historical Study Number 189). Maxwell AFB: Air University, 1959.

Thurston, Professor Robert W. *Life and Terror in Stalin's Russia, 1934–1941*. New Haven, CT: Yale University Press, 1998.

Thurston, Robert W., and Bernd Bonwetsch (Eds.). *The People's War: Responses to World War II in the Soviet Union*. Urbana, IL: University of Illinois Press, 2000.

Timasheff, Nicholas Sergeyevitch. *The Great Retreat: The Growth and Decline of Communism in Russia*. New York: E. P. Dutton, 1946.

Timofeyeva-Yegorova, Anna. *Red Sky, Black Death: A Soviet Woman Pilot's Memoir of the Eastern Front*. Bloomington, IN: Slavica Publishers, 2009.

Tolstoy, Count Leo Nikolayevich. *The Cossacks, Sevastopol, the Invaders and Other Stories*. New York: Scribner's, 1878.

Tolstoy, Count Leo Nikolayevich. *War and Peace*. New York: Knopf, 2001.

Vasilevsky, Aleksandr Mikhaylovich. *Delo Vsei Zhizni (A Lifelong Cause)*. Moscow: Politizdat, 1983.

Vodolagin, M. A. *Ocherki Istorii Volgograda 1589–1967 (History of Volgograd [formerly Stalingrad])*. Moscow: Soviet State Publishing, 1968.

Volkogonov, Dmitri (Harold Shukman, translator). *Stalin: Triumph and Tragedy*. New York: Grove Weidenfeld, 1991.

Von Geldern, James. *Mass Culture in Soviet Russia: Tales, Poems, Songs, Movies, Plays, and Folklore, 1917–1953*. Bloomington, IN: Indiana University Press, 1995.

Voznesensky, Nikolai Alekseevich. *Voennaya Ekonomika SSSR v Period Otechestvennoi Voiny'* (*The Economy of the USSR during World War II*). Washington, DC: Public Affairs Press, 1948.

Werth, Alexander. *The Year of Stalingrad*. New York: Alfred A. Knopf, Inc., 1947.

Werth, Nicolas, Karel BartoÜek, Jean-Louis Panné, Jean-Louis Margolin, Andrzej Paczkowski, and Stéphane Courtois. *The Black Book of Communism: Crimes, Terror, Repression*. Cambridge, MA: Harvard University Press, 1999.

Whiting, Kenneth R. *The Development of the Soviet Armed Forces, 1918–1966*. Maxwell AFB: Air University, 1966.

Wieczynski, Joseph L., (Ed.). *Operation Barbarossa: The German Attack on the Soviet Union, June 22, 1941*. Salt Lake City, UT: Charles Schlacks, 1993.

Witkin, Zara. *An American Engineer in Stalin's Russia. The Memoirs of Zara Witkin, 1932–1934*. Berkeley, CA: University of California Press, 1991.

Yenne, Bill. *Aces High: The Heroic Saga of the Two Top-Scoring American Aces of World War II*. New York: Berkley/Caliber, The Penguin Group, 2009.

Yenne, Bill. *Aces: True Stories of Victory and Valor in the Skies of World War II*. New York: Berkley Publishing, Penguin Putnam Group, 2000.

Yubileinyi Staisticheskii Ezhegodnik. *Narodnoye khozyastvo SSSR za 70 let: Yubileynyy statisticheskiy yezhegodnik* (*The Economy of the USSR During the Last 70 Years: Anniversary Statistical Yearbook*). *Narodnoe Khozyastvo sssr za 70 let*. Moscow: Yubileinyi Staisticheskii Ezhegodnik, 1987.

Zhukov, Georgi K. *The Memoirs of Marshal Zhukov*. London: Cape, 1971.

Zinoviev, Aleksandr (Translated from the Russian By Gordon Clough). *The Radiant Future*. Franklin Center, PA: The Franklin Library, 1981.

Zoshchenko, Mikhail. "Nervnye Iiudi" ("Nervous People") in *Rasskazy Dvadtsatykh Godov* (*Stories of the 1920's*). Letchworth, Hertfordshire, England: Bradda Books Ltd., 1969.

## PERIODICALS REFERENCED

*Aranysas* (a contemporary Hungarian aviation magazine)

*Aviatsiya i Kosmonavtika* (*Aviation and Cosmonautics*)

*Gorkovskaia Kommuna* (a newspaper in Gorky)

*Journal of Decorative and Propaganda Arts*

*Journal of Women's History*

*Minerva: Journal of Women and War* (formerly *Minerva: Quarterly Report on Women and the Military*).

*Modern Language Review*

*Nashi Dostizheniia* (*Our Achievements*)

*New York Times, The*

*Novy Mir* (*New World*) (Russian language literary magazine)

*Ogonek* (Moscow-based illustrated magazine aimed at young adults)

*Pravda* (meaning "Truth," Moscow's leading daily)

*Rabochaya Moskva* (Moscow's workers' newspaper)

*Slavic and East European Journal*

*Soviet Life*

*Soviet Russia Today*

*Technology and Culture*

*Time* Magazine

*Vecherniaia Moskva,* (Moscow's evening paper)

*Voina i Revolyutsiya* (*War and Revolution*)

# Index

# Enjoyed *The White Rose of Stalingrad*?
# We think you'll like these:

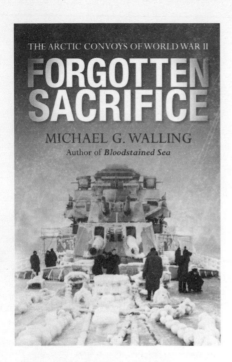

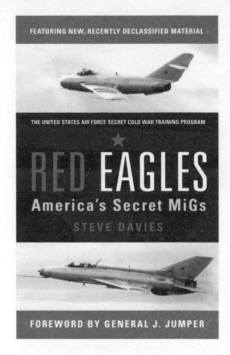

## FORGOTTEN SACRIFICE: THE ARCTIC CONVOYS OF WORLD WAR II

This is the complete story of the Allied forces' Arctic Convoys and the vital role they played in helping Russia repel the Germans. The tale involves torpedo attacks and survival at sea in open boats in the biting cold, as well as Stuka dive bombers, naval guns, and weeks of total darkness in the Arctic winter.

## RED EAGLES: AMERICA'S SECRET MIGS – NEW EDITION

After the failures of the Vietnam War, a squadron was assembled from some of America's best fighter pilots, operating a range of MiG aircraft secured through covert ops. U.S. pilots were thus exposed to the threat they would face in the event of war with the Soviet Union. Packed with recently declassified material, this is the incredible story of America's secret MiG squadron and their missions.